AN INTRODUCTION TO
LAW AND LEGAL
REASONING

AN INTRODUCTION TO LAW AND LEGAL REASONING

Steven J. Burton
Professor of Law, University of Iowa

LITTLE, BROWN AND COMPANY
Boston   Toronto

Library of Congress Catalog Card No. 85-50080

ISBN 0-316-11786-2

ALP

Published simultaneously in Canada

by Little, Brown & Company (Canada) Limited

Printed in the United States of America

For my parents, wife, and children

Summary of Contents

CONTENTS

PREFACE

It is commonly said that the student's primary goal in the first year of law school is to learn how to "think like a lawyer." For the most part, however, law teachers in their classrooms do not deal explicitly and systematically with how lawyers think. The first-year curriculum in U.S. law schools consists largely of courses on selected basic areas of the law, such as contracts, torts, property, criminal law, and civil procedure. The students read examples of legal thinking (mostly as expressed by judges) within the subject of study. The law teacher challenges the student to explain and criticize the examples to shed light on the particular area of law under study. Students are left largely to their own devices to extract from the examples worthwhile lessons about how lawyers think in general.

Many U.S. law schools supplement the standard courses with a general introductory course, usually in the first semester of law school, in which legal thinking may be treated directly. These courses may be called Introduction to Law, Legal Reasoning, Legal Process, Legal Methods, Elements of the Law, or Law, Language, and Ethics. At schools where such courses are not offered, many teachers recommend that students read general books about legal thinking on their own, preferably during or just after the critical first year of study. In my view, confronting legal thinking as such often repays the effort handsomely, though not always obviously.

This book seeks to help students to understand legal thinking in the context of the U.S. legal system. It is intended primarily for beginning law students in general introductory courses or as independent reading. It is suitable for use in many undergraduate law courses. I hope as well that this book is rich enough to be used in some advanced elective courses in law schools and to repay rereading as the years pass.

A book on legal reasoning may strike some persons as an odd venture at this time in the progression of our thinking about law. Some teachers and scholars today doubt that there exists a subject of legal reasoning that merits study in its own right or that law is in any significant way distinct from politics, morality, or psychology. Their doubt has both historical and analytical underpinnings, both of which have influenced the way in which legal education is conducted in the United States.

Historically, U.S. legal scholars often treat our thinking about law in the twentieth century in terms of *legal formalism* and *legal realism*. Legal formalism, in its strong versions, treats law as a system of rules that dictate the results judges must reach in particular law cases by deductive reasoning. Legal realism largely denies the accuracy of legal formalism as a description of how the legal system operates in fact. In its more extreme versions, it asserts that judges decide cases as a product of their emotional or intuitive reactions to the facts of individual cases, rather than through a process of reasoning or with results that could be justified by reasoning.

The conventional wisdom is that legal formalism dominated our thinking about law in the late nineteenth and early twentieth centuries, but gave way to legal realism as a consequence of an outburst of highly influential realist scholarship in the 1920s and 1930s. Efforts to put reasoning back into our thinking about law by "legal process" scholars and others in the 1940s and 1950s, without reviving the discredited legal formalism, had only limited influence. A new version of formalism, known as the positive economic analysis of law, emerged in the early 1970s but again has had only limited influence. A politicized and yet more extreme version of legal realism, known as the critical legal studies movement, emerged in the late 1970s and reinforced the lingering legal realism of law teachers and scholars.

Perhaps it is time to try again to put reasoning back into our thinking about law, though surely no effort will be made here to revive legal formalism and ignore the many valuable insights of legal realists. Dramatic progress has been made in understanding human and scientific reasoning in the last thirty years, largely through the efforts of logicians, philosophers of language, and philosophers of science. The crude notion of reasoning that defines most versions of legal formalism no longer is widely respected as a sufficient explanatory device in any field of intellectual endeavor. The claim that reasoning is not an important part of the legal process no longer is supported by the legal system's inability to operate in fact as indicated by legal formalism in the abstract. This book adapts the new conceptions of human reasoning as necessary to show how legal reasoning plays a major role in the legal process, though it will avoid the jargon of academic scholarship.

Analytically, many teachers and scholars doubt that what is called legal reasoning differs in any material respect from reasoning in other fields. First, they may assert that the kinds of reasoning employed by moral philosophers, literary critics, economists, other social scientists, and even physical scientists are each a part of what goes into good legal reasoning. This is true but does not suffice to deprive legal reasoning of its identity. The purposes for which reasoning is used in law differ from the purposes for which it is used in other settings, and the purposes for which reasoning is used affect its character. As will be seen, legal reasoning can serve the purposes of lawyers and judges well when it would not satisfy the traditional requirements of sound reasoning in more academic endeavors.

It also may be said that the kinds of reasoning employed in the various fields do not differ from one another because all disciplined reasoning is really the same. There is truth in this stronger assertion at a high level of abstraction, where all disciplined reasoning is an exercise of the human mind and can proceed only in those ways that the human mind works. Those ways are called *logic,* and any argument can be analyzed and evaluated for its logic or illogic. All disciplined reasoning also operates on some kind of data—for example, the observations of the scientist or the abstract concepts of the mathematician—and transforms the data from one form into another. Different fields may recognize different observations or abstract concepts as their data, but the reasoning employed to transform the data will be logical in character. Thus, at the highly abstract level of logic and data, all disciplined reasoning is really the same.

The strong claim that legal reasoning is not different from reasoning in other fields is misleading in a significant respect. The characteristics of a field's data and language, as well as the laws of logic, determine the transformations, or "moves," that can or cannot be made within a field. Different kinds of data have different characteristics. Education in a field is necessary to familiarize a practitioner with the characteristics of the data recognized by the field. Each field employs its own vocabulary to describe the data and, thus, a recognized language in which to work. Education also is necessary to familiarize the practitioner with the language of a field and the characteristics of that language. No field, save perhaps symbolic logic, can make all possible logical moves. The reasoning within a field may be distinctive because practitioners in each field can make a distinct set of logical moves in light of the recognized data and language of the field.

More important, few persons employ all of the possible moves with the data and language of a field. Each field has its professional conventions, and most practitioners confine their moves to the conventional. Exceptional practitioners go beyond the conventions and show their colleagues that unfamiliar moves can be made within the field or that the field should be redefined to recognize unfamiliar language or data. Sometimes a move "just won't wash," and what will "wash" in one field may not "wash" in another. The differences in the conventions among the various fields, too, give the reasoning in each field a distinctive identity.

Legal reasoning thus is a subject in its own right analytically for three reasons. First, it operates on its own data — law cases — and allows only those moves that these data permit. Second, it uses a specialized language — legal rules — that has its own characteristics. Third, it is practiced by a community of persons — primarily lawyers and judges — whose conventions are not altogether shared by other communities. Legal education familiarizes students with the characteristics of law cases and legal rules and with the conventions of the legal community concerning the moves that can be made with those materials. This book seeks to facilitate that education.

Steven J. Burton

April 1985

Acknowledgments

It is impossible for me to acknowledge all who contributed to the realization of this book. I should acknowledge some persons whom I know only through their writings, such as William James, Willard Van Orman Quine, and Ludwig Wittgenstein. I am sure acknowledgment is due to some persons whom I do not remember. I can only do my best to mention those who stand out and ask the forgiveness of others.

Thanks are due, first, to my father for more than the ordinary reasons. At the conclusion of the first week of law school, I had decided to drop out in frustration. My father convinced me to give it a month. He had no need to encourage me further. During that month, I located a rabbit-hole through which I fell into the wonderland of the law. It was a course in Law, Language, and Ethics, taught by Professor Christopher D. Stone. This book represents thoughts that he, more than anyone else, stimulated.

Special thanks are due to my best friend, favorite colleague, and beloved wife, Serena Stier. She encouraged me to believe that I might become a good law teacher and scholar. She patiently read every chapter and revision of the manuscript for this book and contributed to its every aspect. My children, Daryn, Max, and Sam Stier, also read the book in manuscript and provided helpful comments.

Many colleagues, practicing lawyers, and students read and commented on the manuscript. Among them were Ronald J. Allen, William G. Buss, Robert N. Clinton, Owen M. Fiss, Thomas Gilbert, Mark A. Hammer, Lisa A. Hausten, Sheldon F. Kurtz, Edward H. Levi, Richard A. Matasar, Peter D. Shane, Burns H. Weston, and the students in my Law, Language, and Ethics and Legal Methods classes during 1984. I also profited from conversations with Dorsey D. Ellis, Jr., Barry D. Matsumoto, and David H. Vernon. Richard R. Heuser and the staff at Little, Brown and Company care about the quality of the books that they make. Working with them was a pleasure.

Research support was generously provided by Dean N. William Hines on behalf of the University of Iowa College of Law and its Law School Foundation. The faculty of the Yale Law School provided hospitality during the summer of 1984, and the European University Institute in Florence, Italy, provided facilities during the spring of 1983. Caroline Tappan assisted in the preparation of the manuscript. Invaluable technical assistance was given, always in a spirit of unflinching professionalism, by my IBM Personal Computer.

AN INTRODUCTION TO LAW AND LEGAL REASONING

INTRODUCTION

A LAWYER'S PRINCIPAL task, among several, is to help a client get somewhere that the client wants to go, using the law to the client's advantage or preventing others from using the law to the client's disadvantage. To perform this task, lawyers often try to predict what a judge (or other adjudicator) will do or persuade someone of what a judge will or should do in particular situations involving the client's interests. Judges decide what the law permits or requires of persons in particular situations that come before a court. Legal reasoning plays a major role in making reasonably reliable predictions, effective persuasions, and responsible decisions that may earn respect as law.

Confusion about legal reasoning leads to confusion about almost everything else in the law because reasoning and communicating reasoning lie at the heart of the law job. Yet it is remarkable how few books have been written to explain directly how lawyers reason. It is more remarkable how few such efforts are directed at beginning law students, who find it so frustrating to learn how to "think like a lawyer." The conventional wisdom is that one learns legal reasoning by doing it. Consequently, the student in the first year of law school proceeds largely by trial and error.

There is much truth in this conventional wisdom. The successful study of law requires patience, persistence, and practice over an extended period of time. A direct explanation of how lawyers think can be helpful to many law students, however, and perhaps to others as well. Of course, no complete and final explanation of legal reasoning is likely ever to be composed. Indeed, much of what will be said in this book speaks only to law and legal reasoning in the U.S. legal system. Nonetheless, we can call certain matters to the reader's attention, draw connections that might not otherwise be noticed, and set law and legal reasoning in a context in which they might make better sense.

A. The Ideal and the Practice

Confusion about legal reasoning often stems from a perceived contrast between the ideal of legal reasoning and its practice. The ideal of legal reasoning consists of those ways in which lawyers and judges perhaps ought to think and communicate their thoughts. The practice of legal reasoning consists of those ways in which lawyers and judges habitually think and communicate their thoughts. Few observers would claim that the practice of legal reasoning conforms to its ideal. Because the ideal is held for many good reasons, the contrast between practice and ideal leaves us troubled in important ways.

In U.S. society, the ideal of legal reasoning reflects a set of values called the rule of law or a government of laws, not of men. Americans are devoted to the principle that the powers of government in a free society are limited by law: The U.S. Constitution provides that "[n]o person shall . . . be deprived of life, liberty, or property, without due process of law."[1] Much of what government does, of course, deprives some person of life, liberty, or property, in one sense or another. A court's judgment, for example, may require one person to pay money or transfer property to another person or the state, may incarcerate a person or otherwise restrict her freedom, or may impose the death penalty. The rule of law requires that all such deprivations occur only in accordance with the law—not arbitrarily or because an individual government official, such as a judge, might for whatever nonlegal reason think it is a good idea under the circumstances.

Legal reasoning is supposed to implement the rule of law by drawing the connection between the law and a particular governmental action that deprives an individual of life, liberty, or property. Faulty legal reasoning signifies a faulty connection and raises the question whether governmental power is being used in ways that are not legitimate. Illegitimate uses of governmental power, such as the decision of a judge who was bribed or who seeks to punish political opponents or to impose personal moral values on others, are frightening in a free and democratic society. They represent oppression and a disjunction between the consent of the governed and the laws that govern.

A traditional, formal approach suggests that legal reasoning is

[1]U.S. Const., amends. V, XIV.

supposed to tell us what specific legal decisions are required by the law, based on objective facts, clear laws, and sound logic. Legal reasoning thus conceived should lead to the same decision no matter who is doing the reasoning so that justice does not vary with the vagaries of human personality. It should enable lawyers to predict with confidence what government officials will do in particular situations, so that clients can be advised reliably or represented effectively, and should enable observers to say with confidence which decisions are right and which are wrong in order to monitor the legitimacy of the legal system.

It takes little exposure to the study of law to begin doubting whether the practice of legal reasoning conforms to this formal version of the rule of law, at least in many situations. A close analysis of almost any legal decision can show it to rest on questionable facts, vague or ambiguous laws, or incomplete logic, leaving the "real" grounds of the decision unclear. Comparisons of decisions reached by different government officials in similar situations often seem to suggest that the officials' personalities, prejudices, or personal values had more to do with the decision than did the law. Lawyers often are uncertain of what government officials will or should do in particular situations and, therefore, of how to advise or represent their clients. Evaluations of decisions often leave observers unable to say with confidence which are right and which are wrong.

Such doubt is troubling in two ways. First, it is hard to see how one can function as an effective lawyer if legal reasoning cannot be relied on to draw a sound connection between the law and a particular official decision. The law game sometimes seems to go on without rules, or with rules that can be changed or ignored at an umpire's whim. Second, it is hard to see why such a game should go on. The law makes some people rich and some people poor, some people free and some people fettered, even some people live and some people die — in the real world. A game that does so arbitrarily is not one that we want to play in a free and democratic society.

Consequently, lawyers and judges often confront a legal problem with conflicting instincts. On the one hand, we try to ascertain how a problem should be resolved in accordance with the traditional, formal ideal of legal reasoning. On the other, we try to ascertain how a problem will be resolved by whatever intuitions we might have about the "real" grounds of legal decisions. The practical implications of each approach differ frequently. We are confused because we find it hard to give up either of these two instincts and do not know what we should do.

B. A Contextual Approach

This book suggests that the successful study of law requires one to develop a third sort of instinct about law and legal reasoning. The practice of legal reasoning seems arbitrary when measured against the formal rule of law and its logical implications. Anything less than certainty in reasoning does not satisfy that standard; everything less than certainty fails the test completely. It will be seen, however, that the formal rule of law is not the right standard of measurement because it is an unrealizable ideal. Human choices in the real world must be made pragmatically from among the available alternatives in light of what we are trying to do in some set of circumstances. From this contextual point of view, the practice of legal reasoning can be explained in a way that suggests how legal reasoning is used to help lawyers function effectively and how the practice of judging justifiably can be accepted as legitimate though it falls short of the formal ideal.

The contextual approach requires, to begin, that legal reasoning be placed in the real-world situations in which it characteristically is used. In the abstract, legal reasoning does not differ significantly from many other kinds of reasoning. It acquires a character of its own in its real-world settings, where it is used by lawyers and judges to deal with certain sorts of problems, is expressed in a specialized language used by a professional community, takes certain principles and goals for granted, and employs artificial devices to circumvent practical problems. Explaining legal reasoning in the context of its characteristic uses has practical implications for lawyers, judges, and the society that they serve.

For example, the chief feature of legal reasoning is that it characteristically is used in the process of anticipating or settling important disputes in advanced societies. People who live in proximity to one another will find themselves at times in disputes, which are controversies in which two or more persons claim incompatible rights. Thus, one person may sell another a cow that both had thought was barren. When the cow turns out to be with calf, the seller may try to get the cow back. The buyer may refuse. Or one person may be hunting foxes and begin to chase one. When another person intrudes, and kills and carries off the prey, the first may demand possession of the fox or payment of its value. The second may refuse. Or one person may be separating fighting dogs with a stick. When that person carelessly hits another person, the victim may request payment of compensation for an injury. The injurer may refuse. These and countless other situations lead two or more persons to differ over practical matters that will not just go away. One person has something that the other person claims should be his, and each may persist in refusing to settle the dispute.

Every society develops methods for settling disputes among its members. Different methods of dispute settlement are employed by different societies in different times and places. In some times and places, disputes in which the parties persist[2] may be settled by organized combat between the parties (duels), their champions (jousts), or their clans (feuds). They may be settled by divination, an appeal by ritual for God's judgment (trial by ordeal; consulting an oracle). They may be settled by appeal to chance (flipping a coin; cutting the cards) or a third person's fiat (father knows best; the divine right of kings). Disputes also may be settled by appeal to a third person's reason, an intellectual search for the right in the matter (an advanced form of law).

Many important disputes in U.S. society can be settled, if need be, by appeal to a third person's reason—by appeal to judges to apply the law. This procedure is thought to be better than the available alternatives because we want disputes in society to be settled in peaceful and justifiable ways. Dispute settlement by law is more peaceful than duels, jousts, or feuds. Dispute settlement by law is more just than trial by ordeal, consulting an oracle, flipping coins, or letting a "wise" man decide. It seems obvious that legal reasoning does enable judges to reach peaceful and justifiable settlements of disputes better than would these available alternatives. What is not obvious is how legal reasoning does so.

C. Scope

This book is organized into three main parts. Parts I and II proceed by way of *explaining* the forms and interpretive methods

---

[2]Negotiation, mediation, and conciliation are methods of dispute settlement that may help the disputants settle their differences voluntarily, but they do not impose a settlement if the disputants persist. They are increasingly important supplements to adjudication in the U.S. legal system.

of legal reasoning, as they are employed by good lawyers and judges in the U.S. legal system. Such an explanation seeks to show how it is possible for legal reasoning to yield reasonably reliable predictions, effective persuasions, and responsible decisions that may earn respect as law. It is different from *describing* what lawyers and judges habitually do because it indulges in judgments about which features of the practice are useful and which are misguided, in light of the objectives sought by lawyers and judges. It also is different from *justifying* the practices associated with adjudication because it refrains from evaluating them by some normative standard, such as the formal rule of law. Part III turns to the problems of justifying the practice of adjudication, in light of the explanation offered in Parts I and II and the values embodied in the ideal of a rule of law.

Part I, Forms of Legal Reasoning, presents and analyzes the two principal forms of reasoning that good lawyers and judges employ. Chapter 1 introduces two basic concepts—cases and rules—that lawyers use to predict what a court will do or persuade someone of what a court will or should do, and that judges use to make decisions. Chapter 2 introduces and analyzes the analogical form of legal reasoning, which is most closely associated with reasoning from cases for these purposes. Chapter 3 introduces and analyzes the deductive form of legal reasoning, which is most closely associated with reasoning from rules for these purposes. Chapter 4 analyzes how the analogical and deductive forms of legal reasoning interact with each other. Part I shows that the two forms of legal reasoning are useful in a number of ways and are critical to the proper expression of legal reasoning in almost all situations. It also shows that they are not adequate in many cases for lawyers and judges to make good predictions, persuasions, and decisions because the two forms raise, but do not solve, a "problem of importance."

Part II, The Problem of Importance, supplements the forms of legal reasoning with a method of interpretation that addresses the problem of importance. Chapter 5 examines the nature of relations among cases and the implications of those kinds of relations for a workable interpretive method. Chapter 6 introduces the roles of theory and the legal experience in legal interpretation. Chapter 7 highlights the role of the legal community to explain judicial decisions, especially in harder cases. Chapter 8 brings the lessons of preceding chapters to bear on the practical problems of making lawyerly predictions and persuasions. Part II shows that, though legal reasoning does not produce predictions, persuasions, and decisions of unquestionable soundness, it nonetheless produces reasonable and useful predictions, persuasions, and decisions.

Part III, The Problem of Legitimacy, explores the implications of uncertainty and interpretive relativism in legal reasoning in light of the deep commitment to the values embodied in the rule of law in U.S. society. Chapter 9 explains the demand for legitimacy in U.S. society and the traditional model of formal legitimacy, which in recent decades has been subjected to devastating criticism. Chapter 10 examines some alternatives to formal legitimacy, including a fundamentally different approach called "contextual legitimacy." Chapter 11 turns to the implications of contextual legitimacy for a legal system in which judges sometimes make law that has substantial implications for society. Part III suggests that, though uncertainty and interpretive relativism in legal reasoning entail that judges make law, judicial lawmaking in adjudication can be legitimate because it contributes to the contextual legitimacy of the U.S. legal and political system as a whole.

The emphasis in this book on good legal reasoning can be misleading because the legal system in operation is a good bit messier than the picture presented. Not all lawyers and judges are good at their jobs. Not even most good lawyers and judges are very articulate about the forms and interpretive methods they employ; many function well instinctively. The pressures of heavy case loads often lead good lawyers and judges to speak and write in truncated ways, on the assumption that the underlying forms could be made explicit and filled in if the audience balks at the truncated argument. More important, good legal reasoning is not all there is to good lawyering and judging. The successful practice of law and judging involves imagination and common sense, as well as interpersonal, rhetorical, political, and other skills, along with legal reasoning. A complete theory of lawyering or judging would explain the role of legal reasoning in relation to these other skills. I suggest only that legal reasoning plays a major role in good lawyering and judging and that this fact is necessary to make the legal venture legitimate.

I
THE FORMS OF LEGAL REASONING

LEGAL REASONING IS AN intellectual process by which lawyers and judges use cases and rules to solve legal problems. It takes two principal forms: One is analogical; the other is deductive. This part will introduce the two principal forms of legal reasoning and examine their separate and joint capacities to contribute to the solution of legal problems.

The forms of legal reasoning perform important practical functions. Some means of organizing the overwhelming mass of legal materials is essential. The forms help identify the proper starting points for reasoning, locate the relevant materials, and formulate issues to focus predictions, persuasions, and decisions. Poorly formed legal arguments often are dismissed from further consideration because they are less likely to be meritorious. Well-formed legal arguments generally make it possible for lawyers and judges to focus on the same points of controversy and thus to communicate and argue intelligently. Legal reasoning is most effective when expressed with proper form.

The forms of legal reasoning, however, cannot guarantee the soundness or meaningfulness of a legal argument. Many well-formed arguments are wrong, and others are less persuasive than competing well-formed arguments. A form of legal reasoning is like an empty vessel: Its usefulness as a form resides in the space where there is nothing. The value of an argument depends on what is carried in that space. As a vessel can carry wine or water, a form of reasoning can carry sense or nonsense. Thus, the following statements have the same form but not the same value:

> Alpha is like Beta.
> A horse is like a cow.
> Blue is like green.
> A horse is like green.

The soundness or meaningfulness of a legal argument depends in large part on how the forms of legal reasoning are filled in—on the substance or content of the statements in an argument. A major part of legal reasoning is the intellectual process of giving content to the analogical and deductive forms. This process requires an interpretive method of legal reasoning, a technique for transforming legal materials into statements that are meaningful. Part II will develop and introduce a method of legal interpretation and examine its capacity to contribute to the solution of legal problems.

CHAPTER ONE

Cases and Rules

MOST LAYPERSONS probably think of the law as a system of rules. The study of law in U.S. law schools, however, normally begins with the reading of a law case. The law student reads and reasons primarily from cases throughout law school. Thinking about cases is an important intellectual activity throughout one's legal career, though legal rules, too, play a major role in legal thought. Before undertaking the main discussion of legal reasoning, three basic questions will be posed in this chapter: What is a case? What is a rule? Why do we study primarily cases?

A. Cases

As used in this book, a *case* is a short story of an incident in which the state acted or may act to settle a particular dispute. The term is used in other ways for other purposes.[1] The purpose here is to say something useful about legal reasoning, and this definition will help.

Treating a case as a *short story* emphasizes that it has a beginning, a middle, and an end and that the story as we can know it is incomplete. The story begins when the stage is set for two or more persons to find themselves in a dispute or for one person to find himself in a dispute with the community as represented by law enforcement officials. It continues in its initial phase until it is clear that a dispute has arisen and the court system is called upon to settle the dispute. The middle phase commences when one party (the plaintiff or prosecutor) files a complaint against another person (the defendant) with a law court, calling on the court to settle the dispute in favor of the complaining party. It continues according to standard procedures at the trial court level until a trial court judgment is entered. If either party believes the trial judge erred in certain ways, it may appeal to a higher court (an appellate court).

---

[1]For a different perspective, see Fiss, The Forms of Justice, 93 Harv. L. Rev. 1, 28-44 (1979).

The last phase takes place in an appellate court, where arguments are heard by a group of judges who issue a final judgment that settles at least a part of the dispute. The appellate court writes and publishes an essay, called an opinion, that summarizes the facts of the dispute and the proceedings in the trial court, announces a decision on the issues before the appellate court, and gives the reasons for its decision. For the most part, a lawyer's knowledge of decided cases comes from what the appellate courts write in their opinions, which may or may not be wholly accurate stories of the events in question.

Treating a case as a short story of an *incident* emphasizes that every case is unique in all of its particulars. A case involves two or more parties, both of whom are unlikely ever to repeat the very actions that led to the dispute between them. It occurs over a period of time that will not pass again. The events in one case can be described in terms general enough also to encompass other disputes between other parties in other times and places. They can be described in terms specific enough to encompass only the dispute that occurred between these parties at this time and place. Each case, in this narrow sense, occurs once, however it may be described.

Treating a case as a short story of an incident in which *the state acted or may act* emphasizes that we will speak much of two sorts of disputes — disputes in the past that were settled, at least in part, by the coercive dispute settlement machinery of the state (decided cases) and unresolved or foreseeable disputes that might be settled in that way (problem cases). A court is a central part of the state's dispute settlement machinery, but only a part. Administrative agencies increasingly perform comparable decisionmaking functions. Additionally, a court's judgment in favor of the plaintiff in a civil case — generally one in which a private plaintiff calls on a court to settle a dispute — may be enforced against a noncompliant defendant by the sheriff. For example, some of a losing defendant's property may be taken, by force if need be, and sold by the sheriff with the proceeds going to the plaintiff to the extent that the losing defendant failed to pay a money judgment. In criminal cases, the police usually initiate the dispute on behalf of the community, and an official prosecutor calls on a court to settle it. On conviction, a criminal defendant may be fined or incarcerated by the sheriff, using force if necessary. The use of force by representatives of the state usually is not necessary because most citizens are law-abiding by habit and, for others, the threat of force is sufficient to induce compliance with the law. Nonetheless, every request to a court to settle a dispute is a request that the state use force, if necessary, to settle the dispute in favor of the complaining party. The state "acts" whether such a request is granted or denied.

Treating a case as a short story of an incident in which the state acted or may act *to settle a particular dispute* emphasizes the social function of the law and reemphasizes the uniqueness of each case. Formal methods of peaceful dispute settlement are needed because disputes will arise whenever people live in close proximity to one another, and some disputes predictably will not be settled by voluntary negotiations between the disputants. The availability of formal dispute settlement procedures is thought to lessen the level of violence and other disruptions in society by affording the disputants an alternative to fighting. The law courts, by their responses to concrete disputes, also contribute to society's understanding of its values. The law both reflects and helps mold social values, substantially through judicial judgments in cases resolving particular disputes.

B. Rules

To explain why we study primarily cases, the principal alternative subject of study—rules—first should be identified and contrasted. The law schools generally employ a case method of instruction because it is thought to be better than a study primarily of rules. The contrast between cases and rules is not difficult to grasp.

As used in this book, a *rule* is an abstract or general statement of what the law permits or requires of classes of persons in classes of circumstances. Again, the term is used in other ways for other purposes. This definition is even more rough than the definition of a case because rules are notoriously slippery characters. Some would draw distinctions between rules and principles or rules and standards, but these are fine points that need not be troubling for now. What is said of rules is general enough to cover most understandings of principles and standards as well.

Treating a rule as an *abstract or general statement* emphasizes that all rules are cast in language. All language, save perhaps proper names, is and must be general to function as language. Every statement in language, if taken to refer to objects in the world, can refer to both more and less than anyone wanted or wants. That is, our words do double- and triple-duty. Consider the word *bar*. You may want to join the bar but may be barred if you fail the bar and wind up tending bar or selling candy bars. A rule that uses the word *bar,* or any other word, requires interpretation to sort out the various possible referents. Both the ideas in our minds and the realities in the world are more complex than language can be and still be language.

Treating a rule as an abstract or general statement *of what the law permits or requires* emphasizes that a rule is normative and implies an obligation. That is, a rule says something about what people in general ought to do or ought not to do. A rule might include a descriptive part, as when it states the circumstances under which the obligation comes into play. For example, a rule might say that "One who kills another without excuse or justification shall be punished. . . . " The part "One who kills another" purports to describe wholly objective facts. The part "without excuse or justification" is primarily normative because it requires a determination of the rightfulness or wrongfulness of a killing, which usually is thought to require subjective judgment. The part "shall be punished . . . " states the legal consequence that attaches to unexcused and unjustified killings of people by people. The entire rule implies an obligation for persons not to kill other persons wrongfully, though this rule says little about which killings are wrongful or rightful.

Treating a rule as an abstract or general statement of what the law permits or requires of *classes of persons in classes of circumstances* emphasizes that rules apply to situations that may occur in the real world and that no rule applies only to one person in one time and place. Rules operate from a position of generality; that is, any rule applies to a group or class of cases — to more than one (real or hypothetical) case. Rules are supposed to affect what people do by bringing obligation, and often force or the threat of force, to bear to influence their behavior. Rules thus should be announced before people engage in relevant behavior and a case governed by the rule has materialized. Because foresight is limited and language imperfect, a rulemaker effectively is forced to speak in generalities that often are unclear. A statement of what the law permits or requires of one person under one set of circumstances — in one case — would be called an order or judgment.

A rule thus stands in contrast to the cases that it governs. A rule is an abstract or general statement (a single sentence); a case is a short story (an essay). A rule is an abstract or general statement of what the law permits or requires; a case is a short story of an incident in which the state acted or may act. A rule is an abstract or general statement of what the law permits or requires of classes of persons in classes of circumstances; a case is a short story of an incident in which the state acted or may act to settle a particular dispute.

C. What Lawyers and Judges Do in Problem Cases

By the case method of instruction, law students are required in each course to read many opinions in cases decided by appellate courts. They are asked in class to explain why the court acted in the way it did in each case, to analyze the implications of each case for possible future disputes, and to integrate the lessons from groups of cases into a general understanding of each subject under study. The process of analyzing and synthesizing cases seeks to develop in the student a capacity to predict what the courts will do and persuade the courts to rule one way or the other in possible future cases. This implies a study of what judges do and ought to do—a study of judicial reasoning and justice. Though rules play a significant role in law courses, the primary focus of attention normally is on decided cases, which are examples of the law in action, and their possible implications for future problem cases.

A large part of what lawyers do involves the same intellectual tasks of reasoning to predict or persuade from past appellate cases, but a large part involves a wide variety of other skills. Much lawyering is an effort to anticipate possible disputes and then to plan a client's activities so that disputes are not likely to arise or can be settled advantageously if they do arise. Much lawyering is an effort to settle existing disputes by negotiation. Indeed, most of those disputes that reach a lawyer are settled before or soon after they reach a court, and most of those that proceed to trial and judgment are not appealed. Lawyers in practice thus spend the better part of their time planning, counseling, drafting, negotiating, or preparing for trials—anticipating and processing disputes from the law office.

Throughout the dispute anticipating and processing sequence, however, a significant part of what lawyers do consists of predicting what an appellate court would do if a case were to materialize and be taken to the highest available court and persuading some-one of what an appellate court will or should do in that event. That much more is involved than predicting and persuading judicial ac-tion does not mean that predicting and persuading such action are not involved. Some examples will illustrate the point.

Consider a lawyer who is counsel to a business firm that manu-factures and sells a product—say, a chain saw. The seller-client wishes to market a new, improved model and seeks legal advice on whether to include a certain kind of chain guard that would reduce the risk of injuries to operators, but only at some increase in the price of the saw (and consequently some reduction in the client's volume of sales and the amount of its profits). The lawyer will want to determine whether omitting the chain guard makes it sig-nificantly more likely that the seller will be held liable, that is, will be forced to pay compensation to users of the chain saw for in-juries that could have been prevented by a chain guard. The lawyer's prediction of what the law will do in the end—what an appellate court will decide—is a significant element in that deter-mination, even though no lawyer makes consistently correct pre-dictions and several other factors also are significant.

If the lawyer concludes that omitting the chain guard is likely to make no difference before an appellate court, she may be more likely to advise the seller that its decision whether to include a chain guard need not be influenced by legal factors. Further questions will arise if she concludes that omitting the chain guard makes liability more likely: What are the courts likely to do should the seller omit the chain guard but include in the instruction booklet a warning of the danger? Will the courts enforce a contract clause by which the buyers agree to assume the risk of such injuries (a disclaimer of liability)? Will it matter how the language of such a warning or disclaimer is drafted? The lawyer's predictions of judicial action in each variation on the anticipated dispute will influence her plan-ning—counseling advice to the client on whether to include the chain guard and drafting suggestions on language for inclusion in the instruction booklet or contracts of sale.

Assume now that the chain saw is marketed without the chain guard, warnings, or disclaimer, and a buyer is injured in a way that would not have occurred with a chain guard. The buyer seeks compensation for his injuries from the seller, and the seller does not want to pay. At this point, the seller's lawyer may be asked to negotiate a favorable settlement, if possible, while preparing for trial should a lawsuit be initiated.

The lawyer again will want to predict what a court will do, based on the facts then available. The lawyer's advice to settle or not to settle out of court will be influenced by the prediction in the following way, to put a simplified example.[2] If the buyer claims compensation in the amount of $10,000 and the seller's lawyer predicts that the seller has a 70 percent chance of losing for that amount in court, the lawyer probably will advise the seller to settle for any amount less than $7,000. The seller would be better off settling for less than $7,000 now than taking a 70 percent chance of being forced to pay $10,000 later. On the other hand, if the buyer's lawyer predicts that the buyer has a 40 percent chance of winning in court, the buyer's lawyer probably will advise the buyer to settle for any amount more than $4,000. The buyer is better off with more than $4,000 for certain than with a 40 percent chance of getting $10,000 later. Given these stakes and these predictions by the two lawyers, the conditions are ripe for settlement at an amount between $4,000 and $7,000.

The lawyers' skills at negotiation are likely to determine the exact amount of the settlement. Though many factors will influence the negotiation, one will be the lawyers' skills at persuasion. If the seller's lawyer can persuade the buyer's lawyer that the probability of a buyer's victory in court is less than the buyer's lawyer had thought, the buyer's lawyer may be persuaded to advise the buyer to settle for a lower amount. The converse also is true. The lawyers' persuasive skills may make a settlement posible even if their initial predictions did not create the conditions for settlement. As the story of the case unfolds, new information is acquired and new arguments are developed. The lawyers revise their predictions and negotiate further.

Assume now that no settlement was reached and the dispute goes before a trial court. The trial judge will be required to make a large number of decisions, including rulings on pretrial motions, admissibility of evidence, and in some cases instructions to the jury. Each decision affects each party's prospects of winning the

---

[2]This example assumes that the people involved are rational and wish neither to gamble nor to avoid risks unreasonably. For purposes of discussion, it also ignores lawyer's fees and other litigation expenses.

lawsuit. These decisions must be made in accordance with the law. If the trial judge errs either by applying the wrong law or, sometimes, by applying the correct law wrongly in the particular case, the final judgment may be reversed an appeal to a higher court. The lawyers representing the parties will have an opportunity to make arguments to the trial judge on what the law permits or requires in each decision. These arguments by counsel in large part will seek to persuade the trial judge of what the appellate court would decide on the point if an appeal were taken.

Assume now that the case reaches the highest appellate court in the relevant jurisdiction,[3] the end of the dispute anticipating and processing sequence. The lawyers and the lower court judges wanted to predict what judges further along the sequence would do and persuade others of what those judges would do, to avoid moving to the next stage of the sequence unnecessarily. The highest appellate court is not concerned to predict what it will itself do. The highest appellate court is concerned about what it *should* do. Accordingly, those who want to predict what the highest appellate court will do must be concerned also to understand what such courts believe they should do.

The highest appellate court's concern may be said in general to have two components. First, the highest appellate court will care that the law be reasonably stable and predictable so that lawyers and lower court judges can do their jobs well, and people can plan their activities to remain within the bounds of the law. This will lead the court to give weight to conventional understandings of what the law *is* because the lawyers and lower court judges probably will have relied reasonably on those understandings. Second, the highest appellate court will care that the law contribute to a more orderly and just society in light of contemporary social, historical, and cultural circumstances and evolving notions of justice. Thus, the court will be open to arguments that the law should be interpreted or changed better to promote order and justice; it will be concerned about what the law *ought to be* under the circumstances.

These two components, however, are not so easily separable. Because the lawyers and lower court judges know that the highest appellate court may interpret or change the law better to promote

---

[3]In some jurisdictions, there are two levels of appellate courts, in which arguments before the intermediate court will focus on persuading the judges of what the highest court would decide.

order and justice, their reliance on conventional understandings of what the law is will be incomplete. Their predictions and arguments about what the highest appellate court would do in the case, like the court's final judgment itself, probably will be based on the conventional understandings and an evaluation of them in light of contemporary circumstances and evolving notions of justice. It consequently is difficult to maintain a practical distinction between what the law is and what the law ought to be in a case. The lawyers' predictions and persuasions depend in part on what lawyers think the highest appellate judges will think ought to be the law. The appellate decision depends in part on what the highest appellate judges think lawyers (commonly) think is the law as it stands. Consequently, there is an unresolvable tension between stability and change in adjudication at the appellate court level, and resulting uncertainty percolates downward to the trial courts and law offices.

To summarize, much of what lawyers do involves planning a client's activities so that disputes are not likely to arise or can be settled advantageously if they do arise (dispute anticipating). Much of what lawyers do involves negotiating settlements or preparing for trials, while relatively little involves litigation in trial courts and less involves litigation in appellate courts (dispute processing). Yet throughout the dispute anticipating and processing sequence, a significant influence is the lawyers' capacities to predict what the highest appellate court would do in a case and persuade others of what the highest appellate court would do in a case. Because the highest appellate court's concerns are to maintain and enhance both order and justice in society, lawyers' analyses of the law, like the highest appellate courts', will be based on conventional understandings of what the law both is and ought to be, in light of contemporary circumstances and evolving notions of justice.

D. Using Cases and Rules

Expressions of the law take the form of both rules (generalizations) and cases (examples). To develop skill at making lawyerly predictions and persuasions, it is better to emphasize a study of cases than a study of rules. Rules are deceptively simple in appearance. Cases are complex and rich in variety. Consequently, predicting or persuading from rules alone is often unreliable in a world that is more complex and varied than even the cases.

1. Rules in Problem Cases

Rules, it was said, are abstract or general statements of what the law permits or requires of classes of persons in classes of circumstances. Rules are cast in general language and apply to more than one case but less than all cases. A rule itself may say little or nothing about how it should be interpreted and analyzed in a particular case. Using a rule, as a basis for making predictions and persuasions, often requires intensive analysis and considerable interpretation.

Consider, for example,[4] a simple rule that provides that "No person shall sleep in a city park." Imagine two problem cases.[5] In the first, a gentleman was found sitting upright on a park bench at noon, his chin was resting on his chest, and his eyes were closed. The gentleman was snoring audibly. In the second, a disheveled tramp was found lying on the same bench at midnight, a pillow was beneath his head, and a newspaper was spread over his body as if it were a blanket. The tramp, however, had insomnia. Both were arrested under the rule and brought before a court for trial. Would you predict that the gentleman will be convicted and the tramp acquitted? That the gentleman will be acquitted and the tramp convicted? That both will be convicted? That both will be acquitted? There is no fifth alternative. Does your answer follow from the language of the rule itself?

Consider, for a second example, a rule that provides that "No person shall bring a vehicle into a city park." Imagine some possible problem cases. An ambulance was driven into the park to reach a jogger who collapsed with an apparent heart attack. The local Jaycees put a World War II tank in the park as a monument to the town's war dead. Some teenagers held a car race in the park, a go-cart race, a bicycle race, or a roller-skating race. A tree surgeon drove his truck into the park to load and remove the branches of a dead tree under contract with the city. Surely some of these incidents would not be violations of the rule, yet all might plausibly be said to involve a person bringing a vehicle into the park. Consequently, merely *saying* in any of these cases that a person brought a vehicle into a park would not be sufficient to persuade someone that the rule had been trangressed.

---

[4]This example and the next are adapted from Fuller, Positivism and Fidelity to Law: A Reply to Professor Hart, 71 Harv. L. Rev. 630, 662-66 (1958).

[5]The shorthand descriptions of cases may be thought of as "short, short stories," which rely on common images to fill in the details.

In almost any case, knowing the rules leaves more intellectual work to be done because rules are expressed imperfectly and projected into an uncertain future. The language of a rule does not itself determine whether many particular cases come within the class of cases designated by the rule. Whoever states a rule to govern future cases rarely, if ever, will anticipate all of the future cases that might plausibly be described in the language of the rule but that should not be within the class designated by the rule, or that could not plausibly be described in the language of the rule but that should be within the class. Consequently, a lawyer must go beyond the rules themselves to predict what a court will do or persuade someone of what a court will or should do in a particular case. A lawyer must analyze and interpret the rules in light of possible cases. Karl Llewelyn put it more colorfully in his lectures of 1929-1930 introducing Columbia students to the study of law:

> We have discovered in our teaching of the law that general propositions are empty. We have discovered that students who come eager to learn the rules and who do learn them, *and who learn nothing more,* will take away the shell and not the substance. We have discovered that rules *alone,* mere forms of words, are worthless. We have learned that the concrete instance, the heaping up of concrete instances, the present, vital memory of a multitude of concrete instances, is necessary in order to make any general proposition, be it rule of law or any other, *mean* anything at all. Without the concrete instances the general proposition is baggage, impedimenta, stuff about the feet. It not only does not help. It hinders.[6]

2. Decided Cases in Problem Cases

A case, it was said, is a short story of an incident in which the state acted or may act to settle a particular dispute. Decided cases tell a story with a beginning, a middle, and an end—a story that occurred once and resulted in the settlement of a particular dispute by the coercive dispute settlement machinery of the state. Using decided cases, as a basis for making predictions and persuasions in problem cases, involves a perhaps less familiar intellectual process than that seemingly required by rules. Though often difficult to grasp, learning this way of thinking is well worth the effort. Lawyers in practice generally will care less about the law in the abstract than in its practical implications for particular existing or

---

[6]K. Llewelyn, The Bramble Bush 12 (1951).

possible future disputes involving a particular client. Judges generally do not enact rules; they decide cases.

Effective legal planning requires a keen sense of the variety of disputes that can arise in the future. A lawyer engaged in planning a client's activities is engaged partly in imagining the particular disputes that might arise from the client's activities and taking precautions to minimize losses the client may suffer in such disputes. Elegantly drafted contract language, for example, may be worthy of praise for its style but will earn none if a foreseeable dispute arises and was not anticipated in the drafting. The world has a habit of confounding even those with perspicacious insights and vivid imaginations. A study of the cases stimulates and supplements the imagination so that better precautions can be taken for a greater variety of disputes that might arise from a client's activities.

Once a dispute has arisen, the lawyer will be engaged in predicting what the court will do or persuading someone of what the court will or should do in that case. Pyrrhic victories, as when a court accepts a lawyer's preferred general rule but concludes that the client loses under that rule, usually are of little interest to the lawyer and less to the client. To predict what the court will do in one case, a lawyer can look to what courts have done in other, similar cases. To persuade a court of what it should do in one case, a lawyer can point out what courts have done in other, similar cases. A practice of comparing and contrasing cases may have advantages over rules because the cases supply particularities that general rules leave untreated. Cases are the grist for the legal reasoning mill.

Consider again, for example, the rule that prohibits any person from bringing a vehicle into a city park. Assume that a judge must decide whether a tree surgeon violated that rule by bringing his truck into the park to load and carry away dead tree branches under contract with the city. As has been seen, it could be said that the tree surgeon violated the rule because he is a person and brought a vehicle into the park. It also could be said that the city, not a "person" within the meaning of the rule, brought the vehicle into the park through its contract with the tree surgeon. At this point, the language of the rule gives no further guidance. The lawyers and judges must look elsewhere.

Assume further, then, that from a previously decided case we know, or from common sense all involved would agree, that it is no violation of the rule for an ambulance to enter the park to minister aid to a stricken jogger. Assume also that we know or can agree that it is a violation of the rule for teenagers to race cars in the park. Now the question may be posed: Is the tree surgeon's truck case more like the ambulance case or more like the teenagers' racing cars case?

It would seem that one can reach a reasoned answer to the question, though the reasons do not line up to produce that answer as numbers line up to produce a sum. The ambulance case shows that the statute cannot be interpreted literally, as prohibiting all persons from bringing any vehicle into any city park under any circumstances. There is room for interpretation. The teenagers' racing cars case suggests, by inference in light of common sense, that the rule seeks to protect the park and those who seek rest and recreation in the park from noisy and dangerous activities involving vehicles. Like the rule, the city and the tree surgeon were maintaining the park for the benefit of persons who use it. A city park is not a national wilderness area, in which virtually no intrusion whatsoever may be allowed. The short intrusion on the tranquillity of the park is small in relation to the benefits. It would be absurd in this day to require the tree surgeon to carry the tree branches out of the park by manual labor or horse-drawn cart (if that is not a "vehicle"). Accordingly, the tree surgeon should not be punished under the rule as properly interpreted.

From a different perspective, a further reason can be given for emphasizing the study of cases: They force lawyers and judges to think *hard* about justice in society. To a large extent in the U.S. legal system, it is thought that justice will emerge from the arguments of adversaries before a judge. Lawyers not only are engaged in protecting a client's interests but also participate in the search for justice, which likely will concern the court because the judge is disinterested as between the parties and isolated from the political process. Predicting what a judge will do or persuading a judge of what should be done requires the lawyer to appeal to the justice of the case.

Moreover, the action of the state to settle a dispute, the decision in a law case, is coercive action by the state involving at least the threatened use of physical force by the state. The law that determines when that power may be used—when the sheriff may deprive an individual of liberty or property pursuant to judicial decree—also determines the limits of freedom from a major form of state compulsion. The law at the same time defines the legitimate use of force by the state and the scope of individual liberty, in a major respect. It is an effort to rule out arbitrary or oppressive uses of power by the state while allowing justifiable uses of that power. The lawyer is society's expert on when (in what cases) the state may use its coercive powers legitimately.

Cases, much more than rules, press lawyers and judges to think hard about justice, the limits of proper governmental power, and the scope of individual freedom. It is easy to agree, for example, on a general rule that promises should be kept. But should the state enforce your promise to pay me $500 for the Eiffel Tower, should you decide not to keep your promise? Would it make a difference if the Eiffel Tower in mind were a stage prop I had delivered to you for use in a play? Again, should the state enforce your promise to join me for dinner at my lodge, should you decide not to keep your promise? Would it make a difference if I had paid you to give an after-dinner speech? What, exactly, should it mean to "enforce" that promise when the dinner is history?

Cases display the complexities with which the law must deal. Comparing and contrasting cases supply the particularities that are needed for lawyers to predict intelligently what a court will do or persuade a court of what it should do in a particular case, and for judges to make reasoned decisions in problem cases. Comparing and contrasting cases requires hard, rigorous thinking about justice and the proper role of government in a free and democratic society. As one philosopher suggested in a different context:

> Principles and laws may serve us well. They can help us to bring to bear on what is now in question, what is not now in question. They help us to connect one thing with another and another. But at the bar of reason, always the final appeal is to cases.[7]

---

[7]J. Wisdom, A Feature of Wittgenstein's Technique, in J. Wisdom, Paradox and Discovery 90, 102 (1965).

CHAPTER TWO

The Analogical Form of Legal Reasoning

LEGAL PROBLEMS IN THE United States may be governed by the common law, enacted law, or both kinds of law. In a pure common law system, official lawmaking is by judges on a case-by-case basis. Legal reasoning starts with a decided case and largely takes the form of an analogy. In a pure system of enacted law, official lawmaking is by an official body (e.g., a legislature) that enacts general rules (e.g., constitutions, statutes, codes, or regulations). Legal reasoning starts with a rule and largely takes a deductive form. This chapter will present and analyze the analogical form of legal reasoning in a common law context. Chapter 3 takes up the deductive form of legal reasoning in a statutory context, and Chapter 4 examines some relationships between the two forms of legal reasoning.

This chapter will show that the analogical form of legal reasoning makes a significant contribution to the rationality of legal thought. It establishes a framework for analysis that serves in appropriate cases to identify the proper starting points for reasoning, organize the relevant materials, and frame the issues for predictions, persuasions, or decisions. However, the analogical form itself is not sufficient for making good predictions, persuasions, and decisions. It leaves unclear which of the many facts in a case are reasons and will or should lead a court to decide the case one way or the other. The problem of deciding which facts in a case thus are the important facts (the "problem of importance") requires that the analogical form of legal reasoning be supplemented.

A. The Analogical Form

The central tenet of the common law is the principle of stare decisis, which means roughly that like cases should be decided alike. It is sometimes expressed as the doctrine of precedent or the principle of equal treatment under the law. Reasoning under the principle of stare decisis is reasoning by analogy, or by example.

Analogical reasoning is familiar in a number of everyday non-legal situations. For example, when Mother allows Older Brother to stay up until 9:00 P.M. and Younger Brother claims the same treatment, Younger Brother probably is claiming that he is like Older Brother because both are children (a fact). He thinks that therefore they are alike and should be treated alike. When Mother rejects his claim and explains that older children need less sleep than younger children (another fact), she is asserting that there is an important difference between the two children and that therefore they should not be treated alike. For a second example, Mother's view that one simply cannot invite to the wedding Cousin Matilda, who lives in town, without also inviting Cousin Wilbur, who lives in Europe, reflects some underlying belief that the two cousins should be treated alike because they both are cousins. Daughter's response that only persons who live nearby should be invited reflects her claim that Cousin Matilda and Cousin Wilbur are not alike in an important respect and therefore should not be treated alike.

In the abstract, analogical reasoning in any setting requires three steps. First, one must start with a *base-point* situation from which to reason (the treatment of Older Brother, Cousin Matilda) and assume that the treatment of the base-point situation was in some sense correct under the circumstances. Second, one must describe those factual respects in which the base-point situation and the problem situation (Younger Brother, Cousin Wilbur) are *similar* (childhood status, cousinhood status); and those factual respects in which the two situations are *different* (age, geographical proximity). Third, one must determine whether the factual similarities or the differences are more *important* under the circumstances and thus should control the decision in the problem situation.

The second and third steps are made necessary by the simple logic of analogies. No two persons, acts, or things ever will be alike in all factual respects. The claim that two persons, acts, or things are alike is not a claim that they are identical (as in the arithmetical conception of equality). If identical, they would not be two and could not be compared or contrasted at all. Nor will any two persons, acts, or things ever be different in all factual respects. If different in all factual respects, they could not both be persons, acts, or things, and comparing or contrasting them would be pointless. Therefore, analogical reasoning requires careful consideration of both the similarities and the differences between two situations and then a judgment whether the similar respects or different respects are more important under the circumstances.

Analogical reasoning is highly situational, or dependent on context. It is largely pointless to ask whether Older Brother and Younger Brother are alike or unalike in the abstract: They are both. Likeness or unalikeness in an important respect makes sense only in a concrete setting, as in the example involving bedtime. Even then, the ascription of likeness or unalikeness may change with the circumstances. Given the fact of a three-year difference in age, for example, the two brothers may be unalike for purposes of bedtime at ages 3 and 6 but alike for the same purposes some years later. And they may be different for purposes of bedtime while similar for purposes of distributing Christmas presents fairly.

Analogical reasoning in most familiar nonlegal settings also is highly informal. What will count as a base point, or an important similarity or difference under the circumstances, is determined by the individuals involved for whatever reasons they find appealing. Their imaginations are left free rein; their intuitions are left unbridled. Rarely are they quite aware that they are reasoning "by analogy" or are analyzing (1) the propriety of a base point, (2) the factual similarities and differences between two situations, and (3) the relative importance of the factual similarities and differences under the circumstances.

B. The Analogical Form of Legal Reasoning

Legal reasoning in the analogical form is not fundamentally different from analogical reasoning in most familiar nonlegal situations. It is more formal and consequently is more self-conscious, rigorous, and uniform in expression than is reasoning in everyday life. Underlying good legal reasoning of this kind are certain well-accepted rules of the game that help identify the proper base points for argument, a vocabulary and method that encourage rigorous consideration of both similarities and differences between a decided case and a problem case, and a form of expression for framing the issue to be decided when making predictions, persuasions, and decisions. The analogical form, however, does not solve the problem of importance; that is, it does not indicate whether the factual similarities or the differences between two cases are more important under the circumstances and thus will or should lead a court to decide the case one way or the other.

1. Precedents

The first step in analogical reasoning is the selection of a proper base point with which to compare and contrast the problem situation. The doctrine of precedent gives a special status as base points to law cases that were decided in the past by the highest court in the jurisdiction in which a problem case arises.[1] The U.S. legal system includes a federal jurisdiction in which federal courts are primarily responsible for certain matters of national interest, and the U.S. Supreme Court is the highest court for these matters. It also includes fifty state jurisdictions in which state courts carry primary responsibility for most other matters. Each state has a highest court, usually called the supreme court of the state. The cases decided in the past by these courts are the best *precedents* for the decision of future cases within their respective jurisdictions. That is, the precedents of the highest court in a jurisdiction are the most authoritative base points for reasoning in the analogical form concerning legal problems within that jurisdiction.

Of less, but considerable, significance are other cases that can serve as useful base points. The precedents of any court (including foreign courts) may be used as the base point for analogical argument before any other court. If the case is not a precedent of the relevant jurisdiction, it nonetheless may be a well-reasoned decision that the court will find persuasive. Hypothetical cases found in the scholarly literature or the American Law Institute's Restatements of the Law similarly may be used as persuasive base points when reasoning in the analogical form. Additionally, lawyers and judges sometimes use hypothetical cases of their own construction when the result in such cases is not controversial among all relevant persons.

This explanation of the relevant base points in common law adjudication simplifies the rules of the game. For example, it is open to the highest court in a problem case to *overrule* its own precedents. The case that overrules earlier cases then becomes the proper base point for future cases, in place of the earlier cases, thereby effecting a change in the law. Overruling is not a common

---

[1] *Jurisdiction* refers to the scope of a court's power to decide cases lawfully. It may be defined in territorial, citizenship, functional, or other terms.

occurrence, though the possibility is ever-present. The complex relationships among courts are treated in several law school courses in far greater detail than is appropriate to this introduction. It suffices here to understand that legal reasoning proceeds on the basis of formal rules of the game that identify the authoritative and otherwise acceptable base points for legal reasoning in the analogical form.

2. *Factual Similarities and Differences*

The second step in analogical reasoning is the identification of factual similarities and differences between the base-point situation and a problem situation. Legal reasoning in the analogical form uses a vocabulary and rhetoric that emphasizes the need for rigorous attention to both relationships. In controversial cases, which are the problem cases that require lawyerly skill because reasonable arguments are available to both parties, there will be many precedents that are facially similar to the problem case but that seem to cut both ways. By rigorous analysis of the facts of the cases the legal analyst will proceed to identify the many plausible points of factual similarity and difference. A judgment whether the similarities or differences are more important under the circumstances can be made intelligently only after identifying the range of plausible points of comparison and contrast.

A judge or decision *follows precedent* when the facts of a previously decided case are sufficiently similar to those of a problem case for justice to require like treatment of the two cases (unless the earlier case is overruled). A judge or case *distinguishes precedent* when the facts of a previously decided case are sufficiently different for justice to require different treatment of the two cases. There is no reason to presume in advance of rigorous analysis that a facially similar precedent should be followed or distinguished. The principle that like cases should be decided alike implies that unalike cases should be decided unalike if the differences are more important under the circumstances. Stare decisis requires as much that judges distinguish unalike precedents as that they follow like precedents.

In principle, then, the doctrine of precedent requires the judge to treat each relevant authoritative precedent in one of three ways: The judge may follow a precedent, distinguish it, or overrule it. A judge may not in good conscience ignore a relevant authoritative precedent, though this sometimes happens and becomes a ground for criticizing the judge. In their arguments, lawyers similarly are expected to advocate that each relevant authoritative precedent be followed, distinguished, or, less commonly, overruled.[2] Legal arguments are seriously vulnerable if they ignore a relevant authoritative precedent that does not support the point.

Whether a judge should follow or distinguish a precedent depends in part on a careful analysis of the facts of the precedent in relation to the facts of a problem case. The facts of a case consist of a description of the events in the world that set the stage for the dispute, how the parties came to find themselves in dispute, and sometimes what the parties did to try to resolve the dispute on their own. These are all events that normally occur before a court is called on to settle the dispute and mostly can be described in ordinary, nontechnical language. The facts of a case also include a description of the legal proceedings in the lower courts, if any, as necessary to identify the legal point (the *legal issue*) that was or may be appealed to the higher court. The issue on appeal always involves the question whether the trial judge erred in making some particular decision under the factual circumstances in the particular case. The facts and the legal issue establish the context in which the judgment of importance will be made at the third step.

A legal analyst compiles the facts of the problem case, as they have been or may be proved in court, and analyzes them until they are understood with great particularity. A detailed mastery of the legally provable facts is necessary because the presence or absence of a particular fact may become the point on which a precedent is determined to be alike or unalike in an important respect: One does not know which facts will matter, at the early stages of legal analysis. Good lawyers err on the side of compiling more facts in greater detail than they are likely to need in the course of legal proceedings.

The legal analyst using the analogical form then locates (by thoughtful legal research) the facially similar precedents and analyzes the facts of the precedents. Here again, it is necessary to gain a masterful understanding of the facts in great detail, though the facts as summarized in the official reports of decided cases normally are sufficient for this purpose. The lawyer does not yet know

---

[2]The American Bar Association's Code of Professional Responsibility (1976) sets forth a comprehensive set of ethical considerations and disciplinary rules governing the practice of law in those jurisdictions in which it is adopted. Under EC 7-23, a lawyer who knows of "legal authority in the controlling jurisdiction directly adverse" to his client's position must disclose it.

which facts will or should matter when a court decides to follow or distinguish each facially similar precedent. The judge will want to know all plausible similarities and differences before deciding which are more important under the circumstances.

Only then can the analyst identify the factual similarities and differences between a precedent and a problem case. Doing so, of course, is not a mechanical matter of finding identical statements in the descriptions of the cases. Lawyers often summarize the facts in their own language. This allows room for creativity and insight into relationships among the facts that overly technical or thoughtless descriptions sometimes mask. It also allows room for some distortion of the facts, though opposing counsel, higher courts, and fellow judges can be expected to point out such distortions.

Highly rigorous analysis of the facts thus is encouraged by the practice of following or distinguishing all facially similar precedents that are not overruled. Whether two cases will be regarded as alike or unalike in the more important respects depends on the facts of the problem case, the facts of the precedents, and the plausible relationships of similarity or difference between the congeries of facts. Prior to such an analysis of the facts, it should not be thought that a facially similar precedent is more likely to be followed or distinguished in any problem case. Accordingly, mastery of the facts to identify all plausible factual relationships is an essential step in analogical legal reasoning.

3. The Problem of Importance

The third step for analogical reasoning is determining whether the factual similarities or the differences between the two situations are more important under the circumstances. Legal reasoning in the analogical form similarly requires a judgment whether facially similar precedents should be followed or distinguished (assuming away any question of overruling). The judge in a law case, however, is not free to assign importance to the similarities or differences between cases on any ground whatsoever. The judge's duty is to decide that question in accordance with the law. But it is most difficult to give a satisfactory account of what it might mean in common law adjudication to decide *in accordance with the law*. This is where the problem of importance arises.

A natural inclination is to think that deciding in accordance with the law means following the common law rules at this third step and, thus, to depart from the analogical form of legal reasoning. The common law rules are rules announced by judges in their opinions in cases governed by the common law. These rules, one might think, should perform two functions: They should identify the legally important facts in advance of a case and what legal consequences follow if the important facts are present in a case. For example, a common law rule might provide that "If a man dies without a will, then his property shall become the property of his eldest son." The man's death without a will would be a possible fact. The legal consequence of its occurrence would be the transfer of his property to the eldest son. The law would make the judgment of important in advance of the materialization of a case; the important fact would be that of a man's death without a will. The judge in a case would not be free to decide that any other fact is important enough to justify a different legal consequence.

To elaborate, such a common law rule would take the form (or be translatable into the form) of an "if . . . , then . . . " statement. For example: If facts a, b and c are present but fact d is not, then the defendant shall be held liable for the plaintiff's damages. A legal rule in this form would tell an analyst that facts a, b, c and d are important in cases governed by the rule that the presence of a, b and c together with the absence of d shall result in the defendant's liability. The "if . . . " clause would state the necessary and sufficient factual conditions that require invoking the legal consequence stated in the "then . . . " clause. Common law rules often are expressed or may be translated into a form approximating this simple scheme.

This form of expression can be illustrated, and its serious difficulties in common law adjudication exposed, by an extended example.[3] Five hypothetical cases will be described in an order in which they might be decided in a common law jurisdiction. The statement of facts and legal reasoning are given in a simplified form that represents what a court might write in a published opinion. Each story starts with Costello, the original owner of five horses and a somewhat naive and too-trusting friend of Abbott's. Each horse came by theft or fraud into the hands of Abbott, and Costello sought to recover possession of the horse from Abbott or someone who came into possession of the horse after Abbott sold it. To help the reader keep the facts straight, a diagram of the factual relationships in each case appears as Figure 2-1.

---

[3]The illustrations are adapted from Fuller, The Forms and Limits of Adjudication, 92 Harv. L. Rev. 353, 375-376 (1978).

Figure 2-1

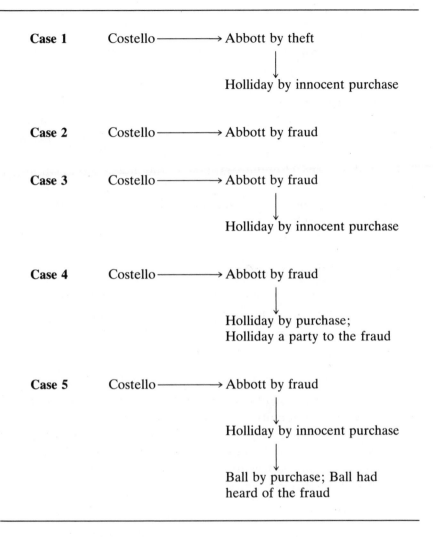

Case 1   Costello ⟶ Abbott by theft
                          ↓
                 Holliday by innocent purchase

Case 2   Costello ⟶ Abbott by fraud

Case 3   Costello ⟶ Abbott by fraud
                          ↓
                 Holliday by innocent purchase

Case 4   Costello ⟶ Abbott by fraud
                          ↓
                 Holliday by purchase;
                 Holliday a party to the fraud

Case 5   Costello ⟶ Abbott by fraud
                          ↓
                 Holliday by innocent purchase
                          ↓
                 Ball by purchase; Ball had
                 heard of the fraud

CASE 1

Abbott stole a horse belonging to Costello and sold it to Holliday, who did not know and had no reason to know it had been stolen from Costello. Costello sued Holliday to recover the horse. Costello won.

The court in Case 1 might give as its reasoning a general rule: A person who purchases property from a seller who did not own the property does not acquire ownership and must return the property to the rightful owner. The court then might apply the rule to the facts of the case: Holliday purchased the horse from Abbott, a thief who did not own it. This evidently yields as a conclusion: Holliday did not acquire ownership of the horse from Abbott and must return it to Costello.

CASE 2

Abbott bought a horse from Costello, giving as payment a forged check on another person's account. Abbott knew the check was forged. After delivering the horse to Abbott, Costello discovered the fraud and sued Abbott to recover the horse. Costello won.

The court in Case 2 might give as its reasoning another general rule: A person who acquires possession of property by fraudulent purchase does not acquire ownership and must return the property to the rightful owner. Application of the rule: Abbott acquired possession of the horse by purchase with a fraudulent check. Conclusion: Abbott did not acquire ownership of the horse and must return it to Costello. So far, so good.

CASE 3

The facts are similar to Case 2, except that Abbott sold the horse to Holliday. Holliday knew that Abbott had bought the horse from Costello, but did not know or have reason to know that Abbott paid with a forged check. Costello sued Holliday to recover the horse. Holliday won.

If the rules announced in the precedents were "the law" that determines the results in future cases, Case 3 would have to go the other way. The combination of the rules announced in Cases 1 and 2 would seem to require that Costello win. Case 2 announces as a rule that people who fraudulently acquire possession of property do not acquire ownership; Case 1 announces as a rule that a person without ownership of property cannot transfer ownership to another. In Case 3, Abbott did not acquire ownership of the horse, under the rule in Case 2. By finding for Holliday, however, the court seems to ignore the rule in Case 1, for it finds Holliday owns the horse when Abbott did not. There are many cases on the books that decide Case 3 for Holliday, in jurisdictions that decide Cases 1 and 2 for Costello and that also recognize a general rule like that in Case 1.

The court in Case 3 could craft a new rule that is consistent with the results in all three cases. It could announce, for example, that an owner of property who loses possession of the property by another's wrongful act may recover possession only from the perpetrator or from a subsequent purchaser if the wrongful act was theft. But surely this is quite a change from the rule given in Case 1. Moreover, this new rule would be announced *after* the decision in Case 3; the judgment of importance would be made by the court in Case 3 rather than by the rule in advance of Case 3. The new rule would not have been on the books for the lawyers to use in predicting what the court would do in Case 3 or persuading the court of what it should do in Case 3.

How reliable, then, would be the rule of Case 3 for predicting or persuading in Cases 4 and 5?

CASE 4

The facts are similar to Case 3, except that Holliday had helped Abbott perpetrate a fraud on Costello. Costello sued Holliday to recover the horse.

CASE 5

The facts are similar to Case 3, except that after buying the horse from Abbott, Holliday sold and delivered it to Ball. Ball had heard rumors of the fraud worked on Costello by Abbott. Costello sued Ball to recover the horse.

The court in Case 3 modified the rule of Case 1 to do justice in Case 3. The court in Case 4 similarly could modify the rule of Case 3 to do justice in Case 4. And the same is true in Cases 5 et seq.

The form of expression that purports to treat the results in common law cases as a consequence of preexisting rules thus does not reflect accurately the process of common law decision. As Professor Edward H. Levi put it, "[t]he rules change as the rules are applied. More important, the rules arise from a process which, while comparing fact situations, creates the rules and then applies them."[4] Judges in common law cases may write as if the law has always been what it has come to be, but this is well known to be a fiction.

An inclination to regard the judgment of importance as a function of preexisting legal rules of this sort is misleading in a further way. Despite its common use in common law cases, this form of expression is not at all compatible with reasoning analogically. Indeed, reasoning by analogy would be analytically superfluous if there were rules of this sort and they worked as their form of expression seems to suggest. Such a rule could simply be applied to the facts of a new case. There would be no need to search out the precedents or analyze the facts of the precedents to identify similarities and differences between the precedents and the problem case. The principle of stare decisis itself would serve no purpose, nor would studying cases be so important. Rather, we would study primarily rules and collect them in textbooks that contain little other than the rules.

To avoid this undesired result,[5] a basic principle of common law adjudication is that a judge is empowered to decide the case before the court and only the case before the court. A judge has no authority at common law to enact an authoritative general rule to govern parties and situations that were not before the court. The judge in Case 1 could not decide how Case 3 must be decided, however broadly she may craft a rule to explain the decision in Case 1. In all likelihood, the judge in Case 1 had not considered the facts of Cases 3 et seq. when crafting the general rule. Its mechanical application in later cases may yield a thoughtless and arbitrary result. Moreover, the parties in the later cases are entitled to their days in court. They should not have their disputes resolved on the basis of the facts and arguments put before the court by others in Case 1 only because the language employed by the court in its opinion in Case 1 was sufficiently general to be so used.

---

[4]E. Levi, An Introduction to Legal Reasoning 3-4 (1948).
[5]See Chapter 1 §D.

This principle is reinforced by the practice of distinguishing between the *holding* of a precedent and its *dicta*. The holding is a statement that captures in a sentence or two the probable significance of a single precedent as a base point for reasoning by analogy in future cases. It summarizes the important facts in the precedent case—the facts that are likely to become a point of important similarity or difference between the precedent and a problem case, largely as perceived by the court in the precedent case. It also states the legal consequence that followed from those facts in that case. A holding technically is less general than a common law rule, which may be stated in a court's opinion but does not contain the particularities needed to convey the short story of the particular case. As will be seen, a common law rule may be used as a major premise in legal reasoning in the deductive form; a holding is used as a base point in analogical legal reasoning.

A holding summarizes what was decided in a single case in which the judge did not and could not decide an entire class of cases. It does not purport to determine the result in other cases involving different parties under different circumstances. Those cases will be decided when they materialize and will be treated in accordance with the holding of a precedent if they then are determined to be like the precedent in important respects. A holding may have broad implications for a class of future cases, but whether a problem case is within that class or not will be decided when the case materializes and is brought before a court.

Common law rules largely are part of the dicta of a case. The dicta include those statements in the court's opinion that go beyond what was necessary to decide the case before the court. Dicta lack the full status of law because they purport to exceed the powers of a common law judge. Dicta can be quite useful when predicting what the court will do or persuading someone of what that court should do in future cases because they often express truthfully the court's inclinations on matters it expects to come before it. But the holding of a case has the privileged states of "the law"; dicta merely forecast, in a vague and less reliable way, what the law is likely to become.

For example, the holding of Case 1 above is that an owner of property who is the victim of a theft can recover possession of the property from a purchaser who bought it from the thief, even if the purchaser did not know or have reason to know that it was buying stolen property. Without casting doubt on the holding in Case 1, the court in Case 3 properly can hold that an owner of property who is the victim of a fraud cannot recover possession of the property from a purchaser who, not knowing or having reason to know of the fraud, bought it from the perpetrator of the fraud. It thus decides that the difference between fraud and theft is an important difference that requires different treatment of the cases. Similarly, the court in Case 4 can hold that a purchaser who helped perpetrate a fraud on the original owner is not like the purchaser in Case 3, which decided only that the owner cannot recover possession of the property from an innocent purchaser—one who did not know and had no reason to know of the fraud. It thus decides that Case 4 is more like Case 2, in which the owner sued the perpetrator of the fraud himself, than it is like Case 3, in which the owner sued a subsequent purchaser who was not complicit in the fraud.

In each case as the law unfolds, the general rule announced in a prior case may be given effect only to the extent that the holding of the precedent and the principle of stare decisis are determined to require. It all depends on the finding of similarity or difference in the more important respects between the facts of the precedent and the facts of the problem case, not necessarily on the announced general rules that stand in substantial part as dicta. The general rule announced in Case 1 ("A person who purchases property from a seller who did not own the property does not acquire ownership and must return the property to the rightful owner") can be disregarded properly in Case 3 because it is dictum insofar as it is more general than the holding ("An owner of property who is the victim of a theft can recover possession of the property from a purchaser who bought it from the thief, even if the purchaser did not know or have reason to know that it was buying stolen property").

The analogical form captures significant aspects of legal reasoning at common law (and, it will be seen, in other settings). The horse trading illustration shows how the analogical form provides a vocabulary and frames an issue for decision and thus contributes to the rationality of legal thought. In Case 5, for example, a judge must decide whether one who, having heard rumors of the fraud, buys a horse from an innocent purchaser who bought it from one who took possession by fraud, is *more like* one who bought a horse fraudulently (Case 2) or from a thief (Case 1), or *more like* one who, not knowing or having reason to know of the fraud, bought a horse from one who took possession by fraud (Case 3). Legal arguments in Case 5 can be expected to address that legal issue,

posed in the analogical form, through an analysis of factual similarities and differences in the cases.

But what does lead a court to determine that, for example, the
difference between fraud and theft in Cases 1 and 3 is an important
difference that requires different results in those two cases? Fraud
and theft are alike in some respects because both are wrongful in
the eyes of the law. But they are unalike in other respects because
fraud at common law most often is a civil wrong, not punished by
imprisonment, while theft at common law is more serious and is
treated as a criminal wrong, punished by imprisonment. The courts
often regard the difference here as more important than the similarity, at least when the subsequent purchaser is an innocent one.
Similarly, the precedents are like Case 5 in some respects because
the original owner is the victim of wrongful behavior in all of these
cases. They are unlike Case 5 in other respects because none involved a purchaser who had heard of the wrongful behavior and
bought the horse from a purchaser who was wholly innocent and
herself would win in a suit by the original owner, as in Case 3. The
resolution of the key issues remains a mystery, so far as the formal
analysis of analogical legal reasoning takes one.[6]

The analogical form of legal reasoning leaves the crucial third
step—the judgment of importance under the circumstances—
wholly unaddressed. As Professor H.L.A. Hart put it:

> [T]hough "Treat like cases alike and different cases differently" is a
> central element in the idea of justice, it is by itself incomplete and,
> until supplemented, cannot afford any determinate guide to con-
> duct. . . . [U]ntil it is established what resemblances and differences
> are relevant, "Treat like cases alike" must remain an empty form.
> To fill it we must know when, for the purposes in hand, cases are to
> be regarded as alike and what differences are relevant.[7]

C. Summary

Thus, analogical legal reasoning—reasoning from cases—is
but a formal version of the analogical reasoning used in everyday
life. It is governed by the principle of stare decisis, the principle
that like cases should be decided alike and unalike cases should be
decided unalike if the differences are important. This form of rea-

---

[6]For further discussion, see Chapters 4 §A, 6 §C.
[7]H. Hart, The Concept of Law 155 (1961).

soning requires three steps: (1) identifying a proper base point, or precedent, (2) identifying factual similarities and differences between a base point and a problem situation, or analyzing the facts to compare and contrast the precedent with the problem case, and (3) determining whether the factual similarities or the differences are more important under the circumstances, or deciding whether to follow or distinguish the precedent.

The practice among lawyers and judges of reasoning in the analogical form establishes a framework of analysis that usefully identifies starting points for reasoning, organizes the relevant materials, and frames the issue for prediction, persuasion, or decision in a problem case at common law. It thus contributes to the rationality of legal thought. But the crucial third step in such reasoning is left unguided. Judging which facts are more important under the circumstances remains mysterious activity, subject to little apparent governance by the analogical form or the rules of the common law.

This key problem—the problem of importance—will be treated more fully in Part II. The next chapter presents and analyzes legal reasoning in the deductive form in an enacted law context. It will be seen that the deductive form shares this problem of importance with the analogical form of legal reasoning. Indeed, the problem of attaching importance to the facts in cases is the central problem of legal reasoning in any form.

CHAPTER THREE

The Deductive Form of Legal Reasoning

LEGAL REASONING IN THE deductive form is most closely associated with reasoning from enacted law, which principally consists of general rules. Such rules are found in a variety of official legal documents, such as constitutions, statutes, codes, regulations, and executive orders.[1] They usually are enacted and published by a group of people who are authorized to make law, such as the Congress, a state legislature, or executive and administrative agencies. For convenience, this chapter will speak primarily of statutes enacted by Congress or a state legislature, though what is said largely applies to other enacted rules (and, as will be seen in the next chapter, common law rules).

Legal reasoning in the deductive form from enacted rules differs from analogical legal reasoning in a number of key respects. First, the enactment of a rule usually occurs before any case governed by the rule materializes. The starting point for reasoning is the rule, not a case. Second, the principle of legislative supremacy, founded on principles of constitutional democracy, generally requires judges to play a subordinate role to the more democratic branches of government, which enact many rules, because the judges generally are less controllable by the electorate.[2] Accordingly, a judge has no authority to modify the language of a duly enacted rule as the case law interpreting that rule unfolds. Its expression remains static, as it was enacted, until the nonjudicial lawmaker amends it or repeals it. Nor may a judge ignore an applicable enacted rule, which displaces any inconsistent common

---

[1]This form of reasoning also is employed with rules "enacted" by private persons in the form of contracts, wills, corporate charters, and the like. What is said in this chapter applies to private law of this kind with some modifications.

[2]The principle of constitutional supremacy and the doctrine of judicial review make out an important exception to this statement. For further discussion, see Chapter 11 §B.

law. Third, the static expression of enacted rules in abstract language leads legal reasoning from such rules to focus heavily on problems of language interpretation. The judicial task largely is to decide on the membership of a particular problem case in abstract classes of cases designated, in principle, by the language of the enacted rules.

A. The Deductive Form

Like analogical reasoning, deductive reasoning[3] is familiar in a variety of everyday nonlegal contexts. A common point of comparison is to the rules of a game. In the board game "Monopoly," for example, it is a rule that any player who passes "Go" receives $200 unless that player is on his way to "Jail." It is easy to determine when a player named Oscar passes "Go," not being on his way to "Jail." Oscar's entitlement to $200 then follows automatically. Deductive reasoning also is used extensively in more serious settings. A teacher may announce that (only and all) students who answer 90 percent or more of the questions correctly on a test will receive an "A." If Martha then answers 92 percent correctly on a test, it should follow automatically that she is entitled to an "A." It follows as automatically that she is not so entitled if she answers correctly fewer than 90 percent of the questions on the test.

In the abstract, this version of deductive reasoning requires three steps. First, having reviewed the factual situation superficially, one must establish a relevant *major premise* (if a player passes 'Go," not being on the way to "Jail," then the player gets $200; only if a student answers correctly 90 percent or more of the questions on a test shall the student receive an "A"). Second, one must formulate a *minor premise* in the language of the major premise (Oscar passed "Go," not being on his way to jail; Martha scored 92 percent on a test). Third, one must use the relationship of the major and minor premises to yield a necessary *conclusion* (Oscar is entitled to $200; Martha is entitled to an "A").

Logicians call this form of reasoning a *syllogism*. The conclusion of a valid syllogism follows necessarily from the premises. Thus,

---

[3]The term *deductive reasoning* is used here to refer primarily to deduction in the form of a syllogism. Other forms of deduction are possible but seem to capture less well the most notable forms of legal reasoning.

MAJOR PREMISE:	All men are mortal;
MINOR PREMISE:	Socrates is a man;
CONCLUSION:	Socrates is mortal.

A syllogism is "valid" if the conclusion must be true *if* the premises are true. In other words, only someone who is crazy or stupid would deny that Socrates is mortal while accepting both that all men are mortal and that Socrates is a man. A syllogism is "sound" when it is valid and the premises in fact are true. A conclusion that is supported by a sound syllogism is true because a logically valid syllogism transfers the truth of the premises to the conclusion. If supported only by a valid syllogism, the truth of the conclusion remains contingent on the unknown truth of the premises.

When used properly, syllogistic deductive reasoning is a powerful form of reasoning—much more powerful than the analogy. No analogical argument as such could yield a conclusion by logical necessity. The deductive form, however, can be easily misused, especially when employed in a real-world settings. It may, by its form, leave the impression that a conclusion is sound when this is far from the fact. Consider the following syllogism:

MAJOR PREMISE:	A foot has 39 inches.
MINOR PREMISE:	Susan has a foot.
CONCLUSION:	Susan has 39 inches.

The conclusion is patent nonsense, though the language of the premises yields the language of the conclusion in perfect mimicry of a proper argument. The major premise is false. The minor premise is uncertain if, for example, Susan in fact has two feet and that matters in the context. The conclusion is not sound, in any event, because the meaning of *foot* is different in the major and minor premises (as, less obviously, is the meaning of *has*). Any one such error robs the conclusion of its soundness.

The conclusions of legal reasoning commonly are expressed in the deductive form. But a syllogism, however logical in appearance, is only as good as its premises and the relationship between them. Legal reasoning in the deductive form is mindful of the potential hazards. Logical validity within this form often is regarded as necessary in legal reasoning, but in itself is of trivial importance. The key problems are (1) adopting a correct major premise; (2) formulating a correct minor premise in the language of the major premise; and (3) using the relationship of the premises to yield a sound conclusion.

B. The Deductive Form of Legal Reasoning

Legal reasoning in the deductive form, like analogical legal reasoning, is more formal than reasoning in most everyday nonlegal contexts. Underlying good legal reasoning of this kind are certain well-accepted rules of the game that help identify the proper major premises from which to reason. The major premises often are crafted to establish specific questions that must be asked in problem cases and the conclusions that might be reached legitimately. This is a valuable contribution to the rationality of legal thought. It will be seen, however, that the problems involved in adopting the premises and establishing a meaningful relationship between them are considerable. All steps require judgments of importance akin to those required in analogical reasoning. Consequently, the necessity promised by the deductive form often proves to be illusory on analysis. The problem of importance is the central problem for legal reasoning in the deductive form, as it is for analogical legal reasoning.

1. The Rule

The first step[4] in deductive reasoning is adopting a major premise that is relevant to the problem at hand. Similarly, the first step for legal reasoning in the deductive form is identifying the legal rules that plausibly may govern the case at hand. Enacted laws themselves generally provide descriptions of the classes of cases to which they might be applied. Careful reading and analysis of the official rules normally will narrow the class progressively. One will isolate a small number of specific provisions on which at least a part of the particular case will be decided, following completion of the second and third steps.[5]

To illustrate, assume a problem case as it might appear to a lawyer from an initial interview with a client in the law office. The following discussion will work through part of a major statute as

---

[4]The division of the analysis into three distinct steps is useful presentationally, but should not be taken to mirror accurately an actual mental process. See J. Dewey, Art as Experience 37-38 (Capricorn ed. 1958).

[5]On occasion, conflicting legal rules may be found that both seem to apply to a particular case. Problems of this sort are discussed in Chapter 7.

the lawyer might. It will illustrate how careful reading and analysis of the statutory text reduces progressively the class of cases with which the lawyer should be concerned and therefore the questions that must be asked to decide the problem case. Note that the discussion begins with the facts before searching for the applicable rule. These facts will be stated wholly in ordinary, nontechnical language and will give only a superficial account of what did happen. After locating a plausibly applicable rule, a lawyer probably would have to search out further facts in greater detail and then formulate minor premises that are suitable for deductive reasoning from the rule. The first impression that a particular rule applies could turn out to be wrong on more complete analysis.

Assume that Franny Farmer grows peaches at her small, family-run orchard in rural Georgia. She contacted Morris Auster, a buyer of produce for distribution in the Atlanta area. Farmer and Auster met on May 28 at the orchard. After inspecting the young fruits, they reached an agreement for Farmer to sell and Auster to buy 200 boxes of peaches per week for three weeks in July, from Farmer's orchard, at a price of $40.25 per box. They shook hands and departed, not having put their agreement into writing. On June 3, rural Georgia was struck by severe rain, winds, and flooding, damaging much of the state's peach crop for the season. Thinking that the shortage of peaches would cause the price to rise, Auster sent a signed letter to Farmer on June 10, stating that it was "to remind you of our agreement for you to sell me 200 boxes of peaches per week for three weeks in July at a price of $40.25 per box." Farmer did not reply. In July she sold all of her peaches to Bernard Berkowitz, at a price of $60.75 per box.

Auster went to see his lawyer. He wants to sue Farmer to enforce the contract. To determine whether it would be worthwhile to litigate, Auster's lawyer needs to predict what a court is likely to do in this case. This is a commercial transaction governed by a statute known as the Uniform Commercial Code (UCC).[6] On consulting the UCC, the lawyer will find many dozens of statutory sections grouped in nine general categories, called *Articles*. Which provisions might govern the Farmer case? Auster's lawyer, for

---

[6]The Uniform Commercial Code has been enacted as statutory law in forty-nine states and the District of Columbia. It was drafted and promoted by two nongovernmental organizations of the nation's leading lawyers, judges, and legal scholars — the National Conference of Commissioners on Uniform State Laws and the American Law Institute.

example, will see that Article 2 is titled "Sales" and will turn his attention directly here.

The lawyer will read the first provisions of Article 2 to determine whether it governs Auster's case. He will find that an early section provides that "this Article applies to transactions in goods" (Section 2-102). In the deductive form, he will ask if peaches are "goods" within the meaning of this provision. This is not a difficult legal issue. A nearby section of Article 2 provides that *goods* means "all things which are movable" and "includes growing crops" (Section 2-105(1)). Probably no one could argue successfully that the peaches in Auster's case were not "growing crops" and therefore "goods" within the meaning of Article 2. It probably will apply. Auster's lawyer will have narrowed the search to the class of commercial transactions involving sales of goods and therefore to the provisions of Article 2 of the UCC. The many rules that govern sales of land, sales of corporate stock, sales of services, other classes of sales, and other commercial transactions will have been excluded from further consideration.

Auster's lawyer then will find it useful to read through Article 2 to narrow further the scope of his problem. On reading another section (Section 2-201(1)), he might be disappointed to find that a class of contracts for the sale of goods must be in writing to be enforceable:

> Except as otherwise provided in this section a contract for the sale of goods for the price of $500 or more is not enforceable . . . unless there is some writing sufficient to indicate that a contract for sale has been made between the parties and signed by the party against whom enforcement is sought.

It might appear from this rule that the Auster/Farmer contract will fall in the class of unenforceable contracts, much to Auster's chagrin. The contract is for the sale of goods at a price of more than $500. Farmer is the "party against whom enforcement is sought" in the action by Auster to enforce the contract. She did not sign a writing of any kind. However, this would be a hasty conclusion because the rule applies "except as otherwise provided" in Section 2-201. One must read on.

The second subsection of Section 2-201 identifies a class of contracts that are enforceable even if they are for sales of goods for the price of $500 or more, and there is no writing signed by the party against whom enforcement is sought. The rule is fairly complicated one. It amounts to saying that some persons who *receive* a writing confirming a deal must object to the confirmation promptly or be precluded from using Section 2-201(1) to defeat enforcement of the deal. Section 2-201(2) provides:

> Between merchants if within a reasonable time a writing in confirmation of the contract and sufficient against the sender is received and the party receiving it has reason to know its contents, it satisfies the requirements of subsection (1) against such party unless written notice of objection of its contents is given within ten days after it is received.

This rule might apply in Auster's case, for Auster sent Farmer a letter to remind her of the deal, and she did not reply. Auster's lawyer might be able to use the rule in Section 2-201(2) as a major premise and formulate a minor premise that both is faithful to the facts and satisfies each element of the major premise. If so, Auster's case would fall within the class of enforceable contracts designated by Section 2-201(2), not the class of unenforceable contracts designated by Section 2-201(1).

The statutory rules identify the issues that must be addressed, often with particularity, and establish a uniform language for legal argument. The rules enable lawyers and judges to reason from a common point of departure and know the conclusions that they might reach legitimately. Accordingly, Auster's lawyer knows from the rules that to get a court to enforce the contract (so far as the requirement of a writing is concerned) he probably must show that the Auster/Farmer contract was "between merchants," that Auster's letter was a "writing in confirmation," that it was "received" by Farmer "within a reasonable time," and so on. Farmer's lawyer knows as well that she can defeat such an argument by showing that the Auster/Farmer contract was not "between merchants" or that Auster's letter was not a "writing in confirmation" or that Farmer did not "receive" the letter "within a reasonable time" and so on. A judge, of course, similarly knows that she must make a finding on each of the several separate issues to decide whether the requirements of Section 2-201(2) were met in Auster's case, at least if Auster's lawyer tries to make this argument.

The rules, however, do not themselves do more than this. These are the functions only of the major premise in the deductive form of legal reasoning. Having identified an authoritative major premise, the lawyers do not know that the Auster/Farmer contract in particular was "between merchants," that Auster's letter was a "writing in confirmation," or that Farmer "received" Auster's letter "within a reasonable time" after their meeting, if she received it at all. Until these and other questions are answered, the lawyers do not know whether the Auster/Farmer contract is enforceable by Auster. It remains to formulate a minor premise and to analyze the relationship of the premises to reach a sound conclusion.

2. The Facts

The second step for deductive reasoning is the formulation of a minor premise in the language of the major premise. Legal reasoning in the deductive form also must characterize the facts and do so in language that is suitable for reasoning validly from a legal rule. Here legal analysts confront a problem of considerable complexity: The facts in any case can be described in a variety of terms. Some characterizations of facts will be noncontroversial and fit the terms of an authoritative rule with little or no discomfort, as Farmer's peaches seem clearly to be "growing crops" and therefore "goods" within the meaning of that term in Article 2 of the UCC. Others, however, will be controversial and fit the terms of an authoritative rule awkwardly or with contradictory implications. In the latter cases, which are the ones that require skill in legal reasoning because reasonable arguments are available to both parties, the correct characterization of the facts cannot be determined from the language of a rule and its logical implications.

Auster's case will be used to illustrate the problems of characterizing facts for use in a legal syllogism. To facilitate concentration on this problem, the issues that were left on the table in the preceding subsection will be simplified. An authoritative rule of some complexity was identified and can be stated in the form of a major premise as follows:

> MAJOR PREMISE: If a contract for the sale of goods is between merchants, and within a reasonable time a writing in confirmation of the contract and sufficient against the sender was received, and the party receiving it had reason to know its contents, and notice of objection to its contents was not given within ten days after it was received, then the requirement that contracts for the sale of goods for a price of $500 or more be indicated by a writing signed by the party against whom

enforcement is sought (UCC Section 2-201(1)) is satisfied against the recipient.

As a practical matter, most of the many elements in the "if . . . " clause of the premise probably would not be controverted by the lawyers in Auster's case. For example, it was stated in the informal version of the facts above that Farmer did not reply to Auster's letter of May 10. That being so, Farmer's lawyer probably could not argue successfully that "written notice of objection to its contents" was given within ten days. Assume further that Auster's letter was a "writing in confirmation of the contract" and was "sufficient against the sender," that it was "received" "within a reasonable time" by Farmer, and that Farmer had "reason to know its contents." Thus, a more manageable, if artificial, major premise can be formulated for subsequent discussion:

MAJOR PREMISE: Only if a contract is between merchants and . . . , then the requirements of Section 2-201(1) are satisfied against the recipient.

One of two possible minor premises must be formulated if the lawyers are to reason from this simplified major premise in the deductive form. Either the Auster/Farmer contract was between merchants, or it was not between merchants. No other minor premises are capable of yielding a valid conclusion by deduction. Assuming that no other provisions in Article 2 are relevant to the question, one of two conclusions are possible. Either the requirements of Section 2-201(1) were satisfied against Farmer, or they were not satisfied against Farmer. Auster will win the point only if the first minor premise is the correct characterization of the facts.

The lawyers and the judge[7] must determine which minor premise is correct. One can assert that either is correct. Absent some sort of argument based on the facts, this does no more than identify a logically possible minor premise that could yield a logically possible conclusion by deduction. Because the opposite minor premise and conclusion also is a logical possibility, such an assertion has no predictive or persuasive value unless supplemented by further argument. Each party has a syllogistic argument of equal logical validity, and they are contradictory:

---

[7]In many cases, a jury also will participate in finding the facts. The jury role is excluded from the discussion to simplify matters.

MAJOR PREMISE: Only if a contract is between merchants and . . . , then the requirements of Section 2-201(1) are satisfied against the recipient.

MINOR PREMISE$_1$: The Auster/ Farmer contract was between merchants.	MINOR PREMISE$_2$: The Auster/ Farmer contract was not between merchants.
CONCLUSION$_1$: The requirements of Section 2-201(1) were satisfied against Farmer.	CONCLUSION$_2$: The requirements of Section 2-201(1) were not satisfied against Farmer.

The problem is to determine whether the Auster/Farmer contract in fact was or was not "between merchants." It is far from obvious which of the two characterizations of the facts is the proper one, as will be seen. The facts of a case simply do not come prepackaged in the language of the applicable rule. A description of facts often requires a choice of suitable language, and this requires interpretation of the language of the rule.

3. The Problem of Importance

The third step in deductive reasoning is using the relationship of the major and minor premises to yield a sound conclusion. Legal reasoning in the deductive form modifies the rigid progression of the formal deductive model. It has been seen that a minor premise cannot be formulated as a logical consequence of an authoritative rule and the facts in a case do not come prepackaged in the language of the rule. Legal reasoning in the deductive form combines the second and third steps both to package the facts as a minor premise and use the premises to yield a conclusion through a single process of reasoning. The result commonly continues to be expressed in the form of a legal syllogism. But it is constructed by judging the importance of the facts in light of a judicial interpretation of the authoritative rule — an interpretation that itself is not a product of deduction but depends on a judgment of importance.

Interpretation, in the narrow sense, is the intellectual process of giving meaning to linguistic symbols, such as the words or combinations of words that are found in legal rules. Interpretation is made necessary by certain common problems of language. Few, if any, words have one and only one meaning such that they refer to some object in the world with certainty. Proper names come closest to that ideal. Most words suffer from a lack of clarity in one or more of several ways. Words may have two or more identifiable meanings. The word *bar* is an example. Such words are called *ambiguous.* Words may have meanings that shade continuously from one to another with no line of demarcation. *Orange* and *yellow* are examples. Such words are called *vague.* And groups of words in a sentence may cause similar problems. In the sentence *The house had a gazebo in the yard which was yellow,* was the house or the gazebo or the yard the thing that was yellow? Such a lack of clarity may be called *sentence ambiguity.* All three forms of lack of clarity can necessitate interpretation of a legal rule and often do.

In everyday life, we normally think of the meaning of a word as its definition. Legal definitions of legal terms can be useful in easy cases. However, interpretation through definitions often transforms the problem of interpreting a rule into a problem of interpreting the definitions of its words, and a problem of interpreting the definitions into one of interpreting the definitions of a definition, and so on. When the last of the available definitions is found, there still may be vagueness or ambiguity in a particular case because of the problems of language.

In Auster's case, the term *between merchants* is defined in Section 2-104(3) of Article 2 of the UCC:

> "Between Merchants" means in any transaction with respect to which both parties are chargeable with the knowledge or skill of merchants.

The case is a bit unusual in that there also is a statutory definition of a part of a definition. *Merchant* is defined in Section 2-104(1) in relevant part as follows:

> "Merchant" means a person who deals in goods of the kind or otherwise holds himself out as having knowledge or skill peculiar to the practices or goods involved in the transaction. . . .

These definitions are helpful in narrowing further the scope of the problem, but they do not solve it. Auster probably is chargeable as a "merchant" because he "deals in goods of the kind." As a middleman between the growers and the Atlanta market, in any year he probably makes several hundred produce purchases and sales and several dozen peach purchases and sales. He is expected to know his trade well, and rightly so. Farmer's lawyer probably could not argue successfully that Auster is not chargeable as a "merchant" as defined.

For the contract to be enforceable against Farmer, however, it is necessary that "*both* parties be chargeable with the knowledge and skill of merchants." It is far from clear whether Farmer is or is not chargeable as a "merchant." She may make as few as one peach sale for a few deliveries in a year. Her orchard was described, you will recall, as a "small, family-run" business. She may not be a very sophisticated business person at all. Perhaps no one would expect that she should be. Farmer might "deal in goods of the kind" or might "otherwise hold herself out as having knowledge or skill" of the kind described. Or she might not.

The definitions are like a rule in a significant respect. The definitions themselves require interpretation because they may suffer from the problems of language. In the first part of the definition of *merchant,* the phrase *goods of the kind* may refer only to peaches or also to fruits, produce, or foodstuffs in a case like Auster's case. This phrase is ambiguous. Moreover, Farmer might deal or not deal in peaches. The word *deals* is vague because it is not known how much or what kind of business activity would make Farmer a dealer; her level of business activity is on a continuum of sorts from the consumer (who is not a merchant) to a big-time middleman like Auster (who surely is). And the phrase *between merchants* means "in any transaction with respect to which both parties are chargeable with the knowledge or skill of merchants," *not* more simply when both parties "are merchants." This suffers from a sort of sentence ambiguity: One who surely "deals in goods of the kind" might or might not be "chargeable with the knowledge or skill of merchants" if she does *not* also "hold [her]self out as having knowledge or skill peculiar to the practices or goods involved in the transaction." The definition of "between merchants" might refer to both parts of the definition of *merchant,* or it might refer only to the second part.

Consequently, legal reasoning in the deductive form confronts the problem of importance: What in particular would be the important facts that would establish whether Farmer is chargeable as a merchant because she "deals in goods of the kind"? Is Farmer more like Auster the merchant, or more like Bessie the consumer, who may make more peach purchases in a year than Farmer makes sales? Is the number of sales or purchases the important fact? The quantities involved? Is the difference between sales and purchases important? Is the fact that Auster both purchases and sells important? Is the fact that Auster and Farmer act for a profit, while Bessie does not, of importance? Is the fact that Auster deals in produce while Farmer deals, if at all, only in peaches important? Similarly, what in particular are the important facts that would establish whether Farmer is chargeable as a merchant because she "holds [her]self out as having knowledge or skill peculiar to the practices or goods involved in the transaction"? Must she say to Auster that she knows well the business practice of sending and responding to confirming letters—the "practices . . . involved in this transaction"? Must she say to Auster that she knows produce well—the "goods involved in the transaction"? Or would it be enough that she introduced herself to him as a business woman who grows and sells peaches in small quantities, or that she has a sign at the entrance to her orchard that announces to the world "FRANNY'S ORCHARDS—EXPERTS IN PEACHES"?

The rules and their definitions stop short of pointing directly at the important facts in the case—the particular facts that establish whether Farmer is a merchant such that the Auster/Farmer contract was "between merchants." The rules and their definitions stop short of providing the needed particularities for resolving the controversy in the case by deduction because the problems of language—ambiguity, vagueness, and sentence ambiguity—require the lawyer to supplement the rule. Moving from a rule, to a definition of the rule, to a definition of the definition, keeps the analysis in the realm of generalities. Eventually in the course of such an analysis, one will exhaust the rules and definitions that purport to determine which argument in a particular case is the correct one by deduction.[8] A judgment of importance then will be required in order to decide which facts are reasons that justify placing a problem case in a class of cases designated by a legal rule.

To help a statutory rule perform its functions, legal reasoning in the deductive form employs a number of source materials other than definitions. These other materials also do not supply the par-

---

[8]Lawyers sometimes consult a dictionary of English language, but it supplies at best another rule, which leads to the same problem one syllogism down the road. It more often supplies a number of definitions among which one must choose. The drafters of statutes often do not intend for the ordinary meaning of a word to be employed, especially when a term has been given a statutory definition that turns it into a term of art within the statute. As in the example, lawyers sometimes are less concerned with a single word than with a phrase or sentence or, as will be seen in Part II, much more.

ticularities that are needed to reach a sound conclusion by deduction and thus to avoid the problem of importance. For example, it often is said that a statute that is vague or ambiguous on its face should be interpreted to give effect to the intention of the legislature. This "intention" is well known to be a fictional thing. A legislature is a group of people; groups themselves do not have intentions, though individuals might. The remarks in debate by a bill's floor leader or the report of a single legislative committee or a statement by a legislator at a hearing each do not of necessity represent the intention of the deliberative body as such. Lacking such necessity, legal reasoning in the deductive form from such statements will not yield a necessarily sound conclusion. Only the language of the rules is approved by the group, and that returns an analyst to the starting point of the difficulties.

Moreover, if a reliable picture of the legislature's intention behind a text could be pieced together, what form would it take? It could be another general statement of what the law permits or requires in a class of cases—a rule or definition—which leads back into the problems of language. It could be an example of the intended effect of the rule in a hypothetical or historical situation, leaving one to reason analogically in a problem case that will be different from the historical or hypothetical situation in some respects and, again, with the problem of importance. Or it could be a statement of the rule's objective or purpose, in the abstract like a rule or in the particular like a case. In any event, the "intention of the legislature" will not supply the particularities that are needed to reason in the deductive form to a necessarily sound conclusion in a controversial problem case.

A number of other kinds of guidance may be available for interpreting a statutory text. We may be told to read a statute as a whole to give it a coherent meaning such that one provision is not interpreted to contradict another. We may be told to consider the legislative history, such as the floor debates, committee reports, and hearings before its enactment. We may be told to interpret a statute in the light of legal history, which is an account of how the common law and other legislatures would treat the problem in other times and places. And we may be told to interpret it in the light of historical, economic, and social circumstances at the time of its enactment.

All of these sources of information often are helpful and in fact are used in good legal reasoning, as will be seen in Chapter 4.

But the commonly expressed commandment merely to "take into account" such a wide variety of things generates considerable frustration. We feel that we have been told to think about everything before doing anything. That is a formula to ensure that we do nothing. We need some sense of what we are *looking for* in the enacted text as a whole, the complex legislative history, the centuries of legal history, or the multitude of historical, economic, and social circumstances at the time of enactment.

Surely none of these sources of information will supply the particularities that are needed to formulate minor premises that would allow one to reason deductively from an unclear legal rule to a necessarily sound conclusion. Some may provide examples of situations (historical or hypothetical) and the "intended" effect of the general rule in those particular situations. Again, that information can be used only analogically. Some may provide statements that are abstract and refer to classes of cases. That, again, will stop short of determining by necessity the membership of a particular case within the abstract class. In either event, the analyst is left with the problem of importance.

The problem of importance requires legal analysts to go beyond the problems of language that inhere in legal rules, definitions, and similar expressions. This should not be surprising. A rule is an abstract or general statement of what the law permits or requires of classes of persons in classes of circumstances—in classes of cases. A rule stands in contrast to a case—a short story of an incident in which the state acted or may act to settle a particular dispute. Thus, the language of an enacted rule, which normally is announced before any case governed by the rule materializes, describes an abstract class. The statement of conditions (the "if . . . " clause) points at the class of cases, not at the particular facts of any problem case.

When a word like *merchant* is copied from the condition part of a major premise and placed in the position of a minor premise, it does not carry with it what is necessary for it to establish the correctness of the characterization of the facts. It fails to point at the particular facts in a particular case but contines to point at a class of cases. Such a use of words leaves the minor premise, so to speak, dangling in the air. The connection between the abstract class and the particular case remains to be drawn; in the example, it remains to determine whether Farmer, in particular, is a member of the class of persons "chargeable as merchants." And it must be drawn by some process of reasoning that is not dependent on other rules or definitions that themselves will dangle similarly. As Oliver Wendell Holmes said long ago, "[g]eneral propositions do not decide concrete cases."[9]

To draw this all-important connection—to decide on the membership of a particular case within a legal class—requires a judgment of importance to identify the particular facts that justify the classification. Legal reasoning in the deductive form does not indicate how to make this judgment in the real-world situations that matter to lawyers and judges. The deductive form of legal reasoning promises a conclusion backed by logical necessity. At least in controversial cases, the problem of characterizing the facts of a case in the language of the rule robs the legal syllogism of its necessity.

C. Summary

Thus, it has been seen that deductive reasoning requires three steps. One must establish a major premise, formulate a minor premise, and use the relationship of the premises to yield a sound conclusion. This form of analysis is called a syllogism. The conclusions of legal reasoning from enacted law (but not only enacted law) ordinarily are expressed in the form of a legal syllogism. One identifies a legal rule that serves as a major premise, characterizes the fact of a case in language that serves as a minor premise, and states a conclusion that appears to follow logically from the relationship of the premises.

The practice of expressing legal arguments in the deductive form serves a number of functions that enhance the rationality of legal thought. The need to reason from an applicable rule makes legal reasoning from enacted law manageable, transforming vague questions of what is "just" into specific questions that often are, as a practical matter, noncontroversial. Even in controversial cases, the rules establish the proper starting points for argument; most lawyers, most of the time, will ask the same questions. The rules also establish a uniform language so that lawyers and judges can know what conclusions they might reach legitimately.

It has been seen, however, that the conclusion of a syllogism is sound only if both premises are true and the meanings of the

---

[9]Lochner v. New York, 198 U.S. 45, 76 (1905) (Holmes, J., dissenting).

language in the premises yields that conclusion by necessity. At least in interesting legal cases, plausible controversy will center on identifying the correct authoritative rule in a complex statute (or other body of law), characterizing the facts of a problem case in the language of the rule, and interpreting vague or ambiguous rules that themselves do not single out the important facts in a particular problem case. These controversies generally cannot be resolved by deductive reasoning from other available rules or definitions. Therefore, the conclusion to a legal syllogism will not be sound as a matter of logical necessity.

Like analogical legal reasoning from cases, legal reasoning in the deductive form from rules has its uses and its abuses. Good legal reasoning neither accepts these forms nor rejects these forms as such, but uses them to benefit from their strengths and supplements them to avoid suffering from their weaknesses. Mastering the proper use of both forms of analysis requires an understanding of their vulnerabilities as well as their contributions. This requires understanding the points in reasoning where a judgment of importance must be made without benefit of an effectively controlling legal rule or definition.

It remains for Part II to confront the problem of importance. First, however, the next chapter will consider the relationships between the deductive and analogical forms. The combination of the two principal forms of legal reasoning contributes further to the rationality of legal thought in cases governed by common law, enacted law, or both, though it does not solve the problem of importance.

Two Forms of Legal Reasoning

To SIMPLIFY THIS introduction to law and legal reasoning, the two forms of legal reasoning have been separated too completely. Legal reasoning in the analogical form is most closely associated with the common law, and legal reasoning in the deductive form is most closely associated with reasoning from enacted rules. But good lawyers also use common law rules in the deductive form and apply enacted rules through analogical reasoning from cases or other similar base points.

This chapter will show that the deductive and analogical forms may be combined and that the combination of two forms of legal reasoning serves some highly useful functions. At common law, reasoning in the analogical form becomes increasingly unwieldy as the number of common law precedents increases. The common law rules help lawyers and judges express themselves economically and organize the precedents, though analogical reasoning from the precedents remains the underlying mode of thought. Reasoning in the deductive form from an enacted text lacks the particularities needed to determine the membership of a problem case within an abstract class. The context of an enacted rule often suggests examples of the rule's intended or accepted effect in historical or hypothetical situations, which can be useful base points for reasoning analogically to interpret and apply the text. However, combining the two forms of legal reasoning does not solve the problem of importance that inheres in each of them.

A. Rules within the Analogical Form

In Chapter 2 it was seen that legal reasoning in the analogical form requires that lawyers and judges in common law cases (1) identify the relevant precedents, which serve as base points for comparing and contrasting a problem case, (2) analyze the facts of a problem case and the precedent cases to identify points of similarity and difference, and (3) decide whether the factual similarities or the differences are more important under the circumstances. The third step is the troubling one. Judges may announce a general common law rule when deciding a case as if the rule controlled the critical third step. But the rule did not dictate the decision in t' case that announced it and does not dictate the decision in future cases within its terms because it largely is dicta. The holding captures in a sentence or two the probable significance of a single precedent as a base point for reasoning by analogy in future cases.

It would be a mistake, however, to think that common law rules serve no useful purpose because they may be changed by appellate courts and do not dictate the decision in problem cases. Legal reasoning in common law cases may employ common law rules as the major premise in deductively formed arguments for convenience in easy cases and to organize the precedents, though the analogical form remains the underlying mode of thought. Unlike enacted rules, common law rules have roots in the case law. A common law rule may be announced authoritatively only in a case for which it is then applicable and in which it is then applied. It must be faithful to all precedents that stand as good law within its coverage. Accordingly, common law rules summarize in abstract terms the holdings of a number of related precedents; the words of a common law rule stand as a symbolic surrogate for a class of precedents.

The class of precedents can be referred to most easily by referring to the words that stand for it. In easier cases, as will be seen, there may be no practical point in articulating a number of obvious analogies when a simple deductive argument from a common law rule will do for all practical purposes. Common law rules thus permit lawyers and judges to express themselves simply when the more complete and accurate form of expression is unnecessary. The language of common law rules also can be used to organize the vast number of precedents into categories, subcategories, and subsubcategories, by associating each word or element of the rule with a different subclass or subsubclass of precedents. Accordingly, the applicable common law rule can help lawyers and judges to locate the precedents from which analogical reasoning should proceed in a case.

1. Easier Cases

To illustrate how common law rules are used in the deductive form when full expression of the underlying analogical reasoning is unnecessary, consider again the line of horse trading cases.[1] All of them concerned the rights of the original owner of a horse (Costello) to recover possession of the horse when possession was taken by a person (Abbott) using wrongful means (theft or fraud). The first three cases held that (1) an owner of property who is the victim of a theft can recover possession of the property from a third party purchaser who bought it from the thief, even if the third party purchaser did not know or have reason to know that the property had been stolen; (2) an owner of property who is the victim of a fraud can recover possession of the property from the person who perpetrated the fraud; and (3) an owner of property who is the victim of a fraud cannot recover possession of the property from a third party purchaser who bought it from the perpetrator of the fraud, when the third party purchaser did not know or have reason to know of the fraud. The court in Case 3 might announce a general rule that summarizes these three holdings: An owner of property who loses possession by another's wrongful act, and seeks to recover possession from the perpetrator of the wrongful act or from a third party purchaser when the wrongful act was theft, is entitled to possession.

It was seen that this common law rule would not be a very reliable basis for making predictions, persuasions, and decisions in some possible future cases. Each common law judge of a highest appellate court has as much authority to announce a new or modified rule as his predecessor had to announce the old one. There are, however, cases where the rule can serve through reasoning in the deductive form to yield a noncontroversial conclusion as a practical matter. Though such a conclusion is not necessarily sound from a logical point of view, it may be acceptable to those concerned for all practical purposes. The simplicity of the deductive form may be the most economical means of expression in such easier cases.

For example, if Abbott steals a horse from Costello and Costello sues Abbott to recover possession of the horse, it seems clear that Costello will succeed. Costello's lawyer may present his argument to Abbott's lawyer in the form of a legal syllogism:

MAJOR PREMISE: Case 3 ruled that an owner of property who loses possession by another's wrongful act, and seeks to re-

---

[1]See Chapter 2 §B.

cover possession from the perpetrator of the wrongful act or from a third party purchaser when the wrongful act was theft, is entitled to possession.

MINOR PREMISE: Costello lost possession of his horse to Abbott by theft, a wrongful act, and seeks recovery of possession from Abbott, the perpetrator of the wrongful act.

CONCLUSION: Costello is entitled to recover possession of the horse from Abbott.

Abbott's lawyer is likely to accept opposing counsel's deductively formed argument and advise Abbott to return the horse, even though Abbott's lawyer knows that this conclusion is not necessarily sound because the major premise is not necessarily true for all cases. The rule relied on by Costello's lawyer is dictum for purposes of Costello's argument because no precedent held that the original owner can recover posession from a thief. Case 2 held only that the original owner can recover possession from the perpetrator of a fraud. Case 1 held only that the original owner can recover possession from a third party purchaser from a thief. In the analogical form, Abbott's lawyer could reason that this case is different from both precedents in some respects even if like them in others. Abbott's lawyer is likely to conclude, however, that it could not be argued successfully that this case is different from Cases 2 and 3 in any important respect. Indeed, this case is a clearer case in which the original owner should recover possession of the horse than is either of the precedents. Consequently, Abbott's lawyer probably would accept Costello's legal syllogism because there is no analogical argument with which to contest it plausibly.

The deductive form of legal reasoning in this case is adequate for practical purposes. As a form for expressing one's conclusion in an easier, noncontroversial common law case, it is short and sweet and to the point. Full expression of the analogical reasoning that yields the same conclusion could show the obvious in a more complex and pedantic way. To do so would be unnecessary, confusing, and time consuming for all concerned.

What makes this case an easier case, however, is not the deductive logic of Costello's argument, however sound it may appear. Under the principles of common law adjudication, the conclusion to that argument could not be necessarily sound. No court can stop the evolution of the common law by announcing a universal rule in a particular case.

Recall Case 4, where Abbott gained possession of Costello's horse by fraud and sold it to Holliday, who had helped Abbott perpetrate the fraud. Holliday's lawyer can formulate a legal syllogism that may appear to be as sound as the one Costello's lawyer used successfully above, using the same major premise:

MAJOR PREMISE: Case 3 ruled that an owner of property who loses possession by another's wrongful act, and seeks to recover possession from the perpetrator of the wrongful act or from a third party purchaser when the wrongful act was theft, is entitled to possession.

MINOR PREMISE: Though Costello lost possession of the horse by fraud, a wrongful act, he does not seek to recover possession from either the perpetrator of the fraud or from a third party purchaser when the wrongful act was theft.

CONCLUSION: Costello is not entitled to possession.

Costello's lawyer, however, would not on this ground advise Costello to give up without litigating. Nor is Holliday's lawyer well advised to rest the case on this reasoning alone, however logical it may appear. It seems more likely that both lawyers will predict that the rule will be modified in Case 4 because it is time for the common law to grow. The lawyers in Case 4, reasoning analogically, are likely to predict that a court would decide that Holliday's situation is in an important respect like Abbott's situation in Case 2. A third party purchaser who helped the perpetrator of a fraud is more like the perpetrator than the innocent third party purchaser in Case 3, who did not know or have reason to know of the fraud. Holliday's lawyer is likely to advise Holliday to return the horse without litigating, despite the available deductively formed argument. Again, this is an easier case. Unlike the preceding example, this one defies the apparent logic of reasoning in the deductive form from a common law rule that was announced in a prior case.

Thus, legal reasoning in some easier cases at common law may be expressed as if the conclusion were the logical consequence of a common law rule. But the form of expression does not mirror the underlying reasoning. The common law rule is a symbolic summary of the precedents in a class. The underlying precedents retain their role as base points for reasoning in the analogical form even after the rule is announced. If the common law rule leads logically to a different result than the relevant precedents lead to analogically, then so much the worse for the common law rule. In common law cases, legal reasoning remains analogical, with all of its strengths and weaknesses.

2. Organizing the Precedents

Common law rules have other useful functions, too. Not the least of these is the way in which the common law rules help organize the sometimes huge number of precedents that may be relevant in current or future controversies. Each common law rule may summarize the holdings of dozens or hundreds of precedents in a single jurisdiction. Reasoning analogically from dozens or hundreds of cases is humanly impracticable. Each rule, however, may be broken down into a number of significant parts. Each part, or element, of a rule then should summarize in a word or phrase the significance of a subclass of the class of precedents that are summarized by the entire rule. The word or phrase will stand as a symbol for the precedents in a subclass. Lawyers and judges can locate (by legal research) or refer (in argument) to that subclass of precedents quickly and easily by using the term that is an element of the rule. The smaller size of the subclass makes analogical reasoning with cases more manageable and focused.

Consider, for example, the general common law rule that governs cases in which a plaintiff seeks compensation from a defendant whose behavior harmed the plaintiff or the plaintiff's property. The traditional lawsuit arising at common law from an automobile accident is a familiar example. The rule, known as the common law negligence rule, may be stated as follows:

> If (1) the defendant was under a duty to use reasonable care to avoid a harm, and (2) the defendant breached that duty by a negligent act or omission, and (3) the breach of duty was a cause-in-fact and (4) a legal cause of (5) damage to the plaintiff's person or property, then the defendant shall compensate the plaintiff for such damages (unless certain exceptions not relevant here apply).[2]

---

[2]The distinction between *cause-in-fact* and *legal cause* (also called *proximate cause*) is not important for present purposes, as long as the reader accepts that there is a difference.

4. TWO FORMS OF LEGAL REASONING   65

In some jurisdictions, there are a few hundred precedents on the books that employ this negligence rule (or its equivalent) in one way or another. Reasoning analogically from each of these hundreds of precedents would be overwhelming, and composing an intelligible argument using all of these precedents would be humanly impossible. To make the thought process manageable, it is necessary to simplify by organizing the large number of precedents in the class into subclasses of precedents, each with fewer members.

The class of hundreds of precedents summarized by the common law negligence rule are organized (roughly) into five subclasses of precedents, each of which is identified in terms of the element of the rule that summarizes the significance of that subgroup. Thus, in shorthand form, under the negligence rule are found the (1) duty cases, (2) breach of duty cases, (3) cause-in-fact cases, (4) legal cause cases, and (5) damage cases. These subclasses are distinguished from one another by the kind of issue that was decided in the cases by the court—by the kind of similarities or differences between that case and its precedents that were the subject of a judgment of importance by the court. The precedents in each subclass should be more like each other (in respect of the issue that was decided) than they are like the precedents in the other subclasses (in the same respect). Often only one of the five elements of negligence was the issue before the appellate court, giving each subclass a separate identity. Some precedents, however, will fall in more than one subclass or be hard to place in a subclass at all, making the system of classification a rough one at best.

The negligence rule suggests that, to recover compensation, the plaintiff in a problem case governed by this rule must show that its situation is like that of the plaintiffs who won in each of five subclasses of cases. Assume that Georgio's car collides with Susan's when Georgio is admiring the scenery instead of watching the road. Susan's lawyer knows that, strictly speaking, five analogical arguments are necessary. It must be shown that (1) Susan's situation is in important respects like the situation of the plaintiffs who succeeded in showing that the defendant had a duty in the cases where that question was decided. It must be shown in addition that (2) Susan's situation is in important respects similar to that of the plaintiffs who succeeded in showing that the defendant breached its duty in the cases where that question was decided. Susan's lawyer similarly must show that Susan's situation is like that of the plaintiffs who succeeded in showing that the defendant's breach of duty was (3) the cause-in-fact and (4) the legal cause of (5) the damage suffered by the plaintiff, in the cases where each of those three questions was decided. Georgio's lawyer can defeat Susan's claim by showing that Susan's situation is unlike those of the victorious plaintiffs, or that Georgio's situation is like those of the victorious defendants, in any one of those five subclasses.

Most problem cases do not require the court to analyze the analogies in all five subclasses. The court in a problem case might state the issue in Susan's case as "whether the defendant's negligence was a legal cause of the plaintiff's injury." This implies that the parties are contesting only the element of legal cause, having accepted that Georgio was under a duty and breached his duty, the breach of duty was the cause-in-fact of Susan's injury, and Susan was damaged. That is, they have accepted that Susan's situation is in important respects like the situation of the plaintiffs who won on the same issues in each of the four subclasses of precedents designated by those four elements of the negligence rule. The court now must decide if Georgio's breach of duty was the "legal cause" of Susan's injury. That is, it must decide if Susan's situation is in important respects like that of the plaintiffs who won on the legal cause issue in the subclass designated the "legal cause" cases.

A subclass often is divided in similar fashion into subsubclasses designated by the elements of yet narrower rules that, in form, define the elements of the general rule. Thus, a further rule or definition may provide that "legal cause," in turn, consists of two or three more specific elements. Each of these elements summarizes the significance of a small subclass of the legal cause cases. There results a sort of pyramidal organization of the hundreds of cases in a single class (negligence) that yields five subclasses (duty, breach of duty, cause-in-fact, legal cause, damage) and a larger number of subsubclasses. The progressively smaller groups of cases are progressively easier to consider in the analogical form when confronted with a problem case. Having isolated one or two subsubclasses that are the subjects of plausible controversy in a problem case, the lawyers and the judge need consider only a relatively manageable number of base points for analogical arguments.

Consequently, an argument at common law can be stated in the form of a legal syllogism in any case:

MAJOR PREMISE: If (1) the defendant was under a duty to use reasonable care to avoid a harm, and (2) the defendant breached that duty by a negligent act or omission, and (3) the breach of duty was a cause-in-fact and (4) a legal cause of (5) damage to the plaintiff's person or property, then the defendant shall compensate the plaintiff for such damages.

MINOR PREMISE: Georgio (1) had a duty to operate his car with reasonable care, (2) breached this duty by failing to maintain a proper lookout, (3) which in fact caused a collision with Susan's car, (4) was the legal cause of injury to Susan, and (5) damaged Susan's foot.

CONCLUSION: Georgio shall compensate Susan for the damage to her foot.

Only in a limited way does this represent a deductively formed argument from the common law rule. The rule establishes deductively that Susan's lawyer must make five successful arguments, assuming away any question of overruling. The common law rules thus identify the general issues in a case, as do enacted rules. The conclusion may be false, or not established to be sound, if Susan's lawyer fails altogether to make one of the five necessary arguments.

Assuming that Susan's lawyer makes all five arguments, however, the soundness of the conclusion cannot be established by deductive reasoning from the rule. The soundness of the conclusion depends on the soundness of the analogies that underlie the minor premise, assuming the major premise to be a correct one. The legal syllogism does not represent the reasoning that is required to decide the soundness of the minor premise; it does not determine the membership of Susan's case in the classes of cases designated by the rule. Rather, the minor premise represents the results of a highly complex network of analogical arguments from a very large number of precedents.

The common law precedents thus are organized in a deductively formed classification scheme described by the common law rules. Like enacted rules, the common law rules refer to classes of cases. Where the enacted rules refer to abstract classes, however, the common law rules refer to classes of precedents. Common law rules are used in the deductive form to express the conclusion in any case economically and to identify the issues in any case; that is, to identify the classes of precedents that must be considered in the analogical form. The common law rules do not determine the membership of problem cases in the classes they describe. At common law, the decision in a particular case remains a matter for analogical legal reasoning.

B. Cases within the Deductive Form

In Chapter 3 it was seen that legal reasoning in the deductive form requires that lawyers and judges (1) identify an authoritative rule that serves as a major premise, (2) characterize the facts of a problem case in language that serves as a minor premise, and (3) interpret the rule in relation to the facts to reach a sound conclusion. At least in controversial cases, however, the conclusion to a legal syllogism based on enacted law cannot be necessarily sound from a logical point of view. The rules refer to abstract classes of cases and do not themselves supply the particularities that are needed to decide a problem case. The membership of a particular case within an abstract class of cases designated by the rule must be decided through a judgment of importance.

Reasoning in the analogical form may be employed by good lawyers and judges to help interpret an enacted rule in relation to the facts of a problem case and thus to decide how the rule applies in a particular case. Enacted rules, however, differ from common law rules because they lack roots in the case law; they supersede earlier decided cases and normally are announced before any problem case governed by the rule materializes. Consequently, no judicial precedents using the rule exist to serve as base points until some time after enactment. Reasoning analogically in a case governed by enacted law requires that other meaningful base points be found with which to compare and contrast a problem case.

The base points that are used when reasoning analogically to interpret and apply enacted law are both real and hypothetical situations. Of course, not just any real or hypothetical situation will shed light on the meaning of the Constitution, for example. There must be some reason for thinking that the base points are examples of what the Constitution permits or requires. There are several kinds of base points that can be employed meaningfully, even though such base points cannot have quite the authority that a precedent does at common law.

The text of an enacted rule is a starting point for finding meaningful base points. The text has a context that includes examples of its "intended" or accepted effect in concrete situations. The context includes the ordinary meanings of the terms used in the text and thus examples that come to the mind of a speaker of the English language. Such examples can be used as base points, though it is usually unnecessary to spell out these analogies. The ordinary meanings tend to be helpful to a lawyer or judge only in easier cases. The cases that require lawyerly skill are those in which analogies with contradictory implications can be drawn from the ordinary meanings of the text. Consequently, a legal analyst often must find base points that are more closely linked to the words of a text, as they are used in the text.

The context also includes precedent cases that interpret and apply the text, noncontroversial hypothetical cases, cases or situations governed by other rules within the same enactment, historical events or situations linked to the enactment of the rule, contemporary historical, economic, and social practices at the time of enactment, and examples given in the legislative history. These features of context, more than the ordinary meanings, may shed light directly on the words of an enacted text, as they are used in the text. The remainder of this section will illustrate how base points found in each of these features of the context can be used to interpret and apply a text.

Consider the freedom of speech clause of the first amendment to the U.S. Constitution: "Congress shall make no law . . . abridging the freedom of speech. . . . " Any lawyer reasoning from this general rule in the deductive form can be seriously misled. For example, the language on its face expresses a prohibition only on certain acts by Congress, but it also effectively prohibits such acts by the states.[3] There is no need to digress to explain how that came about, however, since it is almost universally accepted, at least for the time being. A more straightforward problem will be posed.

Assume two problem cases.[4] In one, a state enacted a penal statute that made it a crime for any person to hang the governor in effigy. Peter Protest was prosecuted under the statute for hanging the governor in effigy, which he admitted doing. Protest was convicted and sentenced to a jail term. He argued unsuccessfully in state court that his conviction was unconstitutional and should be

---

[3]Technically, the freedom of speech clause is "incorporated" by judicial interpretation into the due process clause of the fourteenth amendment, which applies by its terms to the states. See Gitlow v. New York, 268 U.S. 652 (1925); Whitney v. California, 274 U.S. 357 (1927).

[4]This analysis is adapted from Burton, Comment on "Empty Ideas": Logical Positivist Analyses of Equality and Rules, 91 Yale L.J. 1136, 1139-1146 (1982).

set aside because the statute violated the freedom of speech clause. Protest appealed to the U.S. Supreme Court on that ground. In the second case, a state enacted a penal statute that made it a crime for any person to hang the governor. Neil Nihil was prosecuted under the statute for hanging the governor, which he admitted doing. Nihil was convicted and sentenced to a jail term. He argued unsuccessfully in state court that his conviction was unconstitutional and should be set aside because the statute violated the freedom of speech clause. Nihil, too, appealed to the U.S. Supreme Court on that ground.

By coincidence, the two cases reach the Supreme Court at the same time. It is reasonably certain that the Supreme Court would and should set aside Protest's conviction but not Nihil's. It would be expected to do so because a penal statute against hanging the governor in effigy unconstitutionally abridges the freedom of speech, but a penal statute against hanging the governor does not. The problem is to explain the reasoning that would justify these conclusions by, in necessary part, drawing a distinction between the two cases. One cannot justify setting aside Protest's conviction by an argument that as plausibly requires setting aside Nihil's conviction, nor can one justify upholding Nihil's conviction by an argument that as plausibly requires upholding Protest's conviction.

It is not possible to justify the two decisions by reasoning deductively from the text of the freedom of speech clause alone. That might lead to the conclusion that both convictions should be upheld. Neither hanging the governor in effigy nor hanging the governor are *speech*, if *speech* is interpreted in its ordinary sense to mean talking or using words. By this approach, neither act would be protected by the first amendment.

The Supreme Court, however, has given the freedom of speech clause a broader interpretation. In *Tinker v. Des Moines School District*,[5] for example, the Court held that a high school student who wore a black arm band to a public school in 1965 to protest the Vietnam War could not be suspended from school for that reason. This protest was "symbolic speech" within the protection of the freedom of speech clause. In other cases, the Court has said that the first amendment generally protects freedom of expression. Paintings, photographs, music, and other forms of expression thus may be constitutionally protected, along with lectures criticiz-

---

[5]393 U.S. 503 (1969).

ing official policies, campaign speeches, and other more obviously protected forms of expression. *Speech* within the meaning of the first amendment is not given its ordinary meaning.

The two decisions cannot be justified by giving *speech* the meaning *expression* (or *political expression*) and then reasoning deductively from a statement of the meaning of the freedom of speech clause. That would require that both convictions be set aside:

> MAJOR PREMISE: If a state imposes a penalty on a person for engaging in expression, then the penalty shall be set aside as a violation of the first amendment.

MINOR PREMISE₁: Protest's conviction was a penalty imposed for engaging in expression.	MINOR PREMISE₂: Nihil's conviction was a penalty imposed for engaging in expression.
CONCLUSION₁: Protest's conviction shall be set aside.	CONCLUSION₂: Nihil's conviction shall be set aside.

Both hanging the governor in effigy and hanging the governor are ways of expressing one's political views. The latter is but a way to express them forcefully. The mere fact that expression, even political expression, is a part of Protest's situation does not justify setting aside Protest's conviction. The same argument as plausibly justifies setting aside Nihil's conviction.

The two decisions can be more satisfactorily distinguished by reasoning in the analogical form. For example, the enacted rule, the freedom of speech clause, could be interpreted and applied in light of an analogy between the problem cases and a precedent case that interpreted the same enacted rule, such as the *Tinker* case. Thus, the court might defend its decision to set aside Protest's conviction by drawing an analogy between hanging the Governor in effigy and wearing a black armband to protest the Vietnam War. The *Tinker* case and Protest's case are alike in an important respect because both involve expressions of dissenting political views by symbolic means. The differences between wearing a black armband and hanging a governor in effigy probably are not important in this context. The difference between these symbolic expressions and Nihil's act of hanging the governor, however, probably is important because Nihil's act was violent.

Additionally, the Court might reason in the analogical form from noncontroversial hypothetical cases. It might reason that actually hanging the governor is in an important respect different from hanging the governor in effigy because the former is, after all, forceful and a breach of the peace. Hanging the governor in effigy is more like giving a public lecture criticizing the governor's policies. No one would suggest that such a lecture is not protected by the first amendment. By contrast, hanging the governor is more like hanging one's spouse, usually a clear case of murder. Hanging one's spouse, too, is "expression" in some respects. Ask a psychoanalyst. Yet no one would suggest plausibly that the first amendment protects murder.

The Court in Protest's and Nihil's cases might reason analogically from a third kind of base point — cases or situations governed by other rules within the same enactment. For example, the freedom of speech clause of the first amendment is conjoined in that amendment with the freedom of the press clause: "Congress shall make no law . . . abridging the freedom of speech, or the press. . . ." Neither Protest nor Nihil was exercising the freedom of the press in any plausible sense, so that clause does not itself apply. It probably would apply, however, to protect a published political cartoon depicting the governor hanging from a tree, in effigy or in the flesh. The Court in the two problem cases might reason that hanging the governor in effigy is in important respects like such a published political cartoon. Hanging the governor is not. It thus would look to cases or situations governed by other rules within the same enactment and thus within the context of the freedom of speech clause. Such base points would be meaningful when applying the first amendment because the Constitution should be interpreted as a whole to give it a coherent meaning.

Historical events or situations that are linked to the enactment of a rule are another kind of meaningful base point for reasoning in the analogical form to interpret and apply the rule. The history of events that inspired the first amendment is well known and is part of its context. A colonial government's suppression of Peter Zenger's expressions of political criticism, for example, is widely regarded as a prime example of the sort of thing the first amendment was enacted to prevent. The suppression of Zenger's press was referred to during the debates preceding ratification of that amendment and often compared to English practices in the colonies after 1760.[6] The Court might justify its decisions in the Protest

---

[6] Z. Chaffee, Free Speech in the United States 21 (1969).

4. TWO FORMS OF LEGAL REASONING   73

and Nihil cases by reasoning that hanging the Governor in effigy is like what Zenger did but hanging the Governor is not, and all might agree. Some such reasoning might underlie the *Tinker* case. Wearing a black armband to protest the Vietnam War is in an important respect like what Zenger did.

To illustrate additional meaningful base points for reasoning in the analogical form to interpret and apply an enacted rule requires a shift to a different problem case. In 1885 Congress enacted a statute that made it

> unlawful for any person . . . or corporation . . . in any manner what-soever, to prepay the transportation, or in any way assist or encourage the importation or migration of any alien or aliens, any foreigner or foreigners, into the United States . . . under contract . . . to perform labor or service of any kind in the United States. . . .[7]

The Church of the Holy Trinity, a corporation in New York, made a contract in 1887 with E. Walpole Warren, then an alien living in England. The contract required Warren to move to New York and enter into service as the rector and pastor of the church. The church was prosecuted for violating the statute, which prescribed a fine as the penalty for its violation.

The lower court reasoned in the deductive form:

> This suit is brought to recover a penalty of $1,000 imposed by the act of congress of February 26, 1885, upon every person or corporation offending against its provisions by knowingly encouraging the migration of any alien into the United States "to perform labor or service of any kind under contract" . . . previously made with such alien. The defendant, a religious corporation, engaged one Warren, an alien residing in England, to come here to take charge of its church as pastor.[8]

Therefore, the court concluded, the statute had been violated by the church.

The U.S. Supreme Court reversed the lower court's decision in the case.[9] Writing for the Court, Justice Brewer conceded that "the act of the corporation [was] within the letter of this section, for the relation of a rector to his church is one of service. . . ."[10] However, Justice Brewer said that

---

[7]23 Stat. 332 ch. 164 (1885).
[8]United States v. Church of the Holy Trinity, 36 F. 303, 303-304 (1888).
[9]Church of the Holy Trinity v. United States, 143 U.S. 457 (1892).
[10]Id. at 458.

frequently words of general meaning are used in a statute, words broad enough to include an act in question, and yet a consideration of the whole legislation, or of the circumstances surrounding its enactment, or of the absurd results which follow from giving such broad meaning to the words, makes it unreasonable to believe that the legislator intended to include the particular act.[11]

Justice Brewer made two related analogical arguments to justify the Court's conclusion that performing pastoral services in New York was not performing "labor or service of any kind in the United States," within the meaning of the statute.

Justice Brewer considered "contemporaneous events, the situation as it existed, and as it was pressed upon the attention of the legislative body,"[12] to identify the perceived problem that the statute was designed to address. He found that

[t]he motives and history of the act are matters of common knowledge. It had become the practice for large capitalists in this country to contract with their agents abroad for the shipment of great numbers of an ignorant and servile class of foreign laborers, under contracts, by which the employer agreed, on the one hand, to prepay their passage, while, upon the other hand, the laborers agreed to work after their arrival for a certain time at a low rate of wages.[13]

Justice Brewer said that it was this situation that led a group of citizens to petition Congress for relief by passage of the statute. The practice of importing "cheap immigrant labor" was a prime example of the problem to which the statute was directed. Consequently, the Court could use the situation created by the notorious practices described above as a base point for comparing and contrasting the situation created by the church's contract with Warren.

Justice Brewer also considered the legislative history of the statute. He found that the responsible Senate committee recommended enactment to the full Senate but in its report expressed a preference for amending the language to substitute the words *manual labor* or *manual services* for the expression *labor and service* wherever it appeared. The committee did not so recommend, the report said, because the committee expected the statute to be interpreted by the courts to include only those whose labor or service

---

[11]Id. at 459.
[12]Id. at 463.
[13]Id. at 463 (quoting United States v. Craig, 28 F. 795, 798 (1886)).

is manual in character and the committee wanted a quick adoption of the statute in the final days before adjournment of the Congress. It thus would appear that the Senate contemplated prohibiting the importation of manual laborers, but not others.

Justice Brewer found as well that the report of the responsible committee in the House of Representatives had said that the statute

> seeks to restrain and prohibit the immigration or importation of laborers who would have never seen our shores but for the inducements and allurements of men whose only object is to obtain labor at the lowest possible rate, regardless of the social and material well-being of our own citizens and regardless of the evil consequences which result to American laborers from such immigration.[14]

The legislative record thus disclosed that both houses of Congress had before them as the prime example of the statute's object the recent importations of manual laborers. The Court could use the situation described in the legislative history as a base point for comparing and contrasting the situation created by the church's contract with Warren.

The Court concluded that the situation involving the church's contract with Warren was not like the situation involving "cheap immigrant labor" in the more important respects. Justice Brewer quoted further from the House committee's report to describe the important features of the situation involving "cheap immigrant labor":

> "[T]hey come here under contract to labor for a certain number of years; they are ignorant of our social condition, and that they may remain so they are isolated and prevented from coming in contact with Americans. They are generally from the lowest social stratum, and live upon the coarsest food and in hovels of a character before unknown to American workmen. They, as a rule, do not become citizens, and are certainly not a desirable acquisition to the body politic. The inevitable tendency of their presence among us is to degrade American labor, and to reduce it to the level of the imported pauper labor."[15] . . .

It was never suggested that we had in this country a surplus of brain toilers, and least of all, that the market for the services of Christian ministers was depressed by foreign competition.[16]

---

[14]Id. at 465 (quoting Cong. Rec., 48th Cong., p.5359).
[15]Id.
[16]Id. at 464.

Consequently, the Court concluded:

> So far, then, as the evil which was sought to be remedied interprets the statute, it also guides to an exclusion of this contract from the penalties of the act.[17]

In other words, Justice Brewer identified from contemporary historical, economic, and social practices and from the legislative history a meaningful base point for reasoning by analogy in the problem case. "Cheap immigrant labor" is the prime example of a situation within the prohibition of the statute. He identified the similarities between that situation and the problem case: Both involved contracts to bring aliens over to perform labor or services in the United States. He also identified the differences between the two situations: Warren's arrival would not "degrade American labor." The Court concluded that the differences were more important than the similarities under the circumstances. Accordingly, the decision of the lower court was reversed despite its superficial logic; the Church of the Holy Trinity did not violate the statute.

It has been seen, then, that analysis of enacted law begins in any case with the language of the authoritative rule—the text. This starting point usefully identifies the issues that must be decided and establishes a uniform language for analysis and argument. The rule itself, however, stops short of determining the membership of a problem case within the abstract class of cases designated by the rule. The decision in a particular case governed by an enacted rule often is made by reasoning in the analogical form to interpret and apply the text.

Because enacted rules lack roots in the case law, such analogical reasoning requires that lawyers and judges look for base points in a number of settings that are related to the enactment—the context. In addition to the examples suggested by the ordinary meanings of the words of an enactment, there are at least six features of the context that may contain useful base points. First, one may use judicial precedents applying the same enacted rule, much as one would use precedents at common law (the *Tinker* case).[18] Second, one may use noncontroversial hypothetical cases

---

[17]Id. If the language of the statute and parts of the Supreme Court opinion strike you as poor English, be assured that I agree.

[18]Note, however, that the force of precedent need not be the same in common law, statutory, and constitutional cases. See Levi, The Sovereignty of the Courts, 50 U. Chi. L. Rev. 679 (1983).

(giving a lecture criticizing the governor's policies; hanging one's spouse). Third, one may use cases or situations governed by other rules in the same enactment (the published political cartoon). Fourth, one may use historical events or situations that are linked to the enactment of the rule (what Zenger did). Fifth, one may use contemporary historical, economic, and social practices at the time of enactment (importation of "cheap immigrant labor"). Sixth, one may use the legislative history (same). There is, of course, no guarantee that conflicting analogies may not be drawn from these many sources, or that any or all would be helpful in every case.

The similarity between the last four items on this list and the list of things that should be considered when interpreting a statute, in Chapter 3 at page 54, should not go unnoticed. It was said of the earlier list that an analyst needs some sense of what is being *looked for* in the enacted text as a whole, the complex legislative history, the centuries of legal history, the multitude of historical, economic, and social circumstances at the time of enactment. It now can be said that, among other things, the analyst is looking for examples of what the statutory rule permits or requires—concrete situations, whether historical or hypothetical, that would be members of the abstract class to which the statutory rule refers. Such examples or situations can be used meaningfully as base points for reasoning in the analogical form to interpret and apply a statutory rule in a problem case. Such base points may supply the particularities that are needed to think intelligently about the membership of a particular case within a class, though there remains the problem of importance.

C. Excursus on the Problem of Legitimacy

Another troubling problem that is raised by the analysis of legal reasoning should be identified and considered briefly. From the discussion of analogical reasoning when applying enacted law, it may seem that the courts have an extraordinary power to expand or restrict the apparent meaning of a duly enacted law. In the examples, the Court expanded the freedom of speech clause to cover expression or political expression when the enacted rule said "speech." The Court restricted the immigration statute to cover only manual labor and services when it said "labor or services of any kind." Yet it was said in Chapter 3 that the principle of legislative supremacy generally requires judges to play a subordinate role to the more democratic branches of government because the judges are less accountable to the electorate. Similarly, the principles of consitutional democracy require the judges to subordinate their personal views to the requirements of the Constitution.

It should be clear that the use of analogical reasoning is essential to the intelligent application of an enacted law in many cases. A very liberal use of analogical reasoning, however, can have the effect of elevating the judiciary to a far more powerful position than many observers consider legitimate in the U.S. system of government. This "problem of legitimacy" will be the subject of Part III.

In this excursus, we observe that the courts' willingness to expand or restrict enacted laws by the liberal use of analogy often is limited. The problem of legitimacy sometimes leads the courts to refuse to apply an enacted law as called for by an intellectually appealing analogical argument, but instead to apply the enacted law using the ordinary meaning of the text. This may result from a judicial belief that the ordinary meaning of the text is a part of its context and that examples suggested by the ordinary meaning sometimes are the better base points for reasoning by analogy to interpret and apply the text. The judges also may believe that the more democratic branches of the government should be persuaded by an intellectually more appealing analogical argument, in light of whatever political and other considerations may be relevant, before the courts should accept it. The courts may decline to usurp the functions of the other branches when the analogical argument seems less to establish what the enacted law permits or requires than to establish what it ought to permit or require.[19]

In *McBoyle v. United States*,[20] the defendant was convicted of violating the 1919 National Motor Vehicle Theft Act,[21] which prohibited any person from knowingly transporting a stolen motor vehicle across state lines. McBoyle had transported from Illinois to Oklahoma an airplane he knew to have been stolen. The statute defined the term *motor vehicle* as follows:

> The term "motor vehicle" shall include an automobile, automobile truck, automobile wagon, motorcycle, or any other self-propelled vehicle not designed for running on rails.[22]

---

[19]This is not the place to consider the highly complex practices of judicial restraint in constitutional cases. See Chapter 11 §B.

[20]283 U.S. 25 (1931).

[21]41 Stat. 324 (1919).

[22]Id. at §2(a).

An airplane is not commonly called a motor vehicle, and probably does not fall within the definition of "motor vehicle" if one reasons in the deductive form, using the ordinary meaning of the words.

One could argue analogically that an airplane should be treated as a "self-propelled vehicle not designed for running on rails." A stolen airplane is in important respects like an automobile or truck for the purposes of this statute. Automobiles and trucks probably were the subject of this federal enactment because they so easily could be taken outside the state in which they were stolen, causing difficulties for law enforcement by the states because a state's enforcement jurisdiction generally does not extend to the territory of other states. Federal law enforcement authorities face no such difficulty because their enforcement jurisdiction extends throughout the United States. Because a stolen airplane easily can be taken outside the state in which it was stolen, it is in an important respect like the automobile or truck that is clearly within the statute's prohibition.

Justice Holmes, writing for the U.S. Supreme Court, seemed to acknowledge the persuasive force of this analogy. He refused, however, to uphold McBoyle's conviction:

> [T]he statute should not be extended to aircraft, simply because it may seem to us that a similar policy applies, or upon the speculation that, if the legislature had thought of it, very likely broader words would have been used.[23]

Justice Holmes reasoned that the word *vehicle* calls up the picture of a thing moving on land, in everyday speech. He said that

> it is reasonable that a fair warning should be given to the world in language that the common world will understand, of what the law intends to do if a certain line is passed.[24]

For this reason, Justice Holmes applied the statute in light of the examples suggested by the ordinary meaning of the words. He refused to expand its coverage beyond its apparent meaning by following the alternative analogy.

Justice Holmes's approach to the statute in *McBoyle* stands in contrast to Justice Brewer's in *Church of the Holy Trinity*. It also stands in contrast to Justice Holmes's approach in other statutory cases.[25] The effect of a decision like Justice Holmes's in *McBoyle* is

---

[23]283 U.S. 25, 27 (1931).
[24]Id.
[25]E.g., Johnson v. United States, 163 F. 30 (1908).

to assign responsibility for considering the intellectually more appealing analogical argument to the legislative branch of government. If the legislature is persuaded, in light of political and other considerations, it can amend the statute or enact another to prohibit the interstate transport of stolen airplanes. The effect of a decision like Justice Brewer's in *Church of the Holy Trinity* is to assign responsibility for considering the intellectually more appealing analogical argument to the courts. If the courts are persuaded, in light of legal considerations, they can interpret the statute to prohibit the importation only of manual laborers.

It is tempting to think that either Justice Holmes's approach in *McBoyle* or Justice Brewer's approach in *Church of the Holy Trinity* is legitimate and that both cannot be so. This would be a mistake. As there are kinds of statutes that generally are not interpreted liberally in the analogical form, there are others that generally are interpreted in that way.

The restrained judicial role exemplified by Justice Holmes's opinion in *McBoyle* is thought to be appropriate to several kinds of statutory cases. Criminal statutes like the one in *McBoyle* are prime examples of kinds of law that should not be expanded by the liberal use of analogies.[26] As Justice Holmes pointed out, it is of special importance in criminal matters that the rules give reasonable notice to the public of what will constitute an infraction. Keeping to the ordinary meaning of the words may be thought to further that end. Some spending statutes are another example. The power of Congress to control the federal budget is basic to the U.S. system of government. The judiciary generally hesitates to intrude on Congress's prerogative to authorize expenditures of taxpayer's dollars for expressly delineated projects. Moreover, some courts occasionally follow a "rule" of interpretation that requires a court to follow the plain meaning of a statute that is clear and unambiguous on its face, though it may be questioned whether such statutes really exist.[27]

The more expansive judicial role exemplified by Justice Brewer's opinion in *Church of the Holy Trinity* also is thought to be appropriate to several kinds of statutory cases. Commercial

---

[26]Note that Justice Brewer did not *expand* the criminal statute in *Church of the Holy Trinity*.

[27]See generally Murphy, Old Maxims Never Die: The "Plain Meaning Rule" and Statutory Interpretation in the "Modern" Federal Courts, 75 Colum. L. Rev. 1299 (1975).

cases, like Auster's case discussed in Chapter 3, are prime examples of the kinds of cases where the courts would shirk their duty if they refused to engage in analogical reasoning to resolve the dispute. Commercial matters do not occupy a position of priority on the legislative agenda, and the state legislatures often want the courts to guide the development of an area of the law with considerable independence, as they traditionally have in commercial matters. Similarly, cases involving statutes that protect minority rights, such as the civil rights laws, are widely (but not universally) thought to require a more active judicial role. It is one thing to say to the U.S. Department of Justice, as Justice Holmes effectively did in *McBoyle,* that they should make their analogical argument to the Congress. It is quite another to say the same thing to a lone victim of racial or other similar discrimination. Recourse to majoritarian institutions at times may be illusory to redress the rights of a minority.

It is not my purpose to delineate a theory of when the courts should apply statutory rules in light only of analogies suggested by the ordinary meanings of the words, leaving other analogies to be considered by the more political branches of government, and when the courts should consider all analogies themselves.[28] Enough has been said to suggest that the two approaches both play and should play major roles in statutory cases. Which approach a court will employ in a particular case often is difficult to predict, though it may be crucial to predicting the decision in the case. The choice of approach is often informed, to a large extent, by a judge's conception of the legitimate judicial role in relation to the legislature's. That role is not the same in all statutory cases. In fact, however, the judges often subordinate their role to that of the legislature, as did Justice Holmes in *McBoyle.*

D. Summary

It has been seen that the deductive and analogical forms of legal reasoning may be combined in cases governed by both common law and enacted law. Common law rules may be used in the deductive form to express the conclusion in easy cases economically. They also are used in the deductive form to identify the issues that must be resolved by organizing the subclasses or sub-

---

[28]For further discussion, see Chapter 11 §C.

subclasses of precedents that should be used as base points for analogical arguments in a problem case. However, legal reasoning in the analogical form remains the underlying mode of thought. Similarly, analogical reasoning may be used to help interpret and apply an enacted rule in a problem case. The analysis of enacted law begins with the text. It often is necessary to look to the context to find base points that can be used meaningfully to reason analogically in a problem case.

It should be apparent that the combination of analogical and deductive forms of reasoning is useful in many cases but does not solve the problem of importance. Legal reasoning, when confined to these two forms, sends the legal analyst back and forth between them in a regress, as when we stand between the barber's mirrors. If one starts with the analogical form, reaches the problem of importance, and shifts to the deductive form, a similar problem of importance will arise in the different form. Conversely, if one starts with the deductive form, reaches the problem of importance, and shifts to the analogical form, a similar problem of importance again will arise in the different form. The two forms of legal reasoning may be two ways of expressing the same thought: One can say that cases are "like cases" or that they are "members of the same legal class," but mean the same thing. Whichever form of expression is used, however, the soundness of the thought is not established by the form of expression.

Accordingly, the two forms of legal reasoning must be supplemented in order for lawyers and judges to make good predictions, persuasions, and decisions in problem cases. One cannot conclude that legal reasoning really is analogical. Nor can one conclude that legal reasoning really is deductive. In some respects it is both, and in some respects it is neither. Part II addresses the respects in which it is neither—the problem of importance—and seeks to develop a workable method of legal interpretation for treating this crucial problem.

II

THE PROBLEM OF IMPORTANCE

THE PROBLEM OF importance is the problem of determining which of the many facts in a case will or should lead a court to decide the case one way or the other because they count as reasons. It arises in the analogical form of legal reasoning when lawyers and judges must decide whether the factual similarities or differences between two cases will or should matter in reaching a legal decision. It also arises in the deductive form when lawyers and judges must decide which facts justify placing a problem case in a class of cases designated by a legal rule. Lawyers and judges must confront the problem of importance to make meaningful predictions, persuasions, and decisions. Because the problem cannot be avoided by appealing to rules or cases in the analogical or deductive forms, the two forms of legal reasoning must be supplemented.

Confronting the problem of importance in legal reasoning requires a workable method of legal interpretation. As used in this book, an interpretive method is a way to evaluate the facts of a problem case to determine that some facts are or should be legally important while other facts are or should be irrelevant. It is not merely an effort to find the "intention" of a lawmaker or the "meaning" of a word or phrase, but a broad-gauged intellectual effort to treat legal problems meaningfully in their full legal contexts. To be workable, an interpretive method should be useful to lawyers and judges in their everyday professional lives. Whether their predictions, persuasions, and decisions are expressed in the analogical or deductive form, or a combination of the two, it is the method of interpretation that determines how the forms will be filled in and therefore the conclusions of legal reasoning.

One cannot reasonably deny the necessity of an interpretive method. Oliver Wendell Holmes was eloquent in describing the need:

[T]he logical method and form flatter that longing for certainty and for repose which is in every human mind. But certainty generally is illusion, and repose is not the destiny of man. Behind the logical form lies a judgment as to the relative worth and importance of competing legislative grounds, often an inarticulate and unconscious judgment, it is true, and yet the very root and nerve of the whole proceeding. You can give any conclusion a logical form. . . . But why do you [do] it?[1]

One can, however, accept the necessity of an interpretive method and lament it. If Holmes is correct, does it follow that legal decisions are wholly subjective? Does each decision result from the personal moral, religious, economic, or political values of the individual judge? If so, in what sense would lawyers and judges use legal reasoning and have a "rule of law"? In what sense would it be legitimate for the state to use its coercive powers to enforce a judicial decision? These questions are for consideration in Part III. Even if legal reasoning "is not capable of founding exact logical conclusions,"[2] its interpretive method should be understood fully before the implications for legitimacy are evaluated.

---

[1]Holmes, The Path of the Law, 10 Harv. L. Rev. 457, 466 (1897).
[2]Id.

CHAPTER FIVE

Families of Cases

DEVELOPING A WORKABLE method of legal interpretation requires, first, a clear conception of how two or more cases can be like cases and therefore members of the same legal class. A prevalent inclination is to think that like cases must share facts in common such that the presence of those facts signals the proper legal classification of the cases. The common facts then could be described in a legal rule, and lawyers and judges simply would observe whether the facts of a problem case correspond to the words in the rule. If so, the rule would prescribe the appropriate legal consequences. Such a method would mimic the popular conception of scientific reasoning and seems to be implicit in the two forms of legal reasoning.

Alas, the facts of law cases do not organize themselves so neatly. Cases that are alike in legally important respects frequently do not have observable facts in common, such that the presence of those facts signals the proper legal classification of the cases. Rather, like cases are alike as the members of a family are alike. The members of a family may be recognizable as such though they do not share a single nontrivial characteristic in common, and, consequently, the important facts cannot be named in a legal rule. Lawyers and judges as a matter of course recognize the kinship among like cases to a very large extent. A workable method of legal interpretation can be conceived in relation to the conventional practices and dispositions of the legal community, which functions as an interpretive community whose job is to interpret the law.

A. Facts in Common among Cases?

The method of reasoning that seems to be implicit in deductive and analogical forms of reasoning is a familiar one in the modern age. The remarkable successes of the physical and mathematical sciences inspire persons in other fields to follow or adapt the methods of reasoning thought to be employed in the most successful fields. The educated layperson's conception of scientific reasoning usually does not coincide with a scientist's or philosopher's conception; it is a romanticized version of scientific reasoning that tends to dominate thinking about what is rational.[1] The laws of a society, however, cannot be used as a scientist generally is thought to use the laws of nature. A lawyer cannot use legal rules to predict what a court will do as a scientist might use formulas expressing the laws of nature to predict the arrival time of a space ship at the moon; much less could one use that method of reasoning to persuade a court of what it should do or to decide law cases.

The popular conception of scientific reasoning focuses on a potential relationship of correspondence between a word or symbol in a scientific proposition and an objectively ascertainable (observable) fact in the real world. The proposition is supposed to state the conditions under which natural events occur. For example, one may observe that water changes from a liquid to a gas when heated to a temperature of 212° F., using a thermometer to gauge the temperature. Following a number of such observations, one might formulate as a scientific proposition that water always boils when its condition is 212° F. It then can be predicted with some confidence that another volume of water will boil when it is heated to 212° F. — i.e., when the temperature of the water corresponds to the symbol *212° F.* If the water does not boil, one might conclude that the thermometer is broken or that another relevant condition, such as atmospheric pressure, has changed. In the latter case, the proposition might be reformulated to say that water always boils at 212° F. when the atmospheric pressure is the same as at sea level. Predictions then could be made with greater confidence by looking for two observable facts that correspond to the two symbols of the proposition, each of which would state a condition for water to boil, and both of which together would symbolize necessary and (jointly) sufficient conditions for water to boil.

The scientific search is thought to be a search for the objectively observable facts that are common to all instances of water boiling, itself an observable fact. The common facts are described in words (*boils*) or symbols (*212° F.*), organized as necessary and sufficient conditions, in a general scientific proposition. The propo-

---

[1]"It is a commonplace of the philosophy of science that evidence is incomplete, that alternative hypotheses and possibilities can be imagined, that theories are held tentatively until a better one is produced, and so on." R. Nozick, Philosophical Explanations 23 (1981). See also T. Kuhn, The Structure of Scientific Revolutions (2d ed. 1970).

sition is confirmed or disconfirmed by experiment, using techniques of observation to establish relationships of correspondence between the facts of the real world and the words of the proposition. Once confirmed by observation, the proposition popularly is thought to be true.

The two forms of legal reasoning discussed in Part I seem to presuppose a method of legal reasoning that is like the popular conception of scientific reasoning in these respects. The deductive form of reasoning uses major premises that appear to state the necessary and sufficient factual conditions for any case to fall within the class of cases designated by the rule. For example, the common law negligence rule requires a defendant to compensate a plaintiff if the defendant (1) was under a duty to use reasonable care, (2) breached that duty, which breach was the (3) cause-in-fact and (4) legal cause of (5) damage to the plaintiff (subject to certain qualifications omitted for present purposes). This seems to suggest by its form that compensation is required in any case in which these five facts are present and not when one or more of these five facts are not present—that all cases of negligence have in common the presence of these five facts.

The analogical form of legal reasoning seems to contemplate the same method. The commentators often suggest that two cases are alike and should be treated alike under stare decisis if they have material facts in common.[2] Assume that a precedent case includes facts *a*, *b*, and *c* but not *d*, and the court holds that the plaintiff consequently must compensate the defendant. A problem case also includes facts *a*, *b*, and *c* but not *d*. It could be said that the plaintiff should compensate the defendant because the two cases have facts *a*, *b*, and *c* but not *d* in common; therefore, they are like cases that should be treated alike. However, it also could be said as a rule that, for any case, if facts *a*, *b*, and *c* but not *d* are present, then the plaintiff must compensate the defendant. The rule is implicit in the analogy. If analogies did depend on the existence of identifiable facts in common, one could dispense with the analogies and work from the rules in the deductive form.

The inclination to believe that legal interpretation should mimic the popular conception of scientific reasoning should be

---

[2]See, e.g., H. Jones, J. Kernochan & A. Murphy, Legal Method 6 (1980); E. Levi, An Introduction to Legal Reasoning 3 (1948); Landau, Logic for Lawyers, 13 Pacific L.J. 59, 77-78 (1981); Oliphant, A Return to Stare Decisis, 14 A.B.A.J. 71, 72 (1928).

resisted. It would make sense to adapt this version of scientific reasoning to the legal missions of predicting, persuading, and deciding in law cases only if (1) all law cases that are alike in the important respects, or members of the same legal class, have a fact or facts in common, and (2) the facts or facts in common among those cases correspond to the words of legal rules so that, by their presence, they signal the proper legal classification of the cases. It is highly doubtful, to say the least, that facts in law cases so organize themselves and therefore that the language of legal rules could be complete and determinate.

To illustrate, consider two easy cases. The court in each case was asked to decide whether a party to a contract breached the contract by failing to perform the contract in good faith. Though the cases were decided by different courts at different times, the principle of stare decisis presumably requires that such a pair of cases be alike in important factual respects to justify decisions that both parties thus were in breach. Similarly, the common law rule that requires contracts to be performed in good faith presumably would be applied consistently to find both parties in breach only if the important facts in each case establish that it was an instance of bad faith in the performance of a contract.

In the first case,[3] the Vanadium Corporation contracted to purchase from Horace Reddington certain mining rights to land belonging to the Navaho Tribe on their reservation in Arizona. Because federal law required the approval of the Secretary of the Interior before any such rights could be transferred, the contract parties agreed that Vanadium could call off the deal if the Secretary of the Interior did not approve it within six months. Vanadium promptly entered negotiations with two other persons to purchase other mining rights to the same lands, without which use of Reddington's mining rights would be hampered. These negotiations fell through, and Vanadium's interest in the Reddington mining rights cooled. Vanadium refused to give requested assurances to the Secretary of the Interior that it would cooperate with the owners of the other mining rights, withdrew its request for approval of the contract, and asked the Secretary to disapprove its application formally. The Secretary did so. Vanadium claimed that it therefore had the right to call off the deal.

---

[3]Vanadium Corp. of America v. Fidelity & Deposit Corp., 159 F.2d 105 (2d Cir. 1947).

In the second case,[4] Mr. Fry entered into a contract to purchase a residential home in California. As is usual in such contracts, the deal was concluded before Fry had obtained a mortgage loan. He was given a right to call off the deal if he could not obtain a loan on terms described in the contract. Fry was advised by the real estate agent that he could not get a loan on the required terms from a bank, but probably could get one from a mortgage company. Fry delayed for some time before he applied for a loan, and then he applied only to two banks, which denied his applications. He told the real estate agent that he had lost all interest in the home because he had decided to move to Hawaii. Fry claimed that he had the right to call off the deal because he could not obtain a loan as required by the contract.

The courts found that Vanadium and Fry each had breached their contracts because neither had a right to call off the deal. Each court said that the buyer was required by the law to perform its contract in good faith — Vanadium to attempt in good faith to obtain the Secretary of the Interior's approval; Fry to put forward a good faith effort to obtain a mortgage loan on the terms specified. Each court found that the buyer had failed to perform its contract in good faith and therefore was in breach.

Most lawyers and judges would agree that these two cases both are cases in which a party to a contract changed its mind after making a deal and tried to back out, thereby breaching the contract. They are like cases in which the buyers were treated alike, in the analogical form. They also are two cases in which a single applicable rule of law was applied consistently, in the deductive form. The applicable rule of law says that a party to a contract who does not perform in good faith is in breach. Fry and Vanadium each failed to perform in good faith. Therefore, Fry and Vanadium each were in breach. Few lawyers and judges would have difficulty making reasonable predictions, persuasions, and decisions in these cases.

The problem is to explain how it is possible for this to be so. Legal interpretation that mimics the popular conception of scientific reasoning does not offer an adequate explanation. Significantly, there is no single nontrivial fact, in the sense of something that can be observed, that the *Vanadium* and *Fry* cases have in common and that signals their proper classification as breaches of

---

[4]Fry v. George Elkins Realty Co., 162 Cal. App. 2d 256 (1958).

contracts. If it were regarded as a fact that each buyer changed his mind after concluding the deal, and for that reason tried to call the deal off, the search for an observable fact in common would not end. Descriptions of mental states depend on inferences drawn intuitively from observable facts, such as what the subject says or does; the statement that each buyer changed its mind cannot be justified only by pointing to any observable fact(s) that the two cases have in common. Hence, the decisions in the cases cannot be explained satisfactorily by pointing to a common mental state (if that were conceivable) as the common fact that signals a breach of contract in such circumstances.

Rather, we want to point at the facts of each case as an inter-related whole — as a congeries of facts. We almost want to say: "*These* cases are instances of bad faith," or "*this* case is like *that* case," without pointing to any particular fact or facts the presence of which signals the correctness of these statements. Reread the statements of each case, asking of each sentence if its deletion would change your intuition at least to the extent of rendering it more uncertain. No nontrivial fact can be deleted from either case without increasing significantly the probability that the case would be decided differently. In each of the two cases, virtually *all* of the stated facts seem to be important to explain the conclusion. But none of the stated facts in one case is necessary to justify reaching the conclusion in the other case.

Like many cases, the facts in *Vanadium* and *Fry* are not them-selves important apart from their contexts. In each case taken sepa-rately, all of the stated facts seem to be both necessary and (jointly) sufficient to explain the conclusion; that is, all of the stated facts seem to be important. But one cannot universalize from the two cases together to state the necessary and sufficient factual conditions for concluding in any case that a contract party is or is not in breach because it failed to perform its contract in good faith. The absence of any observable fact or facts that both cases have in common precludes such a universalization under this rule. "Good faith" itself is not an observable fact, nor can it be reduced by analysis to neces-sary and sufficient conditions that are observable facts.[5]

Consequently, it is a mistake to think that the laws of a society

---

[5]See generally Burton, Breach of Contract and the Common Law Duty to Perform in Good Faith, 94 Harv. L. Rev. 369 (1980); Burton, More on Good Faith Performance of a Contract: A Reply to Professor Summers, 69 Iowa L. Rev. 497 (1984).

can be used as a scientist commonly is thought to use the laws of nature. Laws of nature are thought to exist in the real world and to explain the facts of the real world insofar as we can observe them. The laws of nature are discovered by techniques of observation, and themselves are objective facts. Laws of nature are not thought to be creations of the human will, designed to serve chosen human ends. The laws of a society, however, are not like the laws of nature thus conceived. It should be obvious that duties, contracts, breaches, legal causes, and rights are not facts that exist in the real world to be observed as the scientist observes the temperature of water or its boiling. A duty cannot be seen, touched, tasted, smelled, or heard, and we have no legal thermometer. There is no observable fact or set of facts that correspond to the word *duty*, or to many other legal words, as a state of water might correspond to *212° F.* or *boiling*. Though the forms of legal reasoning seem to presuppose a method like the romanticized popular conception of scientific reasoning, a workable method of legal interpretation must be different.

B. Family-Style Relations among Cases

The facts and laws that scientific reasoning seeks to understand and make predictions about seem in many instances to be susceptible to scientific methods of reasoning, as popularly conceived. The facts and laws that legal reasoning seeks to understand, and to make predictions and prescriptions about, do not seem to be susceptible to a similar method. This leaves it unclear how else two or more cases can be like cases, or members of the same legal class, and therefore unclear how a workable method of legal interpretation could be conceived. Any method that persists in defining the facts in common among all like cases will misclassify cases like *Vanadium* and *Fry,* while any method that does not substitute a different conception of likeness among cases will not be able to classify cases meaningfully at all. Accordingly, a different conception of how two or more cases can be alike is necessary to set the stage for a workable method of legal interpretation.

It is useful to think that the cases falling within a legal class are alike as the members of a family are alike.[6] No two members of

---

[6]See L. Wittgenstein, Philosophical Investigations §§65-76 (G. Anscombe trans. 1958).

most families will be alike in all respects, nor must any two members of most families be alike in any nontrivial respect. In the nuclear family, the parents usually do not share any observable physical features in common, such that the presence of those features signals their membership in the same family. Two siblings from those parents, however, probably will share some features with each parent and some features with each other. Thus, Johnny may have Father's nose and Mother's eyes. Sarah may have Father's complexion and Mother's chin. Johnny and Sarah may have the same birthmark and color hair. The four persons are recognizable as members of one family even though all four do not have any significant characteristic in common; no observable fact signals their membership in the same family. Necessary and sufficient observable conditions for membership in the family do not exist, but the family is a meaningful idea.

Family-style relations among the members of a class are quite common in many settings. As one philosopher put the idea,

> Consider for example the proceedings that we call "games." I mean board-games, card-games, ball-games, Olympic games, and so on. What is common to them all? — Don't say: "There *must* be something common, or they would not be called 'games' " — but *look and see* whether there is anything common to all. — For if you look at them you will not see something that is common to *all,* but similarities, relationships, and a whole series of them at that. To repeat: don't think, but look! — Look for example at board-games with their multifarious relationships. Now pass to card-games; here you find many correspondences with the first group, but many common features drop out, and others appear. When we pass next to ball-games, much that is common is retained, but much is lost. — Are they all 'amusing'? . . . Or is there always winning and losing, or competition between players?[7]

One form of family-style relations can be conceived as follows: *A* shares characteristics with *B; B* shares characteristics with *C; A* does not share any nontrivial characteristic with *C. A* and *C* may belong in the same classification. Significantly, general principles can be formulated that capture some important facts in *A* and *B* or *B* and *C.* But no universal principle subsumes all of the members

---

[7]Id. at §66.

of the family, which as a whole is a family because of a latticework of interlocking general principles.[8]

Recall the *Vanadium* and *Fry* cases. Lawyers and judges generally would be prepared to conclude that Vanadium and Fry each were in breach because they failed to perform their contracts in good faith, even though the two cases have no important fact or facts in common. How could this be so?

Consider a hypothetical third case. Ms. Vanafry concluded a contract to purchase a retail store from which she planned to sell groceries. As is common in such contracts, Vanafry was given a right to call the deal off if she could not obtain a mortgage loan on terms specified in the contract. Vanafry duly applied for a loan. She then entered negotiations with the owner of the neighboring property in order to purchase it. This was necessary to her plan because she needed a parking lot. Vanafry called off negotiations when the owner of the neighboring property refused to sell but offered a long-term lease. Vanafry had won the state lottery in the meantime and then refused to give the lender requested assurances that she would acquire adequate parking space, withdrew her application for a loan, and requested the lender to make a formal determination that the loan request was denied. The lender did so. Vanafry claims that she has a right to call off the deal because she could not obtain a loan as required by the contract.

The reader will perceive quickly that this hypothetical case seems to have some facts in common with the *Vanadium* case, others in common with the *Fry* case, and yet others that are unique to itself. It seems clear that Vanafry, too, performed her contract in bad faith. The hypothetical *Vanafry* case can link the *Vanadium* and *Fry* cases through two interlocking general principles, which strengthens the intuitive sense that *Vanadium* and *Fry* are akin. It is like a child in a family that links the parents as members of the family. The three cases surely are like cases and members of the same legal class, even though there is no observable fact or facts in all three cases the presence of which signals the proper legal classification of the cases.

---

[8]The distinction in the text between universal and general principles is meant to be a logical one. Functionally universal principles state the conditions under which a legal consequence follows *in all cases*. General principles state the conditions under which a legal consequence follows *in some cases*, including a particular problem case.

The example, of course, is simplified for purposes of illustration. For each legal class of cases, all possible members of the class are related as are the members of a large extended family viewed over many generations past, present, and future. There are an unknown number of possible members, and the members that are known are not necessarily typical of the entire membership. Additionally, each case can be linked to several legal classes, as each person is a member of several extended families whose memberships overlap. Some cases are like stepchildren, adopted children, and children born out of wedlock. Moreover, though legal classes are like families in the foregoing respects, they also are unlike many families in important respects. There is nothing that links cases as genes link most members of most families because membership in a legal class is assigned by human beings (judges). Nonetheless, it often is possible, using hypothetical cases, to fill in the members that would link two or more like cases, as the *Vanafry* case links *Vanadium* and *Fry*. It then may be possible to formulate general principles that subsume two or more like cases and fit into the latticework of principles that makes a family.

The facts and law with which legal reasoning must contend are far different from the facts and law presupposed by popular conceptions of scientific reasoning. The facts are constituted as cases— short stories or congeries of facts in which no one fact itself is significant apart from its context. The rules encompass the cases, rather than any particular fact or facts in common among all cases in a legal class. Two law cases can be alike in important respects though they have no facts in common, and both can be members of the same legal class though no particular fact or facts in either case correspond to a word in a legal rule. Membership in a legal class is in significant respects like membership in a family. It is like membership in an extended family viewed over multiple generations past, present, and future.

C. Toward a Workable Method of Legal Interpretation

Workable legal interpretation must justify placing a problem case in a class of cases while respecting the family-style relations among cases in the class and the resulting indeterminacy of language. This has significant practical implications. Because all cases in a legal class need not have any fact or facts in common as a sign of their proper legal classification, the promise of certainty implicit

in the forms of legal reasoning is an illusory promise. Many problem cases will bear some family resemblances to cases in more than
one legal class, with conflicting legal consequences. It must be
decided which link is stronger because it encompasses the more
important factual relationship. Workable legal interpretation consequently is not capable of mechanically dictating a single correct
result in problem cases. At best, it can aspire to enable lawyers to
make reasonably reliable predictions and effective persuasions
while enabling judges to make responsible decisions that may earn
respect as law for the present and foreseeable future.

The absence of certainty in predictions, persuasions, and decisions might lead some to question whether such legal interpretation
is possible. It might be thought that anything less than certainty in
legal reasoning leaves the judges free to classify cases as a function
of their personal value preferences, rather than "the law." Such a
view not only raises the problem of the legitimacy of adjudication.
As a practical matter it suggests that there can be no reasoned basis
for a lawyer's predictions and persuasions.

However, it should not be doubted that a reasonable method
of legal interpretation is possible. As Roscoe Pound observed:

> It is an everyday experience of those who study judicial decisions
> that the results are usually sound, whether the reasoning from which
> the results purport to flow is sound or not. The trained intuition of
> the judge continually leads him to right results for which he is puz-
> zled to give unimpeachable legal reasons.[9]

This suggests that judges and those who study judicial decisions—
lawyers—share intuitions that often lead them to the same result
in a particular case. Thus, in *Vanadium* and *Fry*, lawyers and
judges generally would agree that the courts properly concluded
that the buyers breached their contracts by performing in bad
faith, even if they would give differing explanations. When cases
are controversial, lawyers and judges often would agree on the
strongest arguments on each side of the question. Something is
operating other than the idiosyncratic value preferences of individuals or reasoning that mimics the popular conception of scientific reasoning.

Pragmatically speaking, the key lies in the fact of widespread
agreement among members of the legal community on what the law

---

[9]Pound, The Theory of Judicial Decision, 36 Harv. L. Rev. 940, 951 (1923).

permits or requires in a wide range of cases within a legal system.[10] The membership of the U.S. legal community includes lawyers and judges most centrally, and in appropriate cases includes legislators, executive or administrative officials, and sometimes others. Their considerable agreement on what the law permits or requires in cases hardly reflects shared personal value preferences; the diversity of moral, religious, economic, and political views among members of the legal community is too great. Rather, it reflects professional intuitions that are developed by legal training and experience and influenced in each case by the conventions of the profession. These conventions consist of the points of general agreement among members of the legal community, reflected in the many easier cases, the language of legal discourse, the practice of refining intuitions in each case through legal research, reflection, and argument, and the commitment to values embodied in the "rule of law" in U.S. society. Conventional practices and dispositions characterize the legal community adequately to treat it as an interpretive community, which in significant respects is different from the people at large or other professional communities. The legal community in relation to a legal system is an interpretive community whose job is to interpret the law, in addition to other functions.[11]

The law in a case will be developed from the legal materials commonly consulted in the course of legal research — case reports,

---

[10]This assertion takes into account all cases that arise or could arise, rather than focusing on the few cases that reach the appellate courts and result in published decisions, much less the fewer reported appellate cases that find their way into law school casebooks or become a subject of scholarly debate. The latter cases are more often controversial, but they do not represent an unbiased sample of the whole. Even among appellate cases, the extent of agreement is striking. Justice Benjamin N. Cardozo, while a member of the New York Court of Appeals, reported: "Of the cases that come before the court in which I sit, a majority, I think, could not, with semblance of reason, be decided in any way but one. The law and its application alike are plain. Such cases are predestined, so to speak, to affirmance without opinion." B. Cardozo, The Nature of the Judicial Process 164 (1921). See also Newman, Between Legal Realism and Neutral Principles: The Legitimacy of Institutional Values, 72 Calif. L. Rev. 200, 204 (1984) (dissenting votes were cast in only 3.7 percent of all cases decided by federal courts of appeal in the year ending June 30, 1983).

It would be a different, and more dubious, observation to suggest that there is widespread agreement among members of the legal community on universal principles that sufficiently explain or justify the results in these cases. See Chapter 7.

[11]See generally S. Fish, Is There a Text in This Class? (1980); Fiss, Objectivity and Interpretation, 34 Stan. L. Rev. 739 (1982); Symposium: Law and Literature, 60 Texas L. Rev. 373 (1982).

constitutions, statutes, administrative regulations, treatises, law review articles, and the like—together with the conventions of the legal community. A lawyer researching a problem case will find the pertinent legal materials useful, even though the rules and cases do not single out the important facts in a problem case mechanically. As will be seen in subsequent chapters, the legal materials, interpreted as indicated by the conventions of the legal community, call a lawyer's attention to the facts in a problem case that are likely to be regarded as important facts by other members of the legal community, including the judges in a particular case. To be skillful, a lawyer who wants to predict what a court will do or persuade someone of what a court will or should do must treat a case largely as the judges would treat it. To be responsible, a judge who decides cases must treat each case in a way that may earn respect as law, at least among other members of the legal community. The decision in a law case in large part results from the interchange of ideas between lawyers and judges, involving most intensely the lawyers and judges assigned to the case, but including in crucial ways other members of the legal community.[12]

A workable interpretive method is "essentially an affair of leading—leading that is useful because it is into quarters that contain objects that are important."[13] The conventions of the legal community can lead the lawyer with a problem case to see the important facts in the case as other lawyers and judges within the same legal system would see them, while preserving flexibility so that the law can respond intelligently to the family-style relations among cases and unforseen congeries of facts. It may not be possible to prove that their predictions, persuasions, and decisions are right in an absolute sense—one surely can imagine different legal systems, with different interpretive conventions, in which even the easiest of cases would be decided differently because different facts would be treated as important facts. In the context of a working legal system, however, the conventions of the relevant legal community are useful pragmatically because they help lawyers and judges to get somewhere that they want to go.

In the aggregate, a workable interpretive method produces predictions, persuasions, and decisions that can be reconciled with

---

[12]For further elaboration, see Chapter 10 §C.
[13]W. James, Pragmatism 141 (Perry ed. 1955) (writing about pragmatism's conception of truth).

the traditions of a legal culture and pass on through the generations those practices that work well to maintain a civilization. Such a method also will modify or discard those practices that no longer work well in light of contemporary circumstances and evolving notions of justice. A culture has made no small achievement if its legal system enables lawyers to make reasonably reliable predictions and effective persuasions, and enables judges to make responsible decisions that earn respect as law for the present and foreseeable future. Legal reasoning only need serve the purposes that it is called on to serve within a legal system.

D. Summary

Thus, law cases that are alike in the important respects, and therefore members of the same legal class, need not have any fact or facts in common such that the presence of those facts signals the proper legal classification of the case. Rather, law cases in a legal class are alike as the members of a family are alike; they are linked by a latticework of interlocking general principles. A romanticized "scientific" method of legal reasoning consequently is not possible. Some uncertainty will exist in any lawyer's or judge's legal reasoning due to the indeterminacy of language and the family-style relations among cases in a legal class.

Pragmatically speaking, such uncertainty need not be disturbing. No lawyer wins all cases, but no competent lawyer is a mere gambler. Lawyers and judges are practical people who pursue practical ends. As will be seen, a workable method of legal interpretation can be conceived in recognition of the fact of widespread agreement among members of the legal community on what the law permits or requires in a wide range of cases. Uncertainty persists, and legal reasoning proceeds in relation to the conventions of an interpretive community. But a lawyer who makes reasonably reliable predictions and effective persuasions can help a client to get somewhere that the client wants to go. A judge who makes decisions that earn respect as law surely helps the society get somewhere that the society wants to go.

Subsequent chapters in this part will focus on three sorts of problems. It remains to be shown how a judgment of importance can be made through a method of legal interpretation that uses the legal materials, together with the conventions of the legal community, to call attention to the important facts in a problem case. This is the topic for Chapter 6. Chapter 7 elaborates on how the differing views of the members of the legal community come together to suggest the proper classification of harder problem cases. How the method of legal interpretation manifests itself within the two forms of legal reasoning will be the subject of Chapter 8.

CHAPTER SIX

The Roles of Theory and the Legal Experience

THIS CHAPTER SUGGESTS that a workable method of legal interpretation depends on a theory about what the law is or should be trying to do and how it might do it effectively. Theories about the purposes served by legal rules and precedents establish a normative perspective from which to approach the facts in a problem case. In the absence of such a perspective, predictions, persuasions, and decisions might be based on any facts[1] that happen to loom largest to one's mind at the time. The theories call some facts to the foreground of the totality of the circumstances, leaving others in the background as context. They lead lawyers and judges to the important facts in a problem case—the facts that will or should influence the actions of judges because they count as reasons.

Theories about the purposes of the laws are tools of analysis that, when properly used, make it possible for lawyers and judges to give reasons for their predictions, persuasions, and decisions in cases. The reasons will be treated as good reasons when the theories supporting them are recognized as relevant normative theories by members of the legal community. To a large extent, it will be seen, members of the legal community recognize as relevant those theories that are embedded in the legal experience—the common law precedents and rules, and the enacted texts with their contexts—as well as commentaries on these legal materials. The legal experience and commentaries reflect the conventional practices and dispositions of lawyers, judges, legislators, and others concerning the law and its implications in families of cases. A synthesis of these conventions in the form of a theory about what the law is trying to do (or sometimes an analysis of these views

---

[1] The text passes over the complex problems of gathering the facts and proving them in court, as well as the role of the jury. The facts that can be proven do not necessarily present a picture that is a complete and accurate account of what did happen. A jury's or other factfinder's finding of facts normally will be taken as "true" nonetheless.

together with a theory about what the law should be trying to do) can help lawyers predict reliably or persuade effectively, and help judges decide responsibly, in particular cases.

A. Calling Attention to Important Facts

The problem of importance is the problem of determining which of the many facts in a case shall be valued for more than their truth. Absent a theory about what the rules and precedents are trying to do, the congeries of facts in a case (the totality of the circumstances) are puzzling. There are so many facts! Each fact by itself is just that—a fact. *Any* fact might be important or unimportant. A fact merits special attention only if it counts more than others (if it is brought to the foreground of the totality of the circumstances). It counts more than others only if it is valued for more than its truth. A fact can be valued for more than its truth if it plausibly accords with a normative theory about what the law is trying to do and how it might do it.

In the legal setting, however, it has been seen that the facts do not accord with the theories because they correspond to the words of a rule that purports to state the necessary and sufficient factual conditions for its use. The method of legal interpretation must respect the indeterminacy of language and the family-style relations among the cases in a legal class. This implies that the theories should leave open the precise identification of the important facts until after a case has materialized, but they should call the attention of different lawyers and judges to more or less the same facts once a case has materialized. We do not understand precisely how theories about law can accomplish both missions. That they commonly do so nonetheless can be shown.

Imagine that you are asked to tell a true story about the Mississippi River.[2] If you are told nothing more, you might be puzzled. You can tell stories about the Mississippi's length, the volume of water it carries, its contributions to irrigation, the drainage basin it serves, the facilities and sites along its banks, its propensity to flood, its role in political boundaries, its effects on human settlement patterns, the traffic it carries, the pollution it carries, its geological history, its role in *Huckleberry Finn,* the hazards of navigating it, and so on. An almost infinite number of facts about

---

[2]This example is suggested by J. White, The Legal Imagination 3-34 (1973).

the Mississippi could be gathered. You may not know where to begin, where to end, or how to organize your story intelligently.

Imagine that you are asked to tell a story about the Mississippi River because you want to transport grain from St. Louis to New Orleans by barge. Given this purpose, you will at once turn attention to the river's length, the navigational hazards one might encounter, and the facilities along its banks for servicing barge transports. These and related facts about the Mississippi will merit special notice in light of your purpose. The facts about its geological history, its contributions to irrigation, its role in political boundaries, and sundry other matters fall away from attention. They are not important in the relevant context, even though true.

By contrast, imagine that you are asked to tell a story about the Mississippi because you want to locate oil deposits. You will turn attention now to its geological history. Given this purpose, you will focus on the transport eons ago of sediments south and into the Gulf of Mexico. Geological theories indicate that there consequently might be some oil in the Gulf. Now *these* and related facts about the Mississippi will come to the foreground of the totality of the circumstances. In light of your purpose, these facts are important. Facts about its length, the hazards of navigating it, the facilities along its banks, its contributions to irrigation, its role in political boundaries, and sundry other matters are left in the background. In the relevant context, those facts are not important, even though true.

The lawyer who first approaches a law case similarly is puzzled. So many facts can be gathered and described in so many ways! Without a theory about what the law is trying to do, it is hard to know where to begin, where to stop, or how to organize a statement of the facts intelligently. With such a theory, the task becomes more manageable and focused.

Suppose that a lawyer is visited by a prospective client, Marilyn Mother. Mother says that she is divorced, works in the home, and until last week had one child. Malcolm Motorist then was driving a truck down Main Street in Springfield. As he approached Chestnut Avenue near Mother's home, her boy entered the street in pursuit of a ball. A collision occurred, and the boy was killed. Mother wants to sue Motorist and wishes the lawyer to represent her. Before deciding to do so, the lawyer will want to get some preliminary idea of what is involved by gathering the relevant facts. He will begin by questioning Mother.

What questions will the lawyer ask? At first he is puzzled. How old was the boy? What was his name? Why was he given that name? Why did he enter the street? Was it nighttime or daytime? Did he look both ways? What was he wearing? Was he a good student? Did Mother see the collision? Is she capable of bearing more children? What kind of truck was Motorist driving? What color was it? How fast was he going? Did he wear glasses? What is his religion? Was he watching where he was going? Did he brake? Were his brakes in good working order? Did he carry insurance? Was an ambulance promptly called to the scene? Did the ambulance reach the hospital quickly? Was medical care properly administered? Absent a theory, any of these facts and many others might be important. The fact that the child was a boy, not a girl, looms as large or as small as any other fact.

Consider the probable effect of two of the several possible normative theories that generally are thought to underlie the rules and analogies in the relevant area of the law. One theory (a *deterrence theory*) supposes that what the law is or should be trying to do in cases like this is to discourage people from behaving unreasonably when they might cause harm to others. It supposes that this goal can be furthered by forcing people to compensate those who are avoidably injured by unreasonably dangerous behavior. This theory calls attention to Motorist's behavior (and the ambulance attendant's, attending physician's, etc.). In light of this simple deterrence theory, important possible facts would be that Motorist was not wearing his glasses, was not watching where he was going, did not keep his brakes in good repair, failed to slow down when he saw the boy's ball roll into the street, and the like. These behaviors by Motorist or by others in similar situations probably should be discouraged by forcing them to pay compensation to their victims, if the law's purpose is to discourage unreasonably dangerous behavior. The fact that Motorist was driving a truck when the collision occurred probably is not very important. By this theory, the law does not seek to discourage people from driving trucks.

By contrast, a second possible theory (a *compensation theory*) supposes that what the law is or should be trying to do in cases like this is to spread the losses resulting from accidents among large numbers of people, rather than to leave the losses on the victim alone. This theory might suppose that persons who are more likely to have insurance should compensate victims who are less likely to have insurance. In light of this simple compensation theory, important facts probably would be that Motorist was driving a truck and the victim was a child. Truck drivers generally carry insurance for this kind of accident. Children do not, and many parents do not carry life insurance to cover such accidents to their children. Motorist's insurance company can pay compensation to Mother and spread the cost among a large group of subscribers. By this theory, it is not important whether Motorist was wearing glasses, was watching where he was going, kept his brakes in good repair, slowed down when a child's ball rolled into the street, and the like.

Assume it were to turn out that Motorist was driving a truck and the victim was a child, and that Motorist was wearing his glasses, was watching where he was going, had just inspected his brakes, braked as soon as any good driver would, and in all other respects was proceeding safely down the street. If the courts employ the first (deterrence) theory, Motorist probably will not be held liable. The facts indicating that he was behaving safely are important because he did nothing that was unreasonably dangerous and should be discouraged. If the courts employ the second (compensation) theory, Motorist probably will be held liable. The fact that he was driving a truck that hit a child is important because Motorist probably is the one in the best position to spread the loss among a large group of people through insurance.

In addition to normative theories, the elements of legal rules themselves are supposed to perform the function of calling the important facts into prominence. Some elements of some rules do a reasonable job of capturing in language the significance of the class of cases for which they stand and consequently perform this function in easier cases. Assume that Motorist had behaved in a less than perfectly safe manner in that he had failed to have his brakes inspected when they were due for an inspection a week before the accident. Assume further that the common law negligence rule governs this case: Motorist is liable if he was under a duty to use reasonable care and breached that duty, which breach was a cause-in-fact and legal cause of damage to Mother.

The language of this rule makes is fairly clear that the lawyer should focus attention on the potential causal relationship between the accident and Motorist's failure to have his brakes inspected. Because Motorist behaved safely in all respects except in failing to have his brakes inspected, that is the only possible breach of duty. The rule tells the lawyer that the breach of duty must be the "cause-in-fact" of the accident if Motorist is to be held liable under this rule. He will not be held liable if the accident would have occurred even if the brakes had been inspected. Accordingly, important facts include whether a defect in the brakes would have been discovered on inspection and whether, if discovered and repaired, the truck would have come to a stop sooner and before hitting the child. In an easy case, there may be no need to resort to the theories underlying the negligence rule in order to apply at least some of its elements.

Often, however, the elements of legal rules do not do a good job of capturing in language the significance of the class of cases for which they stand. The language of the negligence rule, for example, itself does not call attention to the important facts that matter for deciding whether Motorist's failure to have his brakes inspected was a "breach of duty to use reasonable care," assuming that it was the cause-in-fact of the harm to the boy. The language of this element of the rule suggests that less than perfectly safe behavior is not a breach of duty if it nonetheless was reasonable behavior. It does not indicate how much less than perfect behavior is unreasonable.

If the language is interpreted in light of the deterrence theory, attention may focus on the fact that people commonly treat the due date for a brake inspection somewhat casually. A week's delay is not generally regarded as unreasonably unsafe behavior that should be discouraged, and what people generally do in such circumstances probably is important by this theory. However, if the language is interpreted in light of the compensation theory, as courts sometimes do, a different result may be reached. The underlying theory may lead the judge to seize on the imperfect behavior at least to allow a jury to find Motorist liable, if they will. What people generally do in such circumstances is not so important; that the loss probably falls on Mother alone, but could be spread by Motorist, is important. Which theory would be used largely depends on a synthesis of the precedents for which the rule stands. Thus, a theory underlying an element of a rule may be used to help interpret and apply the rule, at least when the language of the rule does an inadequate job of calling attention to the important facts, as is often the case.

A fact or factual relationship has legal implications if its presence in a case helps lawyers and judges determine which decision in the case will further the purposes of the relevant law. Each element of each legal rule, together with its underlying theory, should call attention to important facts in a case, and different elements (and different rules) should call attention to different facts. No word or phrase in a well-crafted rule should remain idle; each should help lawyers and judges locate facts that have legal significance. In the absence of a theory about the law's purposes, attention might focus on any fact in a case. The function of theories underlying the rules and precedents is to establish a normative perspective from which to approach the facts of a problem case — to call the important facts into prominence.

B. General Purposes of Law

Several comments should be made about this special kind of theory, which is about what the law is trying to do or should be trying to do — its normative purposes, policies, or principles and their practical implications in families of cases. Such theory concerns social facts, social values, and the capability of the law to advance social values, and it has practical implications for the judgment of importance in particular cases. This kind of theory depends on what members of the legal community generally will take to be required by an orderly and just society in a case and (some) like cases.

1. Order and Justice

Members of the legal community generally assume that society would be different if the law did not exist. People generally abide by the law due to a habit of compliance and a sense of obligation, or the practical threat of its sanctions (enforced losses of liberty or property imposed for disobedience), or both. People in many situations would not behave in the same ways if there were no formal expressions of what the society regards as minimally honorable behavior and no organized sanctions for misbehavior. We also assume that society generally is better off because the law exists. The laws are thought to encourage valued behavior and discourage disvalued behavior and, accordingly, are normative. If the laws have an effect on society, they should help make it a better society in which to live.

The law thus exists to serve some valued social purpose or purposes. It is assumed that the behaviors of people in society would form some patterns absent particular laws, that society would be better off if the patterns of behavior were changed to conform to some more highly valued pattern, and that each particular law is capable of advancing valued patterns or retarding disvalued patterns of behavior.[3] At a most general level of analysis, this is what the law is trying to do. The abstractness of this broad perspective can be reduced somewhat by identifying two general purposes that underlie the largest part of the law. These, in turn, will help generate less general theories that are of greater practical value in particular law cases.[4]

First, the law should contribute to a more orderly society. People at times will find themselves in conflict in any society with any form of social organization. Serious conflicts sometimes would result in fights, feuds, and the useless destruction of life and property; even nonviolent disputes can be highly disruptive to the disputants and others if left unsettled. Society would be better off if serious conflicts more often were resolved peacefully. An offer to everyone of peaceful dispute settlement procedures, such as adjudication, may induce many persons to seek peaceful resolutions of serious conflicts that are not settled by other means.

The promotion of social order by the peaceful settlement of serious disputes is not the only purpose at this level of generality. A society could settle persistent disputes in a number of peaceful and less costly ways not involving cases, rules, lawyers, and courts or their functional equivalents. Many societies in many times and places have used such alternatives, and some are used in U.S. society for some disputes. For example, we could flip coins, consult oracles, or appoint a "wise" man to rule by fiat, or we could threaten imprisonment for fighting and leave disputants otherwise to work out their differences by negotiation. Much more complex and costly dispute settlement procedures are available when the disputants persist because the law is trying to do more than to settle disputes peacefully.

The law also should contribute to a more just society. It is thought that, absent the law, the distribution of valued liberties, properties, and dignities often would be unfair — a function of the relative power of each person. Society is better off if the strong at least sometimes are restrained from dominating the weak. At least some of the laws probably are effective in helping to give all persons a fair opportunity to pursue their chosen ends, consistent with the liberties, properties, and dignities of others.

---

[3]See R. Danzig, An Introduction to the Role of Law in the Realm of Private Agreement (forthcoming, Foundation Press).
[4]See infra §C.

The values of order and justice seem to be central to any normative concept of law. A system of government that pursued order without justice would tend toward a police state. Mussolini's Italy might be an example. A system of government that pursued justice without order would tend toward chaos. China's Cultural Revolution might be an example. One or the other of these two values may be emphasized in different legal systems, or in a single legal system at different times, but the pursuit of both values seems inherent in the concept of law.

2. Theories Ideal and Pragmatic

Though the general purposes of the law are very obvious and very general, they have practical implications for a lawyer who wants to predict what a court will do or persuade someone of what a court will or should do in a case, as well as for a judge who must decide cases. Members of the legal community hold as an ideal that each legal rule and each law case should further the purposes of the law as a social institution. Rules and cases thus should contribute to the maintenance and growth of a more orderly and just society. We know that we often fall short of these ideals but nonetheless strive for them.

A practical lawyer usefully can assume that the judges are striving to promote the broad ideals of the law. The task of persuasion is to show the judges how a judgment for the client helps to promote the ideals, while a judgment for the opponent tends to hinder the ideals. The task of prediction is to gauge how the client's activities will appear to the judges in light of the ideals. A judge usefully can assume that members of the legal community, as well as the broader society, value a legal system that contributes to a more orderly and just society. Judicial decisions that so contribute will enjoy and merit respect as law.[5]

It may be objected that the ideals of the law are too broad and too vague to be helpful in a particular case. How do we *know* which decision will enhance social order or contribute to a more just society? Is it not necessary first to believe that an ideal Orderly and Just Society somehow "exists" and to answer the questions that philosophers have failed to answer satisfactorily in the millenia since Plato asked them?

---

[5]See Chapter 10 §§B, C.

Two sorts of questions about these matters can be distinguished. The question "What is the ideal Orderly and Just Society?" involves many difficult, if not unanswerable, philosophical questions that may be of little value to practicing lawyers and judges.[6] The question "What will members of the legal community generally take to be required by an orderly and just society in this case and like cases?" asked when a case is presented, is a pragmatic question about the attitudes of people in a legal culture concerning a particular practical problem. The pragmatic question often is of great value to practicing lawyers and judges as long as the community is committed to the ideals of law. The context set by a problem case focuses the theoretical inquiry on aspects that make a concrete difference in the case, leaving wholly theoretical difficulties unattended. The conventions of the legal community are oriented towards cases, using generalizations as a means to the pragmatic end of deciding what will or should be done in a limited context.

The pragmatic question also differs from the traditional philosophical question because it accepts uncertainty and interpretive relativism in law. It directs attention away from abstract theories that purport to be sound in all times and places, in recognition of the indeterminacy of language and the family-style relations among cases. It directs attention toward the conventions of the legal community, which recognize that an important fact in one case need not be important in all other like cases and that importance may change as the social, historical, and cultural context changes. With a particular case in mind, one might long to *know* what is important in the case, irrespective of the conventions of an interpretive community. To have value, however, a lawyer's predictions and persuasions need not achieve certainty but only need enhance a client's prospects as compared to the client's alternatives in some set of circumstances. Judicial decisions only need earn respect as law among the members of a relevant community for the present and forseeable future. Predictions, persuasions, and decisions can serve these purposes if supported by reasons other lawyers and judges will regard as good reasons, which support largely depends on the conventions of the legal community within a society.[7]

---

[6] For a different view, see, e.g., R. Dworkin, Taking Rights Seriously (1978).
[7] For elaboration on the implications of uncertainty and interpretive relativism in law, see Part III.

C. Theories Embedded in the Legal Experience

Given a case, more concrete and useful normative theories can be generated in a number of ways. The most useful theories are embedded in the legal experience — the common law precedents and rules, and the enacted texts with their contexts. Other useful theories can be found in the concurring and dissenting opinions of judges or the secondary literature, including treatises, restatements of the law, and other scholarly publications. These sources, too, draw their theories for the most part from the legal experience, though some advocate legal change.[8] The normative theories underlying the precedents or the enacted texts with their contexts are reliable indications of what members of the legal community generally will take to be required by an orderly and just society in a case and like cases.

Reconsider the principles of stare decisis and legislative supremacy. It can leave a misleading impression to say only that the important facts in a case are a function of the conventions of the legal community. One thing that U.S. lawyers and judges (and many others) think is required by an orderly and just society is that a judge in a case should not make the judgment of importance on the basis of her own value preferences. Rather, the values embedded in the legal experience are, through interpretation of the legal experience in light of the legal community's theories about law, brought to bear in judging the importance of the facts in a problem case. Principles of stare decisis and legislative supremacy reflect conventional practices and dispositions of the legal community, however imperfectly. They are near-central in the U.S. legal system and, together with the legal experience and normative theories embedded in the legal experience, are useful in working out the legal implications of order and justice in cases.

1. Theories Embedded in the Common Law

Recall that the principle of stare decisis requires judges to follow precedent and reason primarily in the analogical form. Having identified the relevant precedents and the factual similarities and differences between the precedents and a problem case, the analogical form leaves judges to decide whether the similarities or differences are more important under the circumstances. It now

---

[8]See Chapter 11.

has been seen that the role of theory is to help lawyers and judges make the judgment of importance by calling attention to the important factual relationships between cases.

Recall also the line of horse trading cases in Chapter 2. Two of them will be used as if they were precedents, for the purpose of discussing a third as if it were a problem case. For the reader's convenience, the facts are repeated.[9]

CASE 2
(Precedent)

Abbott bought a horse from Costello, giving as payment a forged check on another person's account. Abbott knew the check was forged. After delivering the horse to Abbott, Costello discovered the fraud. Costello sued Abbott to recover possession of the horse. Costello won.

CASE 3
(Precedent)

The facts are similar to Case 2, except that Costello discovered the fraud after Abbott had sold and delivered the horse to Holliday, who did not know or have reason to know of the fraud perpetrated by Abbott. Costello sued Holliday to recover possession of the horse. Holliday won.

CASE 5
(Problem)

The facts are similar to Case 3, except that, after buying the horse from Abbott, Holliday sold and delivered it to Ball. Ball had heard rumors of the fraud worked on Costello by Abbott. Costello sued Ball to recover possession of the horse.

In the analogical form, the issue in Case 5 is whether it is more like Case 2, where Costello recovered possession of the horse from Abbott, or more like Case 3, where Costello did not recover possession from Holliday. Case 5 may be more like Case 3 if the fact that Ball bought from an innocent purchaser is more important than the fact that Ball had heard rumors of the fraud. It may be

---

[9]The reader may find it helpful to refer back to the chart at page 33.

more like Case 2, however, if the fact that Ball had heard rumors of the fraud is more important than the fact that Ball bought from an innocent purchaser. The decision in Case 5 turns on whether it is more important that Ball had heard rumors of the fraud or that Ball had bought from an innocent purchaser.

The judge in Case 5 is unlikely to ask only what she personally thinks is important in Case 5. The law would not be orderly if the judges were to make their decisions on such a basis. It is not obvious whether Costello should be more careful about being defrauded or Ball should check on the rumors of fraud and refrain from buying tainted property. Different judges might well come to different conclusions, and the law would be unpredictable. People would find it difficult to plan their transactions to avoid running afoul of the law. In case of disputes, fewer settlements would occur. The court docket would grow, delaying the delivery of justice to all. A society would hardly be orderly if each case were decided on an ad hoc basis in isolation.

Moreover, the law would not be just if judges were to decide each case in isolation on the basis of their own values. The prospect of different decisions from different courts in similar circumstances is disturbing. Basic to almost any theory of justice is the principle of equal treatment under the law, which requires that like cases be treated alike, or that a rule be applied consistently. Dispensing with this principle leaves judges free to indulge their personal values, prejudices, and whims without pause. Consequently, some judges might use the power of the state to oppress the odd, the unpopular or the weak; others might use official power to rob from the rich and give to the poor. One might question whether such a society settled its disputes in accordance with law at all.

The judge in Case 5 is more likely to ask what members of the legal community generally will take to be required by an orderly and just society in Case 5 and like cases. Cases 2 and 3, of course, are like Case 5 in some respects. What the judges decided in those cases (together with the rest of the legal experience) is a fairly reliable indication of what lawyers and judges generally think on the question. The judges in those cases held that the defrauded owner can recover possession of the horse from the perpetrator of the fraud (Abbott), but not from an innocent purchaser from the perpetrator (Holliday). However, that is not all that they effectively decided. Because they made judgments of importance, the judges used a normative theory or theories to decide on their holdings, whether or not they articulated the theories. The judges in the precedent cases thus explicitly or implicitly expressed their views on what the law is or should be trying to do in such cases.

The judge's objective is to decide Case 5 in a way that permits Cases 2, 3 and 5 to be reconciled. This requires a theory to explain how the three cases are decided consistently and may be thought together to contribute to a more orderly and just society. Because Cases 2 and 3 were decided previously by earlier courts, the judge in Case 5 must work presumptively with theories that explain those two precedents. Having used the holdings of the precedents to frame the issue in the analogical form, then, the judge in Case 5 will make the judgment of importance in accordance with a theory of the family of cases.

The normative theories of Cases 2 and 3 are not hard to discern. Preliminarily, it should be noted that the holding in Case 2 "rights the wrong" perpetrated by Abbott on Costello by requiring Abbott to return the horse to Costello, but this will not do as a theory for the decision of Case 5. A theory that the law should "right all wrongs" hardly survives Case 3. Costello was as wronged in Case 3 as in Case 2, but Costello did not recover the horse in Case 3. Something more is going on because the judge in Case 3 did not regard this theory as an appropriate theory for deciding Case 3.

The better theory in Case 2—one that is consistent with Case 3—is that the law in these circumstances seeks to enhance the security of an owner of property as against others with no claim of right. One function of a system of property rights is to encourage owners to invest in the maintenance and improvement of their property and thus to increase the wealth of society. Some people probably would be less likely to spend time, money, and other resources on maintaining and improving property if another person can take the property without the voluntary consent of the investor. In Case 2, forcing Abbott to return the horse allows Costello and others in similar situations to reap the benefits of ownership as expected. Abbott has no claim of right because there is no apparent countervailing reason why the perpetrator of the fraud should retain possession of the horse.

This theory of Case 2 is consistent with Case 3 because there are countervailing reasons why Holliday should retain possession of the horse. Holliday in Case 3 did not know and had no reason to know that Abbott obtained possession of the horse by fraud. She paid a price for the horse and relied reasonably on receiving ownership and possession. Consequently, Holliday should receive the benefit of her bargain and has a claim of right.

Purchasers like Holliday probably would be less likely to buy property if they could lose possession to a prior owner who had been defrauded by another, perhaps long ago. The law seeks to encourage people to buy and sell property, thereby increasing the wealth of society through trade. Allowing Holliday to keep possession of the horse furthers that goal, while allowing Costello to recover possession might discourage some persons like Holliday from entering such trades. The judge in Case 3 need not deny that holding for Holliday might tend to discourage owners like Costello from maintaining and improving their property. As between Holliday and Costello, one of whom will be hurt unfairly, Costello reasonably might have protected himself while Holliday could not. People like Costello should be encouraged to be more careful about detecting fraud in the transactions to which they are parties. Holliday—who did not know or have reason to know of the fraud—stands in greater need of the protection of law.

In light of this theory, Costello has a plausible argument for recovering possession in Case 5. Unlike Holliday in Case 3, it was possible for Ball to protect herself because Ball had heard rumors of the fraud. Consequently, Costello's appeal to the security of ownership is stronger against Ball than it was against Holliday in Case 3.

Ball, however, has a stronger argument than Costello in Case 5. The normative theories embedded in the precedents suggest that the fact Ball bought from an innocent purchaser is more important than the fact Ball had heard rumors of the fraud. The law in these circumstances seeks to increase the wealth of society by enhancing the security of owners and innocent purchasers of property. When these two goals conflict, as in Case 3, the law gives preference to the security of innocent purchasers when the original owner is defrauded by another. The preference for protecting the security of innocent purchasers and thus to promote trade is likely to carry over to Case 5, to Ball's advantage. Otherwise, Costello could effectively impair Holliday's ability to sell the horse to others by giving general publicity to the fraud or spreading rumors. Moreover, it would hamper trade if a potential buyer bore the burden of checking out every rumor of a defect in the title of personal property, running back perhaps many years. Again, Costello is in a better position than Ball or Holliday to protect himself against fraud; Ball and Holliday stand in greater need of the protection of the law.

It could be that a judge writing on a clean slate would reach the opposite result in Case 5, if writing on a *clean* slate were even conceivable. Ball's argument depends in substantial part on the presumption that Case 3 was decided correctly for Holliday. The legal community's practice of stare decisis, however, supports the presumption that Ball should be treated like Holliday if her case is more like Holliday's than it is like Abbott's in Case 2. The law easily could have evolved differently but, having evolved as it did, it is likely to continue along the same lines.

The decision in each common law case thus elaborates on what has gone before, absent overruling. The decision necessarily is creative to the extent that each problem case casts a new light on its legal precedents and presents a question that previously had not been decided. The decision nonetheless is not made for each case in isolation on the basis of the judge's own values. The normative theories embedded in the precedents set the course of the common law on the point. Members of the legal community do not think that the law should change course at a whim. The judgment of importance in most common law cases is a function of the normative theories embedded in the precedents, elaborated as necessary to reconcile each decision in a problem case with its precedents — to show in what way the cases are consistent with each other and may be thought together to contribute to a more orderly and just society.

2. Theories Embedded in the Statutory Text with Its Context

Recall that the principle of legislative supremacy generally requires judges to subordinate their personal views to the enacted views of the people's representatives in the legislature. The rules enacted by legislatures, however, cannot be applied deductively to dictate the conclusion in a case. Determining the membership of a particular case in a class of cases designated by a rule requires a judgment of importance. It now has been seen that the role of theory is to help make the judgment of importance by calling attention to the important facts in a case.

Recall also the case of Franny Farmer and Morris Auster in Chapter 3. Farmer reneged on a deal to sell peaches to Auster, and Auster wanted to sue Farmer to enforce the contract. Section 2-201(1) of the Uniform Commercial Code stood as a possible barrier to Auster's action. It provided that, to be enforceable, a class of contracts for the sale of goods must be in writing and signed by the party to be charged (Farmer). The Auster/Farmer contract was oral. Auster's prospects in court consequently depended on an exception to Section 2-201(1), set forth in Section 2-201(2). This exception might allow a court to enforce the Auster/Farmer contract because Auster sent Farmer a confirmatory letter to remind her of their deal, and she did not object. This would be so, however, only if the contract was "between merchants"—if both parties were "chargeable with the knowledge or skill of merchants" (Section 2-104(3)). Though it is reasonably clear that Auster is chargeable as a "merchant," it is not at all clear that Farmer is chargeable as one for the purposes of this case. A judgment of importance is necessary to determine which of the facts in the case will or should lead a judge to decide that the Auster/Farmer contract was or was not "between merchants."

A judge in Auster's case is unlikely to ask only what she personally thinks is important in Auster's case. The law would not be orderly or just if courts in statutory cases generally made their decisions in this way. It is far from obvious what would be required in an orderly and just society in these circumstances. Different courts might well come to different conclusions—that Auster should have put the deal in writing or that Farmer should have objected to the confirmatory letter.

The judge in Auster's case is more likely to ask what members of the legal community generally will take to be required by an orderly and just society in Auster's case and like cases. The relevant statutory text with its context, including the ordinary meanings of the terms, the text as a whole, the drafting history, the legal history, and the historical, economic, and social circumstances at the time of enactment, are fairly reliable indications of what members of the legal community generally think on the question. The principles of constitutional democracy and legislative supremacy are deeply engrained in the legal culture. What the legislature was trying to do in Article 2 of the Uniform Commercial Code, and specifically in Section 2-201 and the relevant definitional provisions, is of legal significance.

Given a general background in the law of sales contracts, theories of what the legislature was trying to do can be extracted from the statutory text with its context. A judge in Auster's case will elaborate a theory that shows how the decision in the case can be reconciled with the text and context of the statute, and together with those legal materials may be thought to contribute to a more orderly and just society. The judgment of importance in Auster's case will be a function of the normative theories embedded in the statutory materials, elaborated as necessary to decide the case.

It is widely accepted that a central purpose of the law of sales contracts is to encourage people to promise to buy and sell goods, such as the projected exchange of peaches for money between Auster and Farmer. The assumption is that, in the absence of such law, fewer such exchanges would be promised because people would be less willing to rely on others to keep their promises when the time comes. Enforcing contracts may encourage exchange by encouraging some people to keep their promises. Exchange is thought to benefit society because trade contributes to economic prosperity. Accordingly, the law generally enforces promises to buy and sell goods.

As the requirement of a writing for enforcing a class of contracts suggests, however, the law does not enforce all promises to exchange goods. There also is an assumption that, absent the writing requirement in certain contracts, some unscrupulous persons would allege that a promise was made when it was not or that it was made in terms that differ from those used in fact. A traditional belief is that written contracts signed by the person making the promise are less likely to be fraudulent or that a fraud would be easier to discover and prove. The law should enforce only those promises that really were made, and hold persons to the terms of their promises as made, because *voluntary* trade contributes to economic prosperity. Accordingly, some contracts are enforceable only if in writing and signed by the party to be charged.

The first theory suggests that sales contract law generally seeks to protect people who reasonably expect and probably rely on others to keep promises made as part of an exchange. The second theory suggests that sales contract law also seeks to protect people who allegedly made such promises from being forced to keep promises they did not make. Note that the second theory contemplates that some oral contracts that really were made will not be enforced. It usually is easy for the parties to put it in writing, and perhaps it is generally understood in the trades that important contracts should be in writing.

These two theories help to determine whether Farmer is "chargeable as a merchant" such that the Auster/Farmer contract was "between merchants" and that Section 2-201(2) will remove the requirement of a writing signed by Farmer so that Auster can enforce the deal. When Auster sent the letter to Farmer, reminding her of their deal, he probably expected her to reply and object if there in fact was no deal or if he had gotten the terms wrong. Not receiving a reply, he probably relied on a belief that the deal was on and conducted himself accordingly. The theories suggest that this expectation should be protected if it was reasonable—if encouraging people like Auster so to rely would encourage exchange and would not allow the unscrupulous too easily to stick people like Farmer with deals to which they never agreed.

With this background, the more specific theory embedded in Section 2-201(2) can be brought to light. The statutory text explicitly says that the law would consider Auster's reliance to be reasonable only if Farmer was chargeable as a merchant, and a merchant is defined as one who "deals in goods of the kind or otherwise holds [her]self out as having knowledge or skill peculiar to the practices . . . involved in the transaction." The word *otherwise* in the definition suggests that all persons who deal in goods of the kind are deemed to hold themselves out in the manner described. The more pertinent textual definition of "between merchants," requiring both parties to be "chargeable with the knowledge and skill of merchants," confirms that "deals in goods of the kind" should be so interpreted for this purpose. Persons who so hold themselves out—by dealing or by representations—lead others to expect and probably to rely on them to use their knowledge and skill, much as persons who make promises lead others to expect and rely on them to keep the promises. For the purpose of Section 2-201(2), then, a contract is "between merchants" if the parties, by the nature of their businesses or by representations, lead others to expect an objection if a confirmatory letter is received and is not an accurate confirmation of a real deal.

The more specific question in Auster's case, then, is whether, by the nature of her business or by representations, Farmer led Auster reasonably to expect her to object to the confirmatory letter if it were inaccurate. From the facts as stated in Chapter 3, there is no reason to believe that Farmer made such representations. There are facts that characterize the nature of her business: Her orchard was described as a "small, family-run" business; she makes as few as one peach sale for a few hundred boxes in a year. These facts are important because they might suggest that Farmer does not appear to be a sophisticated business person. But other facts are needed to determine whether the deal was "between merchants" for the purposes of this dispute — whether people in such a business by being in that business lead others generally to expect them to object to inaccurate confirmatory letters. Do growers like Farmer generally reply to inaccurate confirmatory letters? Do their buyers generally expect them to reply to inaccurate confirmatory letters?

In all likelihood, almost everyone in business would be expected to answer the mail.[10] Auster's expectation probably was reasonable and Farmer should have objected to protect herself from fraud because honest business persons ordinarily object to inaccurate confirmatory letters. The Auster/Farmer contract consequently would be held to be "between merchants," Section 2-201(2) would apply to this transaction, and the lack of a writing signed by Farmer would not bar enforcement of the contract by Auster.

The normative theory that generates this line of reasoning — that calls attention to the facts concerning the nature of Farmer's business and general trade practices concerning confirmatory letters — is embedded in the text of the relevant provisions of the Uniform Commercial Code and the law of sales contracts. Section 2-201(2) applies only "between merchants"; that is, when both parties are chargeable with the knowledge and skill of merchants in the practices involved in the transaction. The law is trying to protect persons who reasonably expect and probably rely on others to conform to ordinary business practices because they and others are led to do so by those persons. It leaves those who hold themselves out as persons in business to protect themselves from fraud under these circumstances, as by objecting to inaccurate confirmatory letters.

The statutory context is consistent with and supports this interpretation of the text. The text of Article 2 as a whole contains many provisions that look to ordinary business practices as a source of reasonable expectations. For example, Section 1-102 provides that the statute should be liberally construed and applied to promote its underlying purposes, among which are the promotion of commercial practices. Section 1-205 provides that a contract

---

[10]U.C.C. §2-104, Comment 2.

should be interpreted in light of the usages of the trade, which is defined as "any practice or method of dealing having such regularity of observance in a place, vocation or trade as to justify an expectation that it will be observed with respect to the transaction in question." Numerous provisions require the parties to sales contracts to conform to commercially reasonable practices unless otherwise agreed. Moreover, the drafting history of Article 2 and the secondary literature confirm that this statute sought generally to bring the law of sales contracts into conformity with reasonable commercial practices and expectations in a trade.[11] Interpreting the definition of "between merchants" to protect probable reliance on reasonable commercial practices concerning confirmatory letters by people like Farmer thus furthers the purposes of the law in the circumstances of the Auster/Farmer dispute.

The statutory definitions themselves are puzzling if applied to the facts of a case deductively because contradictory conclusions are possible and of equal logical validity. Having generated a normative theory from the text, its context, and the secondary literature, however, reasonably reliable predictions and effective persuasions can be made in a case. The text with its context—in this example the text as a whole and the drafting history supplemented by the secondary literature—reflect what the legislature was trying to do. The principle of legislative supremacy, and the theories of sales contract law involving the protection of reasonable expectations and the promotion of voluntary trade, reflect the conventional practices and dispositions of the legal community as they bear on Auster's case. The judge decides the problem case through a synthesis of the legal experience in light of the legal community's conventions.

Each statutory case thus elaborates on what has gone before—the legislative activities with their product. The decision in a particular case necessarily is creative because no one previously had decided Auster's case, which, like any case, is a unique congeries of facts and may cast new light on the legal experience. The practice of judicial decision nonetheless requires a synthesis of the legal experience as it bears on the problem case. The judgment of importance in statutory cases is a function of the normative theories embedded in the statutory text with its context, elaborated as

---

[11]E.g., U.C.C. §2-104, Comments 1 & 2; Danzig, A Comment on the Jurisprudence of the Uniform Commercial Code, 27 Stan. L. Rev. 621 (1975).

necessary to show how the decision in the case, together with those legal materials, may be thought to contribute to a more orderly and just society.

D. Summary

Thus, skillful legal interpretation—predictions, persuasions, and decisions about the judgment of importance—often depends on theories about what the law is trying to do. The theories do not dictate the result in any case and do not yield certain predictions and persuasions. They are tools of analysis that generate reasons for the actions of lawyers and judges—reasons that will be recognized as good reasons by other members of the legal community. They make it possible for lawyers to make reasonably reliable predictions and effective persuasions and for judges to make responsible decisions that may earn respect as law.

To predict what a court will do or persuade someone of what a court will or should do in a case, a lawyer must understand what the law is or should be trying to do. In the absence of normative theory of this sort, predictions and persuasions might focus on any facts that happen to loom largest at the time. The role of theory is to call the important facts to the foreground of the totality of the circumstances. The important facts are those that count for more than their truth and will or should influence the actions of judges.

Predictions and persuasions largely are based on the premise that judges are striving to further the ideals of law. These ideals suggest that each rule and each case should contribute to a more orderly and just society. Because lawyers and judges cannot *know* what is the one and only Orderly and Just Society or doubt that any such ideal exists, however, they work with what members of the legal community generally will take to be required by an orderly and just society in a case and (some) like cases. This conventionalist approach directs attention to the practices and dispositions of people in the legal culture, who serve as an interpretive community. The conventional practices and dispositions of the legal community have practical implications for the lawyer who wants to predict what those people will do or persuade someone of what those people will or should do in a case.

Members of the legal community generally consider that the judicial role in an orderly and just society is limited by principles of stare decisis and legislative supremacy. Judges who strive to further the ideals of the law do not make the judgment of importance on the basis their own values as they bear on an isolated case. They normally take the common law precedents or the statutory text with its context as given. They work primarily with the normative theories that are embedded in this legal experience, which are reliable indications of what members of the legal community generally think on a question, supplemented by the theories in the secondary literature. These more concrete theories are elaborated as necessary to decide problem cases. The elaborated theory will show how a decision can be reconciled with the relevant precedents or statutory materials and, together with this legal experience, may be thought to contribute to a more orderly and just society.

CHAPTER SEVEN

The Role of the Legal Community

THE PRECEDING CHAPTER highlighted the roles of normative theory and the legal experience in legal interpretation. More realistically, the conventions of the legal community do not support a monolithic body of consistent theories. There are many cases in which only one theory is relevant or several relevant theories have a singular implication. Given agreement on the facts, lawyers are likely to make the same prediction about what a court will and should do in such cases, even if they would give different theoretical explanations. But there also are many cases in which multiple theories have conflicting implications, including some in which controversy centers on the plausibility of a new theory. These are harder cases, in which the predictions of lawyers more likely will differ even when the facts are not in dispute. Harder cases are more often litigated and are of the greatest interest, whether a lawyer is interested in profit, public service, or fun.

The preceding explanation of the roles of theory and the legal experience does not say enough about legal interpretation in harder cases. This chapter will elaborate on that explanation and an analysis of easier cases to shed light on this more complex matter. The difference between harder and easier cases is one of degree. Both are capable of reasonable treatment by lawyers and judges, in light of what members of the legal community generally will take to be required by an orderly and just society in a case and like cases, as indicated by the legal experience and the totality of our theories about law.

A. Easier Cases

As a practical matter, it is not necessary to appeal explicitly to theory to make reasonable predictions, persuasions, and decisions in easier cases. The legal rules themselves may do an adequate job of calling the important facts into prominence, or the underlying theories may converge to suggest a single result such that the theories need not be made explicit. The theories underlying easy cases either way are hidden from view and may seem to be superfluous. However, understanding the underlying role of theory in easier cases is helpful to understanding the more complex and explicit role of theory in harder cases.

Imagine a simple case. Old Man Featherstone was a wealthy landowner. He had no surviving family of his own, but had nieces, nephews, and cousins. He also had a grandson born out of wedlock, whom he barely knew. Featherstone was known to be a bit of a crank. He deeply resented the frequent self-ingratiating kindnesses of his relatives, which were motivated solely by greed. Following his death, the hopeful relatives gathered to hear the reading of the will. They were shocked to find that the Old Man left his entire estate to his grandson. The will was typed in proper form, duly signed by Featherstone, and witnessed by two persons whose signatures appeared.

Some of the relatives were upset enough to consult a lawyer about challenging the will. Assume that the estate would go to two cousins if there were no will or the grandson had died before the Old Man. Assume also that the relevant statute (the *statute of wills*) provides that a person's property shall go to the person or persons named in a valid will and that, to be valid, a will must be signed by the testator (Featherstone), while sane and not under fraud or duress, and in the presence of two witnesses whose signatures appear. To predict what a court will do in the case, the lawyer probably will reason from the relevant statutory rules in the deductive form. Thus, Featherstone's will named his grandson. It was signed by him and witnessed by two persons whose signatures appeared. From the facts as stated, there is no reason to believe that he was insane or a victim of fraud or duress. The will probably is valid, and the grandson will inherit the estate. The case is an easier case.

It may be thought that theory has nothing to do with this case of Old Man Featherstone's will because deduction from the statute is wholly adequate to explain such easy cases.[1] So it appears. But

---

[1] See B. Cardozo, The Nature of the Judicial Process 112-114 (1921); R. Dworkin, Taking Rights Seriously 81, 337 (1978); Hart, Positivism and the Separation of the Law and Morals, 71 Harv. L. Rev 593, 607-608 (1958); N. MacCormick, Legal Reasoning and Legal Theory 100 (1978). Both Dworkin and Hart seem to have had subsequent doubts about the logic of easy cases, but neither has worked

two variations on the facts of this case will show that theory, too, underlies this decision and that many easier cases can be explained adequately only with recourse to theory. Consequently, it appears that deduction without theory does not adequately explain easier cases in general.

For the first variation, imagine that Featherstone left two wills. One gave the estate to two cousins; the other gave the estate to the grandson. The will favoring the grandson bore a date subsequent to the will favoring the cousins. Both wills were otherwise identical, save that the first will was witnessed by two persons whose signatures appeared and the second by three.[2]

Assume that the relevant statutory rules are the same as before with the addition of a rule providing that a subsequent valid will revokes a prior will. The grandson will inherit the estate only if the second will is valid; that is, if it was signed by Featherstone, while sane and not under fraud or duress, and in the presence of two witnesses whose signatures appear. Does the estate go to the cousins or the grandson? The fact of a third witness on the subsequent will is the only possibly significant problem, though it seems as clear as before that the estate will go to the grandson. This, too, is an easier case.

This easier case cannot be explained by deduction from the statutory rule, which requires the will to be witnessed "by two witnesses." The statute does not say "at least two witnesses" or "at most two witnesses" or "two and only two witnesses." "Three witnesses" surely is not the same as "two witnesses." A lawyer would be puzzled if only the rules, facts, and logic were considered. It cannot possibly be deduced either that the will is valid or not valid because it is not known whether the fact of a third witness is important.

Lurking behind the prediction in this case is a normative theory generally recognized by members of the legal community. It could be explained why the third witness is not important, if it were necessary to do so. The lawyer only need ask what the law is trying to do here: Why should two witnesses be required for a will to be valid? It is conventionally thought that several purposes may

---

out the theoretical implications of such a shift. See Dworkin, Law as Interpretation, 60 Texas L. Rev. 527, 545 (1982); Hart, Problems of Philosophy in Law, in 6 Ency. Phil. 264, 271 (R. Edwards ed. 1967).

[2]This illustration is adapted from W. Bishin & C. Stone, Law, Language and Ethics 724-726 (1972).

be served by such a requirement.[3] In theory, the witnessing ceremony serves to bring home to the testator the legal significance
and possible finality of what he is doing; the requirement seeks to
assure that he acts with due deliberation. The witnesses also serve
to reduce the likelihood of some person fabricating a will for
another, on the assumption that it is harder to get two persons to
witness a fraudulent document and escape detection. (Perhaps one
witness will not do because that person could be the perpetrator of
the fraud.) And the witnesses might later provide access to evidence of the testator's mental health when he signed his will and of
other circumstances at the signing. (Perhaps one witness will not
do because of the greater risk that that person will be unavailable
should a dispute arise years later.) Because three witnesses serve
all of these purposes better than two witnesses do, there is no
reason for the third signature to invalidate the subsequent will.
The fact of a third signature is not important in this case.

This conventional explanation of the second case of Old Man
Featherstone's will underlies the first case, along with the deductive explanation. Two witnesses serve adequately to assure due
deliberation by the testator, to reduce the likelihood of fraud, and
to provide evidence of the circumstances at the signing, as determined by the legislature. Whatever purposes the statute might
serve, they have a singular implication in the first case. The court
predictably will decide that the will in the first case is valid (in this
respect) because of both deduction and, implicitly, the normative
theories with their singular implication in the case. The first case of
Old Man Featherstone's will can be explained by both deduction
and theory, but the second can be explained only by theory.

Consider another hypothetical variation. The facts are similar
to the first case of Old Man Featherstone's will, except that the
will leaving the estate to the grandson was in Featherstone's handwriting and was signed by him, but it was not witnessed. Such a
will is called a *holographic will*. Assume that, the preceding year,
the highest appellate court in the relevant jurisdiction held that a
holographic will executed by some other testator was valid even
though not witnessed. The lawyer in this third case of Old Man
Featherstone's will is likely to predict that the holographic will in
this case is valid. This, too, is an easier case.

---

[3]See generally, Gulliver & Tilson, Classification of Gratuitous Transfers, 51
Yale L.J. 1, 5-15 (1941).

It should be apparent that, like the second case of Old Man Featherstone's will, this easier case cannot be explained by logical deduction from the statute of wills. Nor can it be explained sufficiently by analogy from the precedent without calling on a theory.[4] It differs from the preceding easier cases because the plausible theories have conflicting implications under the circumstances and thus generate reasonable arguments for the cousins and the grandson. The absence of a witnessing ceremony probably would weaken the law's effort to assure due deliberation by the testator and provide evidence of the circumstances at the signing. But the fact that the will was in Featherstone's handwriting tends to indicate some deliberation (as contrasted with an oral will) and to reduce the possibility of fraud that could not be detected by handwriting experts. Whether the fact of no witnesses or the fact of a handwritten will is more important under the circumstances depends on how the theories are seen to bear on the case.

This could be a harder case. The court in the precedent case decided the preceding year, however, was presented with this very conflict under similar circumstances. By holding that the holographic will in that case was valid, the court resolved the conflict in favor of the theories that favor the grandson. The lawyer will predict that the third will is valid in this jurisdiction because the court is not likely to rethink its recent decision. The case is an easier case because the theories, as elaborated to decide the recent precedent, point in the same direction for all practical purposes.

Three easier cases have been examined. Only one can be explained by deduction, but all three can be explained by normative theory generally recognized by members of the legal community. Because each represents a kind of easier case that in fact will be found often in the real world, it can be concluded that easier cases in general are better explained by theory, whether or not explicit treatment of the underlying theories is necessary in the course of legal argument.

What makes easier cases easier is the singular implication of the relevant theories in the circumstances of a case. The singular implication may result in two ways: In the first two cases, all relevant theories pointed in the same direction; in the third case, the relevant theories pointed in different directions, but a recent

---

[4]See Chapters 2 and 4. The hypothetical case assumes for purposes of illustration that the precedent is not based on a holographic wills statute.

precedent resolved the conflict. For all practical purposes, given the precedent and stare decisis, the relevant theories had a singular implication in that case as well.

B. A Harder Case

What makes harder cases harder are the multiple and conflicting implications of the relevant theories under the circumstances. Theories may conflict in a case in ways that have not been resolved as a practical matter by the precedents and enactments, as they had been in the third case of Old Man Featherstone's will. Or a previously unaccepted but plausible theory may compete for acceptance against a conflicting accepted theory. In either situation, both sides in harder cases will have reasonable arguments. As will be seen, the judgment of importance in such cases is harder.

Consider a fourth variation.[5] Old Man Featherstone informed his cousins and grandson that his estate would go to the grandson under a duly executed will. Some weeks later, Featherstone discovered that the grandson had concealed the fact that he was heavily in debt because of a gambling obsession. Featherstone confronted the grandson, who told the Old Man to mind his own business. Featherstone threatened to disinherit the grandson, who drew a knife and stabbed Featherstone to death. The grandson was convicted of murder in a criminal court and sentenced to fifteen years in prison. The cousins consulted a lawyer about challenging the will because they did not think a man's murderer should inherit his property under such circumstances.

Assume that the relevant statutory law provides that a person's estate shall pass upon death to the person or persons named in a valid written will, Old Man Featherstone's will was in writing and in all respects valid, no statutory or other enacted rule denies the right of a murderer to inherit from his victim, and the cousins clearly would inherit the estate if there were no will or if the grandson had died before the Old Man. In the deductive form, it might appear that the grandson will inherit Old Man Featherstone's estate. But this conclusion is troubling; most persons would agree that it should be important that the grandson murdered Featherstone to prevent him from changing the will. The problem is to

---

[5]This illustration is adapted from the case of Riggs v. Palmer, 106 N.Y. 506 (1889).

show that *the law* precludes the grandson from taking the estate because the fact is of legal importance.

A consideration of the relevant theories in this case suggests that both sides have plausible legal arguments. The grandson's lawyer can argue that the principle of legislative supremacy requires the court to follow the law exactly as laid down by the legislature. It would promote disorder for the court to guess what the legislature might think about a case it had not thought about. The purpose of the statute is revealed best by its terms, taken literally. The law thus gives the estate to the person named in a valid will, in this case the grandson. This result gives effect to the revealed intention of the testator and avoids any need to guess the intentions of a dead man. Sticking to the written document promotes the orderly passing of property from one generation to another. The legislature should change the law if it needs to be changed.

On the other hand, the lawyer for the cousins can argue that the underlying purpose of the law is to provide for the orderly and just passing of property from one generation to the next. In normal circumstances, giving the estate to the person(s) named in the will serves this purpose well. This, however, is a highly unusual case that requires creative judicial interpretation of the statute to effectuate the intention of the legislature. Allowing one to inherit after murdering the testator to prevent a change in a will would fail to promote justice. A basic principle of the law is that no person shall profit by his own wrong. No reasonable testator could want his estate to go to his murderer, and no reasonable legislature could have intended such a result. Accordingly, it is important that the grandson murdered the Old Man because the law's purposes would not be served if the grandson were to inherit the estate.

This case is a harder case because of the multiple theories with conflicting implications. The grandson's arguments place greater stress on the orderly passing of property from one generation to the next. They emphasize the literal interpretation of the statutory text, the clarity of the testator's written will, and the uncertainty of guessing a dead man's intention. The fact that the grandson murdered the testator to prevent a change in the will is not important by these theories. By contrast, the cousins' arguments place stress on the just passing of property from one generation to the next. They emphasize the unusual circumstances in the case, the probable intention of the legislature, and the injustice of rewarding wrongful behavior. The fact that the grandson murdered the testator to prevent a change in the will is important by these theories.

It will be seen that the multiple and conflicting theories in this hard case of Old Man Featherstone's will all were embedded in the legal experience. Parenthetically, note that harder cases also occur when the implications of the theories embedded in the legal experience differ from the implications of a plausible theory that evaluates the law but has yet to achieve judicial or legislative acceptance. The latter kind of theory most clearly concerns what the law ought to be. It may enjoy considerable support among members of the legal community and may be articulated in losing briefs, concurring and dissenting judicial opinions, or the secondary literature. A case that accepts such a theory and is decided according to its implications is a "landmark" decision. It is likely to overrule established precedents or declare a statute unconstitutional. Such decisions represent dramatic instances of legal change and are worth considerable study.[6] From the standpoint of the method of legal interpretation, however, they do not differ in kind from harder cases like the fourth case of Old Man Featherstone's will. The concern in harder cases is with the conflicting implications of relevant theories, whatever their legal authority.

C. Deciding Harder Cases

It has been seen that easier cases in general are easier because of the singular implication of the relevant theories in the case; harder cases are harder because of the conflicting implications of multiple theories in the case. The next question concerns how the judgment of importance is made in harder cases.

1. Experience and Webs of Belief

The lawyer's predictions of what a court will do and persuasions of what a court should do in a case are aimed at the judges. They cannot be made intelligently without understanding judicial reasoning, which is but a stylized and rigorous version of the reasoning used in everyday life. Beneath the dignified bearing, the black robes, and the air of mystical capacity, judges are human beings who think basically as you and I do. Much depends on intuition, though judicial and lawyerly intuitions are trained by

---

[6]See Chapter 11.

legal education, developed by experience, and refined in each case through legal research, reflection, and argument in accordance with the conventions of the profession. Something useful can be said about judicial reasoning and intuition in harder cases if human reasoning and intuition in simple everyday problem situations first are considered.

Imagine that you and a fellow birdwatcher are walking one afternoon along a path in a park when your friend calls attention to a bird in a tree. She asks what kind of bird it is, and you say, "I believe it is a crow." But your friend says that she thinks it is a blackbird. You argue for a bit, during which you say that you believe yourself to be an expert and perceptive birdwatcher and that you care and understand about these things. The disagreement is left unresolved. That evening, you pick up a copy of the Audubon Society Magazine, which you believe to be careful and expert about birds because of its reputation. You come upon a picture of a bird and believe it is of the same kind as the bird in the park. The caption, to your relief, says "Crow." You feel confirmed in the opinion ventured earlier in the day and believe that you were correct.

By contrast, imagine that the caption below the picture in the magazine had said "Blackbird." Depending on how serious a birdwatcher you are, you would feel somewhat disappointed. In the first situation, all of your beliefs together had a singular implication under the circumstances. You could believe that it was a crow in the park; and that you are an expert and perceptive birdwatcher, the Audubon Society Magazine is careful and expert about birds, the bird in the picture is of the same kind as the bird in the park, and you care and understand about these things. In the second situation, however, your beliefs have conflicting implications under the circumstances. Something must give.

You have several alternatives in the face of this disappointing experience. You can maintain that the bird in the park was a crow, if you drop or modify the belief either that the Audubon Society Magazine is careful and expert about birds or that the bird in the picture is of the same kind as the bird in the park. Or you can decide that the bird in the park was really a blackbird, if you drop or modify the belief that you are an expert and perceptive birdwatcher. Or you can decide that it all makes very little sense, if you drop the belief that you care and understand about these things. However, you cannot maintain that the bird in the park was a crow and, at the same time, hold unmodified all of the identified beliefs that you held before experiencing the bird in the picture with its caption, or maintain that the bird in the park was a blackbird while holding all of these beliefs, or maintain that you care and understand about these things while holding all of these beliefs.

Your beliefs bearing on this matter are like a web of beliefs in which each relevant belief is connected with several others that, in turn, are connected with many of the beliefs that you hold. The web of beliefs is a "seamless web" because no one belief is a necessary starting point, or foundation, from which all other beliefs necessarily follow. Each belief is supported by a complex network of beliefs in which all beliefs ultimately are mutually reinforcing. A change in any one belief has a ripple effect causing changes in a number of other beliefs, and any belief can be changed without producing a tattered web if the necessary consequential changes are made.

Accordingly, which alternative you select in the second birdwatcher situation will be a function of many, if not all, of your other beliefs about yourself and the way the world works. It would be easy for me, for example, to give up any belief I might foolishly have held that I am an expert and perceptive birdwatcher. I can quickly concede that the Audubon Society, which I know only by reputation, is more likely to get it right than I am. I also would not have noticed enough about the bird in the park to assert that it was not of the same kind as the bird in the picture. I want things to make sense and would conclude that the bird in the park probably was a blackbird.

My friend Judy, however, happens to be a professor of biology who specializes in ornithology. Under the same circumstances, she would find it harder to give up or weaken her belief that she is an expert and perceptive birdwatcher, easier to challenge the accuracy of the Audubon Society Magazine, and harder to conclude that her initial belief that the two birds were of the same kind was wrong. She, too, wants these things to make sense, so she might conclude that the magazine had made a printing error. My other friend, Clarence, thinks of himself as an expert in everything and finds it hard ever to admit an error, most of all to himself. He also is proud to serve on the Audubon Society's board of directors. Perhaps he is more likely to conclude that the bird in the park was not of the same kind as the bird in the picture. Lastly, I have a friend named Albert, who is not very smart and quite used to confusion. Perhaps he is more likely to hold contradictory beliefs in this situation and, with a shrug, drop his belief that he cares and understands about these things.

Logically speaking, any person could select any alternative in these circumstances if they were willing to adjust their web of beliefs as necessary to accommodate the alternative selected.[7] For example, I could maintain that the bird in the park was a crow if I were willing either to challenge the accuracy of the Audubon Society Magazine or to assert that the bird in the park was not of the same kind as the bird in the picture. In the same circumstances, Judy could conclude that the bird in the park was really a blackbird if she were willing to drop her self-image as an expert and perceptive birdwatcher and ornithologist. These are logical possibilities because we each would hold a coherent web of beliefs; at least, the beliefs would be consistent, and there would be an absence of apparent anomalies.

Pragmatically speaking, however, we are likely to select the alternative that requires the fewest adjustments to maintain the coherence of our webs of beliefs. Moreover, we try to conserve those beliefs that are most likely to work well pragmatically — those beliefs that, if acted on, have not and likely will not produce disappointing experiences.[8] I am likely to conclude that the bird in the park probably was a blackbird, though maintaining that it is a crow is as possible logically. My beliefs about my birdwatching skills are lightly held and easily given up; I have had few experiences from which to develop much attachment to them. My beliefs about the reliability of reputations of groups like the Audubon Society are more deeply held; I would much prefer to alter my belief about my birdwatching skills, which requires me to alter very few other beliefs that I depend on, than to alter my beliefs about relying on the reputation of such groups as the Audubon Society. By contrast, Judy's beliefs about her own birdwatching expertise are more deeply held than her beliefs about the good reputation of the Audubon Society. Judy is less likely to alter her beliefs about

---

[7]See generally, W. Quine & J. Ullian, The Web of Beliefs (1970); Quine, Two Dogmas of Empiricism, in From a Logical Point of View 20 (W. Quine ed. 1961).

[8]*Pragmatism* is used here in its philosophical sense, not in its lay sense of "muddling through." The emphasis thus is placed on ideas or beliefs that have discernible consequences in the real world when taken seriously by people. See generally W. James, Pragmatism (Perry ed. 1955). See also L. Festinger, A Theory of Cognitive Dissonance (1957).

her own expertise, which has proven reliable through years of experience, because it would require her to alter her web of beliefs radically. She is not nearly as dependent as I am on relying on the reputation of groups like the Audubon Society. She is likely to maintain that the bird in the park is a crow, though conceding that it is a blackbird is as possible logically.

Thus, we confront situations in everyday life where our beliefs converge to suggest a singular implication, as in the first bird-watcher situation. We also confront situations where our beliefs diverge and have conflicting implications, as in the second bird-watcher situation. The latter kind of experience leads us to review our webs of beliefs and adjust them as necessary to accommodate coherently the experience, preceding experiences, and expected future experiences, so as to enhance our ability to act effectively in the future. We try to make the fewest adjustments necessary to accommodate experience while maintaining the coherence and pragmatic value of our webs of beliefs.

2. The Legal Community

The birdwatcher situations are comparable to easier and harder cases. The first birdwatcher situation is like easier cases because all relevant legal theories converge to suggest a single result in the case. Harder cases are like the second birdwatcher situation because a number of relevant legal theories have conflicting implications in such cases. However, the judicial response to a harder case may be more predictable than a layperson's response to the second birdwatcher situation. Among a judge's core beliefs are those concerning judicial responsibility. The judicial decision must be accommodated coherently with the judge's deep commitment to the ideals of law and all that they entail.

Before being confronted with the facts of a harder case, the judge probably held a web of beliefs about law. For example, the judge in the fourth case of Old Man Featherstone's will (where the grandson murdered the Old Man) probably would include among the relevant legal theories that the purpose of the law in such circumstances is to provide for the orderly and just passing of property from one generation to the next, that the law should give effect to the revealed intention of the testator and avoid guessing a dead man's intentions, that the courts should follow the law as laid down by the legislature, that statutes work best in normal circumstances but require creative interpretation to effectuate the intention of the legislature in unusual circumstances, and that a basic principle requires that no person shall profit by his own wrong. The previously decided cases might be reconciled in light of these theories or, more realistically, the cases that had arisen previously might not have brought their conflicting implications to attention. On being confronted with the problem case, however, the judge becomes aware of the conflicting implications of these theories in the case.

This disappointing experience leads the judge to review her web of beliefs about law to determine which parts shall be adjusted to accommodate a decision in the case as coherently as possible. Logically speaking, the judge can conclude either that the grandson shall inherit or not if she is willing to make the necessary adjustments to her beliefs about law. Pragmatically speaking, the judge will try to conserve as many as she can of the beliefs that have worked well. But the judicial response to a case differs from a layperson's response to the problems of everyday life. Most important, the layperson considers a belief to work well if it comports with *his* past experiences and probably will not lead to future disappointing experiences *to him*. The judge considers a legal theory to work well if it comports with *the legal community's* past experiences and will not lead to disappointing experiences *to the legal community*. She will try to make the fewest adjustments necessary to accommodate a decision in the case coherently with the precedents and legislative materials (the legal experience) in light of the legal community's explanations and evaluations of what has gone before (the totality of our theories about law).

To elaborate, as laypersons we hold a wide variety of goals and beliefs and generally are free to form beliefs as we wish. We form and retain beliefs that have the most practical value in pursuing our personal goals, whatever they may be — those beliefs that work for us as individuals. A judge, however, on taking the oath of office in good faith assumes a responsibility to further the ideals of law. The judge's web of beliefs about law thus will place the values of order and justice at the center, where they can support the remainder of the web, which works out the implications of those values for the principles, rules, and cases in the legal system. To have pragmatic value in pursuing order and justice, such a web of beliefs must reflect what members of the legal community generally will take to be required by an orderly and just society in cases.[9] Consequently,

---

[9]See Chapters 5 §C, 6 §B.

the judicial web of beliefs seeks to incorporate the legal experience and the totality of the legal community's theories about law as a coherent and pragmatically valuable whole.

The conscientious judge faced with a harder case will endeavor to reach the decision that requires the fewest adjustments to maintain or enhance the coherence of the law, given the centrality of order and justice, in light of the conventions of the legal community. The harder case reveals anomalies within the judge's web of beliefs about law and requires the judge to abandon or modify one or more beliefs. The judge's responsibilities narrow the range of response from what is logically possible. The judge confronts the case as a representative of the legal community, and the decision must be accommodated coherently with the collective experience of the legal community. The values and theories that are used to organize the legal experience are those of the legal community. The judge will prefer to abandon or, more often, modify those beliefs that less well reflect the conventions of the legal community so that lawyers and judges are disappointed as little as is feasible.

The judicial opinion in the case of *Riggs v. Palmer*,[10] from which the harder case of Old Man Featherstone's will is adapted, illustrates well the operation of this conventionalist perspective on judicial reasoning. Not surprisingly, the New York Court of Appeals held that a person who murders a testator to prevent the testator from changing his will may not inherit property under the will, notwithstanding a statute of the kind described above. The interesting part is the court's reasoning in support of this conclusion.

After stating the facts in that case, Judge Earl, writing for the court, noted the grandson's argument that the will was made in proper form and must have effect according to the letter of the law. He conceded that the relevant statutes, if literally construed, gave the property to the murderer. He then embarked on an extensive discussion of the principle of legislative supremacy.

Judge Earl abandoned the theory that regards the literal interpretation of a statutory rule to be required by the principle of legislative supremacy in all cases, if he ever had recognized it among his beliefs about law. He retained the theory requiring a statute to be interpreted to give effect to the intention of the legislature. Judge Earl thus maintained the principle of legislative supremacy, which is basic to a system of statutory law, by recogniz-

---

[10]115 N.Y. 506 (1889).

ing one version of it and rejecting another. Further, he explained in effect that the rejected version of the principle of legislative supremacy generally is not taken by members of the legal community to be required by an orderly and just society in this case and like cases.

To show that the literal interpretation of statutes in all cases is not regarded as basic to a system of statutory law, Judge Earl quoted extensively from eminent legal writers on statutory law:

> It is a familiar canon of construction that a thing which is within the intention of the makers of a statute is as much within the statute as if it were within the letter; and a thing which is within the letter of the statute is not within the statute, unless it be within the intention of the makers. The writers of laws do not always express their intention perfectly, but either exceed it or fall short of it, so that judges are to collect it from probable or rational conjectures only, and this is called rational interpretation. . . . [11]

Judge Earl cited or quoted from no fewer than five legal treatises to this effect, evidencing the legal community's conventional attitude. He also reported two proverbial cases that exemplify the operation of this theory of statutory interpretation:

> There was a statute in Bologna that whoever drew blood [i.e., engaged in sword-play] in the streets should be severely punished, and yet it was held not to apply to the case of a barber [i.e., a surgeon] who opened a vein in the street. It is commanded in the Decalogue that no work shall be done upon the sabbath, and yet, giving the command a rational interpretation founded upon its design, the Infallible Judge held that it did not prohibit works of necessity, charity or benevolence on that day.[12]

In light of such authority, Judge Earl was saying in effect, it is hard to believe that many lawyers and judges reasonably expect judges to follow the literal interpretation of a statute in all cases. Abandoning that version of the theory of legislative supremacy would not greatly disrupt the totality of the legal community's theories about law.

This left it necessary to determine what the legislature "intended" in the circumstances of this case and like cases.[13] The

---

[11]Id. at 509.
[12]Id. at 511.
[13]Recall that this "intention" is widely understood to be a fictional thing. See Chapter 3 §B.

thought that the legislature might have intended the murderer to inherit under his victim's will did not fit well within Judge Earl's web of beliefs about law:

> What could be more unreasonable than to suppose that it was the legislative intention in the general laws passed for the orderly, peaceable and just devolution of property, that they should have operation in favor of one who murdered his ancestor that he might speedily come into the possession of his estate? Such an intention is *inconceivable*.[14]

Moreover, Judge Earl thought that application of a certain maxim of the common law (a kind of very general principle) was relevant to the "orderly, peaceable and just devolution of property":

> No one shall be permitted to profit by his own fraud, or to take advantage of his own wrong, or to found any claim upon his own inequity, or to acquire property by his own crime. These maxims are dictated by public policy, have their foundation in universal law administered in all civilized countries, and have nowhere been superseded by statutes.[15]

He gave a number of analogous cases exemplifying the application of the maxim. In one, decided by the U.S. Supreme Court, it was held that a person could not collect under an insurance policy according to its literal terms when he murdered the insured to make the benefits payable.[16] Justice Field in that case had written for the Court:

> It would be a reproach to the jurisprudence of the country, if one could recover insurance money payable on the death of a party whose life he had feloniously taken. As well might he recover insurance money upon a building that he had willfully fired.[17]

In other cases, Judge Earl reported, the courts held without statutory basis that a will would be set aside if procured by the fraud or undue influence of the person in whose favor it would operate.[18] Here, the effect of Judge Earl's argument is to suggest by analogies

---

[14]Riggs v. Palmer, 115 N.Y. 506, 511 (1889) (emphasis added).

[15]Id. at 511-512. Judge Earl cited four treatises on foreign law to support his assertion that the maxim has its foundation in "universal law administered in all civilized nations."

[16]N.Y. Mut. Life Ins. Co. v. Armstrong, 117 U.S. 591 (1886).

[17]Id. at 600.

[18]Riggs v. Palmer, 115 N.Y. 506, 512 (1889) (citing two cases).

that members of the legal community generally should expect judges in cases like these to apply the principle about not allowing a person to profit from his own wrong even in the face of the literal terms of an applicable statute and a will.

Judge Earl's difficulty in accommodating a decision for the grandson coherently with the collective experience of the legal community, including the law's commitment to the above-quoted maxim and the presumed wisdom of the cited precedents, is further revealed by a number of hypothetical cases he posed in the analogical form:

> Here there was no certainty that this murderer would survive the testator, or that the testator would not change his will, and there was no certainty that he would get this property if nature was allowed to take its course. . . . If he had met the testator, and taken his property by force, he would have had no title to it. Shall he acquire title by murdering him? If he had gone to the testator's house, and by force compelled him, or by fraud or undue influence had induced him to will him his property, the law would not allow him to hold it. But can he give effect and operation to a will by murder, and yet take the property? To answer these questions in the affirmative, it seems to me would be a reproach to the jurisprudence of our state, and an offense against public policy.[19]

Thus, the grandson's argument depended on the theory that the principle of legislative supremacy requires a literal interpretation of a statute in all cases. That theory, however, conflicted with the theory about the probable intention of the legislature and the principle reflected in the maxim. More important, it cannot be reconciled with the many real and hypothetical cases Judge Earl discussed. In his opinion, it seems, the theory of literal statutory interpretation does not work well; if recognized, it would cast doubt on much of the legal experience, displace a larger number of accepted theories about law, and lead to disappointing experiences for the legal community. His citations to legal writers and cases support his belief that this theory is not thought to have much pragmatic value in contributing to a more orderly and just society in this case and like cases.

Judge Earl had relatively less difficulty accommodating a decision for the other relatives in this case. In his opinion, it seems, the theories of "rational interpretation" and the maxim are more

---

[19]Id. at 512-513.

strongly supported by the legal community in similar circumstances, as evidenced by the many cases he discussed. Retaining
these theories and therefore holding for the other relatives con-
serves the theories that were thought by the legal community to
work well. So holding maintains greater coherence in the law and
leads to fewer disappointing experiences than the available alternative. Accordingly, a decision for the relatives was thought better to
contribute to the orderly and just passing of property from one
generation to the next, where the implications of order and justice
were a function of the conventions of the legal community, as
indicated by the legal experience and the totality of our theories
about law.[20]

It should be clear that there was nothing inevitable about the
result in *Riggs v. Palmer*. It was as possible logically for Judge Earl
to retain the theory requiring a literal interpretation of all statutes
and to hold for the grandson. If it were not, the case probably
would not have been litigated. What led to his decision favoring
the other relatives was the conflict between plausible theories and
Judge Earl's effort to maintain as well as possible the coherence
and pragmatic value of the law in its entirety, given the centrality
of order and justice. A judgment for the grandson could be fit into
the legal experience and the totality of the legal community's theories about law only at the cost of abandoning widely supported

---

[20]This approach to easier and harder cases is comparable to Professor Dworkin's approach to hard cases. See R. Dworkin, supra note 1, at 81-131. However,
Dworkin's treatment of easy cases places far greater emphasis on deduction from
legal rules than this treatment of easier cases. See note 1 and accompanying text.
At least in the original, fully developed version of his theory, the treatment of
hard cases is necessarily dependent on the existence of a large number of settled
rules that themselves sufficiently govern easy cases.

More important, Dworkin would have judges in hard cases follow principles
that figure in the "best" justification of the legal experience, where the "best"
justification is a grand theory that (1) is not inconsistent with a substantial part of
the legal experience and (2) among those theories, is most justifiable in moral and
political philosophy even if less consistent with the legal experience than an alternative theory. R. Dworkin, supra note 1, at 118-130, 206-222, 340. The approach
in this book emphasizes the judge's responsibility to the legal community's conventions of language, argument, and judgment, which seek to work out the implications of order and justice in cases. This approach does not claim that there is a
"single right answer" in virtually all harder cases and accordingly acknowledges
that judges sometimes must make contributions to the legal experience. See
Chapter 10, §C. But the contributions seek to enhance the coherence of the law in
its entirety in the eyes of the legal community, rather than to conform in theory to
one or another political or moral philosophy. See also Fried, The Artificial Reason of the Law Or: What Lawyers Know, 60 Texas L. Rev. 35 (1981).

theories that were thought often to work well in similar circumstances. A judgment for the other relatives could be accommodated at the cost of abandoning a lightly held theory that was thought not to work as well in similar circumstances.

D. Summary

Judicial methods of interpretation in law cases are complex. We are far from the simple versions of deductive and analogical reasoning that give legal reasoning its form of expression and leave an analyst so dissatisifed. The judge does not decide a case by confronting the facts with a single rule or precedent in mind or with wholly personal value preferences. The judge confronts a case in light of a web of beliefs about what members of the legal community generally will take to be required by an orderly and just society in a case and like cases, as indicated by the legal experience and the totality of our theories about law.

In easier cases, these theories, and the precedents or legislative materials they explain or evaluate, converge to suggest a single result in the case. In harder cases, they diverge to suggest contradictory results in the case. As a practical matter, the judgment of importance in harder cases depends on which decision requires the fewest adjustments to accommodate the decision coherently with the facts of the case and the legal experience in light of the totality of the legal community's theories about law. Decisions that thus can be accommodated are in accordance with the law in its entirety and contribute to the pursuit of a more orderly and just society through law.

CHAPTER EIGHT

Form and Method

ONCE THE JUDICIAL decision in harder cases is viewed as suggested in the preceding chapter, a number of practical questions can be posed: How does a judge cope with the huge mass of information within the legal experience and the totality of the legal community's theories about law? How do lawyers develop a case and influence which decision a judge will settle on as the best decision? What, if any, role do the analogical and deductive forms of legal reasoning play in facilitating use of the method of legal interpretation thus conceived? This chapter will use these questions to develop further, and probe the practical implications of, a conventionalist conception of legal interpretation. It will be seen that the lawyers in a case play the key role in presenting a case to a court so that the judges are faced with a manageable problem. Capable lawyers consequently can have a substantial influence over the way in which a judge will perceive a case. The forms of legal reasoning help lawyers use the legal experience and the totality of the legal community's theories about law to make reasonably reliable predictions and effective persuasions, even in many harder cases.

A. How Judges Get Started

To speak in the abstract of the legal experience and the totality of our theories about law is to speak of the law in its entirety, including the vast numbers of common law rules and precedents, enacted texts with their contexts, and commentaries on those materials by lawyers, judges, legal scholars, and others. Observing that judges decide harder cases in accordance with the law in its entirety may appear to be a truism with no practical implications. It may appear to enjoin lawyers and judges to think about everything before doing anything and thus effectively to ensure that they do nothing. For the extent of the law is too vast for any one person to know it all or use it all at any one time. A lawyer or judge would be disabled from acting if the law in its entirety must be reviewed and digested before action could be taken in a case.

To make law and legal reasoning manageable, it is necessary

for lawyers and judges to select from the law in its entirety those parts that are most germane to their predictions, persuasions, and decisions in a particular case. The aspects of the law that bear most directly on a particular decision should be called to attention. But other aspects of the law should not be excluded from consideration because the whole is necessary background for the intelligent understanding of its parts. The forms and interpretive methods of legal reasoning together should bring into prominence the most relevant aspects of the law, leaving the rest in the background as the context for thought.

Because of the practical need for manageable decision legal reasoning should be viewed in its real-world contexts, not in the abstract as a matter only of logic and rules or principles. Legal rules and principles conflict frequently in the abstract; when properly used, their implications in particular cases are much less often puzzling. Lawyers in fact make their predictions and persuasions in light of what a judge will or should do in a case. Judges in fact make their decisions in cases that have materialized and come before the court. The courts' procedural forms put limitations on how a case can be brought to a court for decision and how lawyers must present the case before decisions of certain sorts can be made properly. The context set by the case has the effect of refining the focus of legal reasoning for each judicial decision in each case.

For example, a civil lawsuit is initiated—is a case before a court—when the plaintiff files a complaint with a court. In the federal courts and many state courts, a complaint must set forth, among other things, "a short and plain statement of the claim showing that the [plaintiff] is entitled to relief," together with a request for relief, such as the payment of money by the defendant.[1] The defendant then is required to respond in one of several ways. Among them is a defendant's right to ask the court to rule that the plaintiff's complaint "fail[s] to state a claim upon which relief may be granted."[2] If the court so rules, the plaintiff's complaint is dismissed and the lawsuit ends immediately; otherwise, the parties proceed to the next step in litigation. A court will dismiss a complaint on this ground, for example, if it does not provide sufficient information to give a defendant's lawyer a reasonable idea of what facts and law might sustain the plaintiff's lawsuit so that the defendant has a fair opportunity to prepare a defense.

---

[1]Fed. R. Civ. Proc. 8(a).
[2]Fed. R. Civ. Proc. 12(b)(6).

Thus, to bring a case before a court requires that the plaintiff's lawyer announce at the outset, albeit in a truncated way, the legal basis of the plaintiff's claim. In effect, the plaintiff's lawyer must point to a part of the legal experience and assert that that part of the legal experience entitles the plaintiff to the relief requested. It is not necessary at this early stage of litigation for the complaint to set forth a detailed legal argument, or even to cite precedents or legal rules. But the complaint does need to inform the court and the defendant, in a succinct way, of the facts pointing to a general area of law that might allow the plaintiff to prevail. A complaint that gestures at the law as an entirety without alleging facts constituting a legal claim would be dismissed for failure to state a claim upon which relief may be granted.

To illustrate, consider a case involving a property owner in the role of defendant and a trespasser in the role of plaintiff.[3] The property involved was an unoccupied farmhouse that contained personal property. Over a ten-year period, the farmhouse had been broken into and damaged a number of times, and some of the defendant's possessions had been taken. The defendant set up a booby trap, involving a shotgun, in the bedroom. The plaintiff was shot and seriously wounded in the lower leg after entering the house and opening the door to the bedroom. The plaintiff had pleaded guilty to a minor criminal trespass charge, but then brought a civil action against the defendant for damages involving personal injuries, medical expenses, and loss of earnings occasioned by the shotgun wound. Other facts will appear below.

A lawyer for the plaintiff might file a complaint in proper form as follows:

IN THE DISTRICT COURT
OF THE STATE OF WILLARD
IN AND FOR LUDWIG COUNTY

Terry Tress,	
Plaintiff	COMPLAINT
v.	Civil No. 85-1949
Oscar Olner,	Trial by Jury Demanded
Defendant	

---

[3]The illustration is based on Katko v. Briney, 183 N.W.2d 657 (Iowa 1971).

The plaintiff, Terry Tress, states for his complaint against defendant, Oscar Olner, as follows:

1. On or about July 16, 1967, plaintiff, Terry Tress, was shot by a spring gun trap set by defendant, Oscar Olner, in an unoccupied house owned by the defendant.

2. Defendant, Oscar Olner, erected the spring gun trap with an intention to cause death or serious bodily injury to persons entering the premises.

3. Defendant was not privileged to use deadly force or to erect the spring gun trap.

4. As a direct and proximate cause of the defendant's wrongful acts, plaintiff Terry Tress's leg was seriously injured, and plaintiff was prevented from working for some time, suffered great pain of body and mind, and incurred expenses for medical attention and hospitalization in the sum of twelve thousand, seven hundred, and twenty dollars ($12,720).

WHEREFORE plaintiff, Terry Tress, demands judgment against defendant, Oscar Olner, in the sum of twelve thousand, seven hundred, and twenty dollars ($12,720) plus interest from the date the cause of action arose together with his costs and expenses of prosecuting this action.

In most jurisdictions, this complaint states a claim upon which relief may be granted. By its allegations, it effectively invokes certain well-known rules and precedents in the common law of torts. All common law jurisdictions recognize a claim for battery, which is an intentional causing of a harmful or offensive physical contact to the person of another without excuse or justification. If the defendant's lawyer were to ask the court to dismiss the complaint for failure to state a claim upon which relief may be granted, the plaintiff's lawyer could cite the common law rules and precedents in a brief in opposition to the defendant's request.

Only then would the judge be in a position to decide the question. The judge would not, however, be in the position of thinking about everything before doing anything. The complaint and the rules and precedents cited in the parties' briefs would be before the court. These documents would call the judge's attention to parts of the legal experience that, in the lawyers' opinions, are relevant to the case. Reasoning would focus on the cited rules and precedents, though the judge could draw as well on her own research and general knowledge concerning the law of torts and related criminal or property law, theories of compensation and responsibility, rules and theories of civil procedure, and sundry other aspects of the legal experience and the totality of the legal community's theories about law. The decision would be a manageable one because the lawyers will have presented the case in a manner that poses a discrete question and proposes a reasoned decision.

In this respect, the judicial decision on a defendant's request to dismiss a complaint for failure to state a claim upon which relief may be granted is typical of almost all judicial decisions. Such decisions are made in a context with structure. Courts generally act in concrete cases at the specific request of a party, and the request must frame a legal issue with some particularity. The possible requests that a party can make are fixed in advance by the procedural forms. Each party is afforded an opportunity to present arguments that will call attention to aspects of the legal experience and the totality of the legal community's theories about law. The lawyers thus construct a framework for the judicial decision by taking the initiative to bring into prominence the most relevant aspects of the law in its entirety, leaving the rest in the background as the context for thought.

B. How Lawyers Get Started

The lawyers start the ball rolling for the judges, but no one similarly starts the ball rolling for the lawyer. Clients come to the law office with an often vague sense that they have been wronged. They rarely provide the lawyers with much more than a bare, often biased or misleading summary of the facts of a dispute. They may be unclear about their objectives and, in any event, rarely know whether the law permits or requires what they want to do, much less what law is relevant. The lawyer must start by developing the facts, based on a web of beliefs about law and an intellectual capacity for bringing that knowledge to bear in a concrete dispute through legal reasoning.

Imagine, for example, that the plaintiff in the spring gun case summarized above had started the initial interview with his lawyer by asking whether it was legal for someone to booby trap an abandoned farmhouse with a gun. A competent lawyer would know immediately that answering the question yes or no would be poor legal advice. His pre-existing knowledge of the law would be sufficient for him to have at least a vague idea that there are some precedents in which defendants who set traps that injured other persons were convicted of crimes and others in which such defendants were acquitted; some precedents in which plaintiffs injured by traps recovered damages for battery and others in which injured plaintiffs did not recover. He also would have some notion that these precedents often involved the common law rules concerning battery and a property owner's privilege to use force in self-defense or the defense of property. The client's question will call the lawyer's attention to these parts of the legal experience. With a moment's reflection, the lawyer will know that more information is needed before competent legal advice can be given.

The needed additional information is of three kinds. The lawyer first needs to know why the client wants to know whether it is lawful to set a spring gun. Based on the simple first question asked by the client, the lawyer would not know whether the client wants to set one or to sue someone who set one. Second, the lawyer needs to know a great deal about the facts that have led or might lead to a dispute that could come before a court. Third, the lawyer needs to know a great deal about the law that will determine what a court will or should do in a case. The second and third kinds of information are interrelated because the law determines what facts are relevant to the lawyer's predictions or persuasions while, at the same time, the facts determine what law is relevant. Thus, the lawyer must begin a process of (1) gathering facts to narrow the focus of legal research, (2) conducting preliminary legal research, (3) gathering more facts in light of the research, and (4) conducting further legal research in light of those facts.

So the lawyer will begin by questioning the client to develop a preliminary picture of the relevant facts. The hard part is to know what questions to ask. It is here that the lawyer's general knowledge of the law, together with skill at using the analogical and deductive forms of legal reasoning, are necessary to get started. Though many lawyers ask good questions instinctively, a good question can be the product of an hypothesis concerning a possible analogical or deductive relationship between the problem case and the precedents or rules that the lawyer has reason to think might be found within the legal experience. That the question arises from an hypothesis bears emphasis because, at the early stages in developing a case, it may even be likely that any one hypothesis will turn out to be wrong when a full picture of the facts and the law is compiled. The initial questioning of a client is like a fishing expedition—there may be some reason to believe that a good fishing spot has been located, but one never knows whether the fish will be biting.

To illustrate, consider the following imaginary transcript of part of an initial interview in the spring gun case:

Client (C): Is it legal for someone to set a trap with a gun in a farmhouse?

Lawyer (L): Why do you want to know?

C: I was shot by one.

L: Please continue.

C: I want to sue the guy who set it.

L: Tell me how it happened.

C: I just opened the door to the bedroom and the thing went off. It nearly blew my foot off.

L: I'm sorry. Are you OK now?

C: I can walk all right. It still hurts. I was in the hospital for forty days. In surgery twice. They almost had to take it off.

L: You were lucky. What were you doing in the farmhouse?

C: Well, I was picking up some old jars and bottles. I'd been there before.

L: Whose farmhouse was it?

C: Turns out it belongs to a guy named Olner.

L: Did you know that before you went in?

C: No. I thought the place was abandoned.

L: Why?

C: I don't live far from there, and I've passed it lots of times. It's all boarded up, overgrown—has been for years. I didn't think I was doing anything wrong by going in and taking some things no one cared about anymore.

L: Do the police know you went in?

C: Sure. They busted me for burglary. I pleaded to a lesser charge, and they fined me fifty bucks.

L: Do you know if they charged Mr. Olner?

C: Don't know.

L: Did you see any "No Trespassing" signs before you went in?

C: No.

L: Did you see any signs warning of the trap?

C: No.

L: Did you look through the windows before going in?

C: Couldn't. They were all boarded up.

L: How did you get in?

C: I—and my friend—we tore a board off. There was no glass in the window, so it was easy.

L: Then what happened?

C: Joe, my friend, went into the kitchen to look around. I saw this chair propped under a door handle, so I got curious. I moved the chair and turned the door handle. That's when it happened. Boom.

L: That thing could have shot some kid on a lark!

C: Sure.

L: Was anyone else in the farmhouse?

C: Just Joe. He took me to the hospital.

L: Have you spoken with Mr. Olner since this happened?

C: Yeah. He came to the hospital once. Said he wanted to see the bastard who was driving him and his wife nuts. He's a nasty customer.

L: Do you have a family?

C: Wife and one kid.

L: Do you work?

C: I pumped gas at Shelly's station for four years before this happened. Couldn't work for three months. I'll start again next week.

Notice that some of the questions that the lawyer asks are similar to questions a layperson might ask but, significantly, others are not. Those that are not similar are a product of the lawyer's training and experience—his general knowledge of the law and skill at using the analogical and deductive forms of legal reasoning. Thus, where a layperson might pass by the client's seemingly innocent comment that he was in the house to pick up some old jars and bottles, the lawyer asks a series of questions revealing that the client was a trespasser and thief. As will be seen, the precedents concerning a property owner's right to use force in defense of his property sometimes allow an owner to use greater force against a thief than a mere trespasser, though when asking the question the lawyer may hypothesize in the analogical form only that the law might so distinguish such cases. Similarly, where a layperson might not think to ask whether there were any "No Trespassing" signs, signs warning of the trap, or other ways for an intruder to become aware of the trap before being shot, the lawyer might ask such questions because of an hypothesis that the common law rules might permit the use of traps to scare off intruders but not to cause them death or great bodily harm. Where a layperson might not think to ask whether there were any persons other than the intruders present in the house, the lawyer might hypothesize that the cases and rules then might allow Olner to claim that force was used lawfully in defense of people when it could not be used lawfully in defense of property only.

Having developed a preliminary account of the facts by questioning the client, much work remains to be done before good legal advice can be given. Except for the very accomplished specialist working within an area of expertise, lawyers normally will not know the relevant rules and precedents with sufficient detail to give reasonable legal advice with only momentary reflection. They will have to read or reread the cases, statutes, and legal commentaries with the particular problem case in mind. This legal research will be guided by the forms of legal reasoning: The legal materials are organized by a deductively formed scheme, and the lawyer's hypotheses concerning what might be suggested by the rules, and precedents within classes designated by the rules, will lead him through the library. Then he will develop more facts (including the other party's point of view) in light of the legal research and employ a method of legal interpretation to think hard about the case.

The general knowledge of the law that every competent lawyer possesses, together with intellectual skill in using the forms of legal reasoning, is sufficient for the lawyer to get started and develop the case to a large extent. However, general knowledge and skill in using the forms of legal reasoning are not themselves sufficient to enable the lawyer to make reasonably reliable predictions or effective persuasions. Good legal advice and good avocacy require a judgment of importance. As will be seen, the lawyer's skills at reasoning in the analogical and deductive forms must be supplemented by a capacity to pierce through the forms of legal reasoning to its interpretive method and thus to make predictions and persuasions using the legal experience and the totality of the legal community's theories about law.

C. Predicting and Persuading in Harder Cases

Having developed the facts and conducted legal research, the lawyer in a case will be in a position to make a reasonably reliable prediction of what a court will do in order to decide whether to advise the client to litigate, settle, or drop the matter. The lawyer's prediction, however, is a function in part of how the lawyer thinks a judge will respond to the persuasive arguments presented to the court by the lawyers on each side. A lawyer's argument is likely to be more persuasive to the extent that it presents the more coherent argument, taking into account the relevant facts and legal experience in light of the totality of our theories about law, without overwhelming the judge. Consequently, before giving sound legal advice to a client, the lawyer for each party must compose an argument and anticipate the opponent's argument, and must evaluate how a judge (and, in appropriate cases, a jury) is likely to respond to each argument. The power of the initiative can give both lawyers opportunities to exercise substantial influence over the way in which a judge will perceive a case and thus over the decisions the judge is likely to reach.

The components of the judicial decision are (1) the facts of the problem case, (2) the legal experience, including the common law precedents and rules, and enacted texts with their contexts, and (3) the totality of the legal community's theories explaining and evaluating the legal experience. Each of these three components consists of a potentially vast array of bits of information that, in interesting cases, can be combined in a number of plausible ways. The task of an advocate is to use these bits of information to compose a picture of the case that shows how a decision for the client can be accommodated coherently within a judge's web of beliefs about law. An advocate does so effectively by (1) calling attention to particular facts, parts of the legal experience, and aspects of the legal community's theories; and (2) integrating these bits of information into a coherent legal argument that supports a decision for the client in the case.

When an advocate mentions a fact, cites a precedent or rule, or explains how a theory bears on the case, the advocate calls particular bits of information to attention. They then will be perceived by the judge, when they otherwise might not be noticed. The judge's perception of a bit of information constitutes an "experience" of the kind discussed in the preceding chapter.[4] If at all conscientious, the judge will feel obligated to respond to this experience in one way or another. It may be denied that the bit of

---

[4]See Chapter 7 §C.

information merits attention, as by denying that a fact is adequately supported by the evidence, that a precedent is an authoritative base point for analogical legal reasoning, that a rule is an applicable rule in the case, or that a theory is embedded in the legal experience. Or it may be accepted that the bit of information merits attention, in which case the fact, case, rule, or theory is there to be dealt with and cannot be ignored. Each bit of information that merits attention may lend support to the decision requested by one party or to the opposite decision. How the information will be treated depends on how all of the relevant bits of information are combined.

An effective advocate can influence the integrative process, in addition to calling attention to the bits of information that go into the process. The information often can be described in different terms that evoke different connotations or associations. Treating a point in detail tends to draw out the attention paid to that point. Placing a bit of information in a broader or narrower context can affect its perceived meaning or significance. Juxtaposing one bit of information to another can call attention to relationships of compatibility or anomaly. The advocate can use intellectual and rhetorical skills to tell a short story that shows how the bits of information fit together to support a decision for the client, and can criticize an adversary's argument by pointing out facts or laws that challenge the coherence of the adversary's presentation.

To illustrate, assume that the jury at a trial in the spring gun case found the defendant liable and awarded damages to the plaintiff. The defendant appealed, claiming that the trial judge erred in the instruction to the jury. This instruction had said that an owner of premises is prohibited from willfully or intentionally injuring a trespasser by using force that either takes life or does great bodily injury, and that use of a spring gun or similar booby trap for the purpose of thus harming trespassers is unlawful, even if the trespasser is violating the law. It added that such a use of force would be privileged only when the trespasser was committing a felony of violence or one punishable by death, or where the trespasser was endangering human life by his act.

The arguments of the two lawyers on appeal will present the appellate court a summary of facts supported by evidence in the trial record, citations to and brief summaries of the common law rules and precedents relevant to the court's decision, and explanations of why the law requires a decision for their respective clients under the circumstances. In this case, like any harder case, plural but plausible versions of the facts, the legal experience and the theories are possible. Consider, first, sketches of the statements of facts that each of the lawyers could compose, with support in the trial record[5] and without contradicting the facts stated by opposing counsel.

The defendant's lawyer might present the facts as follows:

Oscar Olner, the defendant, testified that the farmhouse in this case belonged to his wife and had been in her family for several generations. It contained furniture and other valuable possessions, including a collection of antique jars and bottles. She visited the farmhouse to enjoy the collection frequently. The house had been broken into and vandalized repeatedly in recent years. To stop the intrusions, Mr. Olner nailed the doors and some windows shut, boarded up others, locked the doors, posted seven "No Trespassing" signs, and complained on numerous occasions to the sheriff. When all of these efforts proved futile, he placed a gun in a bedroom and wired it so that it would shoot downward and toward the door if anyone opened it. He said he first aimed it straight at the door but later, at his wife's suggestion, pointed the gun down in a way he thought would only scare an intruder. He testified that he "didn't want to injure anyone."

The plaintiff was injured while making a second visit to the defendant's farmhouse to enter unlawfully and steal Mrs. Olner's antiques. He entered by tearing a plank from a porch window and was injured when he came to a closed bedroom door, removed a chair braced under the door knob, and opened the door. This action triggered the gun. The blast went through the door and struck the plaintiff just above the right ankle.

---

[5]All of the facts that appear below were stated as fact in the majority or dissenting opinion in Katko v. Briney, 183 N.W.2d 657 (Iowa 1971). EC 7-26 of the American Bar Association's Code of Professional Responsibility (1976) states that the law prohibits the use of "fraudulent, false, or perjured testimony or evidence. . . . A lawyer should, however, present any admissible evidence his client desires to have presented" unless the lawyer knows or should know that it is legally prohibited.

The plaintiff's lawyer might present the facts differently:

Terry Tress, the plaintiff, was shot by the defendant because, over the preceding ten years, a number of trespassing incidents occurred at the defendant's unoccupied farmhouse. The defendants over the years boarded up the windows and doors and posted a few "No Trespassing" signs on the land. The nearest remaining sign was thirty-five feet from the house at the time of the incident. On June 11, 1967, following one such trespassing incident, the defendant set a shotgun trap in the north bedroom. After cleaning and oiling his 20-gauge shotgun, the power of which he was well aware, the defendant took it to the old house where he secured it to an iron bed with the barrel pointed at the bedroom door. It was rigged with wire from the doorknob to the gun's trigger so that it would fire when the door was opened, no matter who opened it. The defendant at first pointed the gun so that an intruder would be hit in the stomach but, at his wife's insistence, lowered it to hit the legs. He admitted doing so because "I was mad and tired of being tormented," though he "didn't want to injure anyone." He gave no explanation of why he used a loaded shell, set it to hit a person already in the house, and posted no effective warning. The bedroom window was covered so that no one could see the trap.

Terry Tress lived with his wife and child and worked regularly as a gasoline station attendant nearby. He had observed the old house for several years, knew it was unoccupied, and thought it was abandoned. In 1967 the area around the house was covered with high weeds. The plaintiff had been there with a friend and found several old bottles and fruit jars, which he took home. On a second trip, he and his friend entered the house through a window that was without glass. As he started to enter a bedroom, the shotgun went off striking him in the right leg below the knee. Much of the leg, including part of the tibia, was blown away. Only with his friend's help was he taken to a hospital for emergency surgery, and he remained in the hospital for forty days.

These two versions of the facts leave very different impressions of the case. The defendant's account portrays the plaintiff as a heartless burglar depriving the defendant's poor wife of her family heirlooms. The defendant appears as a vigilant, if frustrated, husband defending his wife's property from persistent and anonymous vandals. By contrast, the plaintiff's account portrays the plaintiff as a hardworking family man with an interest in collecting old jars and bottles. The plaintiff appears as a cold and vengeful man seeking to punish a stranger violently, whether or not that person was responsible for past intrusions. One might be tempted to characterize the difference as one involving the goodness or badness of the principal players, and this is a part of what is involved in good advocacy. But the two versions at the same time bring into prominence facts that are relevant to the properly legal issues involved.

A sketch of how the defendant's lawyer might present the legal experience follows:

The jury should have been instructed that the plaintiff in this case could not recover if the defendant set the spring gun in his dwelling house with the intent to repel, but not seriously injure, a felonious intruder. In Scheuerman v. Sharfenberg, 163 Ala. 337 (1909), the plaintiff had been badly hurt by a spring gun while burglarizing the defendant's storehouse. The court assimilated the storehouse to a dwelling and held that the plaintiff could not recover because he was injured while committing a felony. In Hooker v. Miller, 37 Iowa 613 (1873), the court held that a plaintiff who was injured by a spring gun while trespassing in the defendant's garden could recover, but placed emphasis on the fact that the plaintiff was not committing a felony and did not trespass in a dwelling house. Many cases have held that a property owner is privileged to use reasonable force, including devices, to repel an invader even if there is no threat to human life or safety. E.g., Allison v. Fiscus, 156 Ohio 120 (1951).

The plaintiff's lawyer might present the legal experience differently:

The trial court's instruction was correct to limit the defendant's privilege to use force to situations in which there is a threat to human life, whether or not the intruder is a wrongdoer. A property owner is privileged to use mechanical devices that inflict great bodily harm only if he would be entitled to use such force in person. State v. Childers, 133 Ohio St. 508, 515 (1938). One person is not privileged to use deadly force or force likely to do great bodily harm to protect property, even from burglary, absent an accompanying threat to the life or safety of a person. People v. Ceballos, 12 Cal. 3d 470, 479 (1974). In Hooker v. Miller, 37 Iowa 613 (1873), the court held that a vineyard owner was liable for damages resulting from a spring shot gun although the plaintiff was a criminal trespasser and there to steal grapes. Accord, Bird v. Holbrook, 130 Eng. Rep. 911 (1825).

These two sketches of the legal experience also leave very different impressions.[6] The defendant's account places its emphasis on the precedents that allow a property owner to use force to protect his dwelling and focus attention on the criminal conduct of the intruder. The facts as stated above by the defendant's lawyer call attention to the defendant's effort to protect his property, using force only after taking a number of less aggressive measures unsuccessfully, and to the plaintiff's intention to steal valuable antiques from the farmhouse. By contrast, the plaintiff's account places its emphasis on the precedents that limit a property owner's privilege to use force to protect property when there is no threat to human life or safety, and that give little or no weight to the criminal conduct of the intruder. The facts as stated above by the plaintiff's lawyer call attention to the plaintiff's reasons for believing

---

[6]Under EC 7-23 of the American Bar Association's Code of Professional Responsibility (1976), a lawyer who knows of "legal authority in the controlling jurisdiction directly adverse" to his client's position must disclose it. If the spring gun case arose in Iowa, for example, both advocates would be ethically obligated to disclose the case of Hooker v. Miller. Note how each legal argument does so, but treats it in a way that seeks to support the client's position.

that the farmhouse was abandoned and, without denying that the plaintiff trespassed, treat his adventure almost as a misguided lark. The defendant is portrayed as acting recklessly, without concern for the circumstances under which a person may be shot, if not with a malicious intention to seek revenge for the past intrusions.

A court thus would be faced with two versions of the facts and the legal experience, both of which are plausible. The defendant's version fits the facts and the legal experience together compatibly, as does the plaintiff's. The court's decision depends on which version fits better with the remainder of the legal experience and aspects of the legal community's theories about law. Consequently, the parties' advocates are well advised to continue their arguments to show how their versions can be accommodated coherently with the legal community's normative theories about law.

Thus, the defendant's lawyer might continue along the following lines:

There is no doubt in this case that the plaintiff was a wrongdoer — a thief who entered the defendant's dwelling house without permission. The defendant acted in defense of his valuable property, after taking a large number of nonviolent measures unsuccessfully, and with no wrongful intention to harm intruders unnecessarily. The common law tradition upholds the right of a homeowner to protect his dwelling by the use of force, including deadly force. W. Prosser, Handbook of the Law of Torts 116 (4th ed. 1971). "The principle that controls is that the right need never yield to wrong, where the justification of self-defense has shown the defendant to be in the right and the plaintiff in the wrong. To deny the use of deadly force necessarily allows the plaintiff to profit from his own wrong even when the defendant is able to stop him." Epstein, Intentional Harms, 4 J. Legal Stud. 391, 419 (1975) (citation omitted).

The plaintiff's lawyer again might continue differently:

The law has always placed a higher value on human safety than on mere rights in property. W. Prosser, Handbook of the

Law of Torts 115 (4th ed. 1971). Consequently, "spring guns and other man-killing devices are not justifiable against a mere trespasser, or even a petty thief." Id. at 116. See also 2 F. Harper and F. James, The Law of Torts 1440-1441 (1956). It makes no difference that the plaintiff entered a farmhouse because the privilege to use greater force to defend a dwelling exists only when there is a threat to the safety of persons residing therein; in this case, the farmhouse was unoccupied. See People v. Ceballos, 12 Cal. 3d 470 (1974). It makes no difference that the plaintiff was a trespasser because the foundation of the law is "not the criminality of the act or the turpitude of the trespasser." Hooker v. Miller, 37 Iowa 613, 615 (1873). The privilege of a property owner to use force against an intruder is limited to force that is proportional to the nature of the intrusion; "it would seem clear that no interest which is merely one of property can be equal or superior to the interest which both the individual and society have in life and limb." Bohlen and Burns, The Privilege to Protect Property by Dangerous Barriers and Mechanical Devices, 35 Yale L.J. 525, 528 (1926).

Each of the lawyers thus would appeal to a normative theory and argue that the theory is embedded in the legal experience such that it explains the decided cases better than the alternative theory. Moreover, they effectively would argue that the favored theory better represents what members of the legal community generally would take to be required by an orderly and just society in this case and like cases. The defendant's theory calls attention to the wrongfulness of the plaintiff's conduct and requires no balancing of the interests at stake; by contrast, the plaintiff's calls attention to the value of human life as compared to property and requires a balancing of interests. In retrospect, it should be apparent that the facts and legal experience presented by the defendant fit well with the defendant's theory, as the facts and legal experience presented by the plaintiff fit well with the plaintiff's theory. Each argument has a coherence of its own and is supported by facts in the trial record, precedents on the books, and normative theories recognized by members of the legal community.

From these sketches of arguments, it not obvious how a court would or should decide this case: It is a harder case.[7] It is possible, however, that full argumentation would show that one argument or the other can be accommodated more coherently with the facts, the legal experience, and the totality of the legal community's theories about law. That is what the lawyers would seek to show in their full arguments, and it is on this basis that the lawyers would make their predictions and advise their clients whether to litigate or settle. If judges decide harder cases as suggested in the preceding chapter, the lawyer who succeeds in presenting the more coherent argument, taking into account more of the relevant facts and legal experience in light of the totality of our theories about law, will make the more persuasive legal argument. The lawyer who succeeds in anticipating the arguments on both sides of the question, and evaluating them in relation to the conventions of the legal community, is in a good position to make reasonably reliable predictions with which good legal advice can be given.

D. Summary

As shown in Part I, the analogical and deductive forms of legal reasoning perform a number of useful functions. They contribute to the rationality of legal thought by establishing the starting points for legal reasoning, organizing the mass of legal materials to facilitate legal research and analysis, and framing the issues for consideration so that lawyers and judges can communicate effectively. In interesting cases, however, the forms are not sufficient to enable lawyers to make reasonably reliable predictions and effective persuasions or to enable judges to make responsible decisions that may earn respect as law. Because the forms, together with the cases and rules, often allow plural but plausible versions of the facts and the law, the forms must be filled in through an interpretive method that draws on the conventions of the legal community. Legal reasoning commonly is expressed in the analogical and deductive forms, but in crucial ways this represents the outcome of legal reasoning rather than its method.

Logically speaking, the analogical and deductive forms them-

---

[7]The decision of the Iowa Supreme Court will be found in Katko v. Briney, 83 N.W.2d 657 (Iowa 1971), but the result is less important for this discussion than the plausible legal reasoning supporting each party.

selves point toward such an interpretive method because the forms themselves imply the need to consider the law in its entirety in each case. The analogical form of legal reasoning not only requires that each problem case be decided as like cases have been decided; it also requires that each case be distinguished from all other cases that might require a different result. The deductive form of legal reasoning not only requires that each case be decided as required by a rule of law; it also requires that all other rules that might require a different result be shown not to be applicable. Because one cannot negate the possible implications of all other cases and rules exhaustively, the forms point at all other precedents and all other rules in a way that points at the law in its entirety.

The analogical and deductive forms consequently facilitate a method of legal interpretation requiring a coherent account of the facts in a case and the legal experience in light of the totality of the legal community's theories about law. Given a general knowledge of the law, the forms raise the questions that call attention to parts of the law in its entirety so that more of the relevant legal experience and theories can be taken into account. They guide research and analysis of the facts and the law, to reveal the bits of information with which the lawyer must work. They suggest relationships that may show compatibilities or anomalies among the facts, experiences, and theories, and that point the way toward decisions that can be more coherently accommodated with the law in its entirety.

What the forms and interpretive methods of legal reasoning do not do is to dictate which decision is right in a scientifically objective and mechanical way. For each case, the lawyers and judges start with their webs of beliefs about law, in which order and justice are the central values and the remainder of the web incorporates what they know of the legal experience and the totality of the legal community's theories about law. Through legal research and analysis, they refine their professional intuitions and develop legal arguments that bring the legal materials and recognized normative theories to bear on the problem case. The goal is to compose a legal argument that most coherently accommodates a decision in the case with what members of the legal community generally will take to be required by an orderly and just society in the case and like cases, as indicated by the legal experience and the totality of our theories about law.

III

THE PROBLEM OF LEGITIMACY

IT HAS BEEN SEEN THAT THE forms of legal reasoning do not
produce predictions, persuasions, and decisions in cases with
unquestionable soundness. The unavoidable problem of importance, which results from the indeterminacy of language
and the family-style relations among cases, precludes a mode
of thought that could produce absolute certainty. Legal precedents do not themselves dictate the results in problem cases
because each problem case differs from its precedents in
some factual respects; to make a good analogy, it must be
decided whether the differences between the cases are important differences requiring that the cases be decided differently. Legal rules do not themselves dictate the results in
problem cases because the general language of the rule desig-
nates classes of cases; to reach a good conclusion, it must be
decided which particular facts in a case are important and
justify its legal classification.

To make a judgment of importance, the analogical and
deductive forms of legal reasoning must be supplemented by
a workable method of legal interpretation. Such a method
draws on an interpreter's web of beliefs about what members
of the legal community, as an interpretive community, generally will take to be required by an orderly and just society in
a case and like cases. Lawyers and judges make reasonable
predictions, persuasions, and decisions in light of which decision in a case can be better accommodated coherently with
the facts and the legal experience in light of the totality of
the legal community's theories about law.

A particular legal decision thus may be right or wrong in
relation to the conventional understandings of the legal community. However, it does not follow that the decision is right
or wrong in any stronger sense. The decision also can be
evaluated in relation to various moral, religious, economic,
and political interpretive communities or abstract normative
theories. The same decision may be right in relation to the

conventional understandings of the legal community, but wrong in relation to other interpretive contexts. Though theories about law often draw on interpretive methods or theories from other domains, there often remains a significant disjunction between legal and other normative views.

A skeptic might respond that this picture of legal reasoning is troubling because there is something illegitimate about a legal system in which order and justice are relative to a professional community's conventional understandings, which sometimes leave room for significant judicial lawmaking in the course of adjudication. The concern might be that individual judges or an elite professional community can use the power of the state to impose their personal value preferences on others without adequate justification—to maintain the wealth of the wealthy, to take from the rich and give to the poor, to abuse the dignity of people, or otherwise to dominate under a mere cloak of legitimacy. The skeptic might claim that the U.S. legal system does not satisfy the requirements of a rule of law, or a government of laws, not of men, because the rightness of its decisions cannot be proven.

This part will explore the implications of uncertainty and interpretive relativism in law and legal reasoning in light of the undoubted commitment to order and justice, and other values embodied in the ideal of a rule of law, in U.S. society. It will be seen that the skeptic's critique rests on an outmoded, formal model of the rule of law—one that could not be realized in any working society under any imaginable circumstances. The pragmatic question is not whether law and legal reasoning fall short of a formal ideal. They surely do. The pragmatic question is whether alternatives are available and would better serve the purposes that law and legal reasoning are called on to serve in the U.S. legal and political system.

CHAPTER NINE

Formal Legitimacy

I⊤ HAS BEEN SEEN THAT uncertainty and interpretive relativism in legal reasoning do not mean that lawyers and judges make their predictions, persuasions, and decisions on the basis of mere hunches or arbitrarily. The judgment of importance depends on a judge's opinion as to which decision in the case can be better accommodated coherently with the facts and the law as interpreted by members of the legal community. Different judges can (and do) reach different decisions in the same case and give plausible reasons for their decisions. But the conventions of the legal community generally provide enough common ground for lawyers to make reasonably reliable predictions and effective persuasions, and for judges to make responsible decisions that may earn respect as law, in a wide range of cases.

In U.S. society, however, law and legal reasoning are called on to do much more than only to help lawyers and judges pursue their professional goals. Legal reasoning is supposed to draw the justifying connection between the law and a particular governmental action that may deprive a person of life, liberty, or property. Such a justifying connection is needed to show that each judicial decision is in accordance with the law and thus is a legitimate exercise of official power. Uncertainty in legal reasoning implies that there is logical room for judges and other government officials to abuse their power while offering mere rationalizations for their actions. The dependency of legal reasoning on the conventions of the legal community implies a power in the legal community that requires justification.

Legitimacy matters as long as we want to maintain individual liberty and a democratic government of limited power. This chapter explains the classical approach to the problem of legitimacy in adjudication, which commonly treats the demand for legitimacy as a demand that judicial reasoning satisfy a formal model of the rule of law. After explaining the demand for legitimacy, the chapter considers two classical conceptions of how a judicial decision might be justified within a formalist framework. As will be seen, however, no theory is capable of establishing the legitimacy of adjudication in practice, *if* the demand for legitimacy is taken to mean that judicial reasoning practices must satisfy the requirements of strong legal formalism. The next chapter will explore alternative interpretations of the demand for legitimacy.

A. The Demand for Legitimacy

The U.S. legal system does not exist to authorize the persons who hold the reins of official power to use it for their personal ends. The individual who stands before a judge presumptively is entitled to dignity and autonomy. The community wants to know *by what right* the individual sitting behind the bench uses the power of the state to take another individual's liberty, his property, and even his life. This demand for legitimacy requires that judicial decisions be justifiable uses of the power of the state. The need to justify the exercise of judicial power is among the most deeply held theories about law in U.S. society, reflecting a commitment to liberty and a democratic government of limited power.

The law in major respects is an effort to rule out arbitrary and oppressive uses of the coercive powers of the state. The police, for example, are agents of the state and are justified in using force, if necessary, to limit an individual's freedom by lawful arrest if they have probable cause to believe that the individual has violated the criminal law. The police are not authorized to arrest an individual because they do not like the individual, disapprove of the individual's life-style, believe the individual to be an immoral person, or oppose the individual's political views.

It is less obvious that the question whether a similar use of force by the state would be justified lies behind almost every judicial decision. Imagine a case in which a landlord seeks to have a tenant evicted from an apartment because the tenant is in arrears on the rent. The landlord cannot use force to evict the tenant lawfully, but must go to court to get a judicial decree enforcing the lease by ordering the tenant to vacate the premises. If the tenant defies the decree, the landlord can get a court order instructing the sheriff to evict the tenant from the apartment; if the tenant persists in defiance, the sheriff then is justified in effecting a removal forcibly. Though the threat of forcible eviction induces almost all holdover tenants to comply with a court order peaceably, those who resist will find themselves on the wrong end of a sheriff's revolver. It would not be justifiable for a judge to empower the sheriff to use force to take a person's life, liberty, or property for any reason or no reason at all. The judicial power can be used legitimately only if it is used to enforce the law.

The demand for legitimacy accordingly places judges under a duty to decide cases in accordance with the law, not as a product of personal values not validated by the law. When a judge's decision is in accordance with the law, it is not the individual behind the bench but the society's law, acting through that individual, that is responsible for any deprivations. Further, the demand for legitimacy implies that unjustifiable judicial decisions are not legitimate uses of the powers of the state. It would seem to follow that such abuses of official power should not be tolerated—that illegitimate adjudication should be abandoned. The problem is to determine what it means for judges to decide cases "in accordance with the law," and therefore what would count as an adequate justification of a judicial decision.

The classical interpretation of the demand for legitimacy treats it as a demand for *legal formalism* in adjudication. Legal formalism posits an abstract formal model of legal justification. Judicial reasoning practices then could be assessed in relation to the abstract model. The main model of formal legitimacy is based on the legal syllogism and relies on logic to exclude all personal value preferences from the judicial decision. In this model, deciding cases in accordance with the law requires sound legal syllogisms to support each judicial decision in every respect.

A simple version of formal legitimacy supposes that, to be legitimate, a judicial decision in a problem case must be the single decision that follows logically from the authoritative legal rule or rules. To be authoritative, a legal rule must follow logically from other authoritative rules that ultimately are grounded in some foundational authorizing principle. The foundational principle would define the rules that define the decisions that judges can reach legitimately. A more complex version of formal legitimacy recognizes that determinations of importance must be made in order to derive judicial decisions from authoritative rules, or to derive authoritative rules from legitimating foundations. It may insist, however, that the determination of importance itself be a logical product of authoritative principles that, in turn, rest on some foundational authorizing principle.[1] The more complex logical relations between a decision, the authoritative rules, authoritative principles, and an ultimate legitimating foundation would leave no logical room for a judge's personal value preferences to intrude in legal reasoning.

For example, the principle of constitutional democracy may be said to be a legitimating foundation supporting the U.S. legal system. The specific textual provisions of the Constitution, and laws made by democratic processes as provided in the Constitution, would be among the authoritative rules. By the simple version of formal legitimacy, courts would be required to justify each decision by logical reasoning only from the constitutional text or constitutionally enacted rules. By the more complex version of formal legitimacy, the courts may make a determination of importance to interpret the constitutional text or duly enacted rules, provided that it is justified by logical reasoning from authoritative principles. The principles would be authoritative only if logically derived from the principle of constitutional democracy or another consistent legitimating foundation.

The prevalent use of a deductive form of legal reasoning from enacted rules, common law rules, and legal principles reflects judicial consciousness of this model. It often leaves the impression that judicial decisions are dictated by authoritative rules or principles deductively, leaving no logical room for judicial shenanigans. If the practice were coincident with this appearance, the judge would have no room for choice with which to produce an arbitrary or oppressive decision based on considerations outside the law. Judges surely would decide cases in accordance with the law, and it could be said that we have a government of laws, not of men. Consequently, the pretense of the deductive form of legal reasoning often is taken to define legitimacy for adjudication in the U.S. legal system.

What was said in Parts I and II about the forms and interpretive methods of legal reasoning, as well as the conventional wisdom concerning judicial reasoning practices, suggests that legitimacy is a serious problem if it is defined by legal formalism. By this strong standard of legitimacy, it will not do to claim that a judicial decision is legitimate because the judge thought that the decision could be

---

[1]See, e.g., Bork, Neutral Principles and Some First Amendment Problems, 47 Ind. L.J. 1 (1972); Wechsler, Toward Neutral Principles of Constitutional Law, 73 Harv. L. Rev. 1 (1959).

better accommodated coherently with the facts and the legal experience in light of the totality of the legal community's theories about law. Such legal reasoning has no foundational authorizing principle but, rather, is composed from a web of beliefs about law in which, ultimately, all beliefs should be mutually reinforcing and pragmatically valuable when acted upon. Though principles of legitimacy, stare decisis, and legislative supremacy stand together near the center of our webs and support many of our beliefs about law, it is logically possible to drop or modify even these principles if we were willing to make the necessary adjustments to the remainder of the web. The forms and interpretive methods of legal reasoning do not satisfy the strong requirements of legal formalism because any decision is logically possible.[2]

The demand for legitimacy, together with legal formalism as a common model of legitimacy, requires consideration of whether foundations are available that might be better able to satisfy these strong requirements for legal justification than the explanation of legal reasoning presented in Parts I and II. The next section examines two classical approaches that employ legitimating foundations that may be thought to generate legitimacy in particular cases, as required by legal formalism. It will be seen, however, that no known or imaginable legitimating foundation is capable of satisfying such strong requirements. Consequently, it will be necessary to question whether a different interpretation of the demand for legitimacy should replace legal formalism.

B. Formalist Theories of Legitimacy

There are two classical formalist responses to the problem of legitimacy in adjudication. One, to be discussed first, treats moral principles as a legitimating foundation.[3] The other, discussed next, bases the legitimacy of laws and judicial decisions on principles of democracy that serve as an ultimate legitimating foundation for judicial reasoning.[4] Neither view solves the problem of legitimacy

---

[2] See Chapter 7.

[3] There are a number of more sophisticated theories of (methodological) natural law that do not fall within the formalist school of thought. See, e.g., R. Dworkin, Taking Rights Seriously (1978).

[4] There are a number of more sophisticated democratic theories that do not fall wholly within the formalist school of thought. See, e.g., J. Ely, Democracy and Distrust (1980).

in adjudication if legal formalism is taken to be the meaning of legitimacy.

1. Moral Legitimating Foundations

A first classical response to the problem of legitimacy in adjudication bases the legitimacy of all law made by human beings on its conformity to a higher law made by God or inherent in the nature of things. It often is called a theory of *natural law* because it assumes or asserts the existence of foundational principles that are not made by human beings. It more often is equated in modern times with the moral law, though not necessarily with conventional morality, which consists of the moral experience of people and the totality of their widely shared theories about morality. In a strong version, this response claims that the only legitimate judicial decisions are those that can be justified directly under the moral law, sometimes going so far as to consider laws enacted by democratic institutions to be illegitimate (and invalid) if not justifiable by the moral law. In a weaker version, this theory claims that the judgment of importance must be justified directly under the moral law, but allows humanly made (positive) rules of law to frame the issue for moral decision.

Legal reasoning differs from reasoning from the moral law in significant respects. Legal reasoning is reasoning from specialized social convention—from the practices of a society that are accepted as law, including the practices of the courts and legislatures, and the dispositions of lawyers and judges, if not the general populace. As Professor H.L.A. Hart said, "The proof that 'binding' rules in any society exist, is simply that they are thought of, spoken of, and function as such."[5] This calls attention to the conventional practices and dispositions of people and, more specifically, to the conventional practices and dispositions of the members of the legal community within a society because those persons most often think, speak, and give effect to the law. Legal reasoning thus is explained best with reference to the legal experience (practices) and the totality of our theories about law (dispositions of members of the legal community). Accordingly, legal reasoning is what passes as acceptable legal reasoning among members of the legal community—reasoning that influences the predictions, persuasions, and decisions of lawyers and judges in practice.

---

[5]H. Hart, The Concept of Law 226 (1961).

Reasoning from the moral law, in the strict sense required by legal formalism, would not be reasoning from social convention. One would not equate what any person or limited group of people think is morally right with what is, in truth, right. Genocide was practiced in Hitler's Germany and apparently accepted by much of the then-contemporary community. Cannibalism and slavery once were practiced and widely accepted in some societies. By almost any current conception of morality, however, these social practices are morally wrong. From a moral perspective, one must be wary of thinking that none of our own practices are widely accepted in the contemporary setting, but morally wrong. The human experience makes it unwise to so lack humility that we deny our moral fallibility.

Principles of the moral law must be standards that exist naturally so that they are capable of condemning a social convention that is not moral, however widely it may be practiced and accepted by people in a particular community. Reasoning from the moral law, in the strict sense, is reasoning from foundational principles of right and wrong that are not made by people through their social conventions or otherwise. It is reasoning from principles that (somehow) exist independently of human practices and dispositions.

The problem of legitimacy in adjudication, as classically posed in terms of legal formalism, cannot be solved by justifying judicial decisions with reference to the moral law as thus conceived. To justify legal rules, or the application of the rules in a case, on these moral grounds requires that the rule or application be dictated by the moral law. An appeal to moral law, like an appeal to any other law, satisfies the requirements of legal formalism only if it provides a foundation from which can be derived authoritative rules or principles and their applications in cases. The logical derivation must be tight enough to leave no room in judicial decisions for arbitrary or oppressive uses of the coercive powers of the state by the individual persons who hold the reins of official power.

This would require, first, that the moral law exist naturally and that what it says can be known. Doubt about the existence of a moral law in this sense now is so widespread that there is no need to belabor the point that many people will consider that this first (and necessary) requirement cannot be met. Even those who sincerely believe that a moral law exists rarely assert that they know with certainty what it says. They may believe sincerely in one or another moral system or proposition, but normally have sufficient humility to admit a significant risk of error.

Even if a moral law existed and it could be known what it said, however, what it permits or requires in a particular case often would remain puzzling. Before moral laws can dictate the decision in a case logically, they must take the form of a general statement whether it is called a rule, a principle, or a standard. They must take a form that is suitable for use as the major premise in a moral syllogism. It then would be necessary to formulate a minor premise that characterizes the facts in a case and that is capable of yielding a sound conclusion, as it is to use a legal syllogism. Though it thus may be possible to reason from the moral law in the deductive form, however, the choice points in the legal syllogism would recur in the moral syllogism, and a judgment of importance would be necessary. Alas, there is no reason to think that a moral judgment of importance can be made with reference only to general statements of the moral law with any less difficulty than a legal judgment of importance can be made with reference only to legal rules and principles.

Additionally, a moral judgment of importance would be even more troublesome because a deductive (or analogical) form of moral reasoning would lack an appropriate method of interpretation. In reasoning from the moral law, one could not satisfy the requirements of legal formalism by making a judgment of importance in light of which decision can be better accommodated coherently with the moral experience and the totality of our theories about morality. As has been seen, what people have done in the past is no sure guide to what is morally right, and what contemporary people think is morally right is no sure guide to what is, in truth, right. To satisfy the requirements of legal formalism, a moral judgment of importance cannot be founded on social practices and dispositions that themselves are not known to be right by the moral law.

An appeal to the moral experience and the totality of our theories about morality is an appeal, not to the moral law, but to conventional morality. It is an appeal to what past and contemporary people do and think about moral matters. Many individuals form their moral beliefs in accordance with their personal views of a moral law, but few assert that they have a privileged view of the moral law that makes their views the only correct views. Even when moral views are widely shared among the members of a community, the shared views are not equated with the moral law. To mark this distinction, such views are treated as conventional morality, signifying that the views are to be respected because they are held sincerely by people.

Conventional morality also cannot legitimate adjudication as required by legal formalism. It is too contingent on contemporary circumstances and notions of rightness to validate itself as a legitimating foundation. Moreover, it does not follow from the fact that a person's behavior is not regarded as moral by the moral conventions in a society that the state should use its coercive powers to deprive that person of liberty or property. For example, conventional morality requires persons to keep their promises, including a neighbor's promise to remove an unsightly shrub from her property, but may not comprehend legal action to enforce all promises. Much of the moral sense of the community creates no more than social pressure for individuals to conform or is highly deferential to each individual's personal moral code.

However valuable conventional morality may be to individual persons and as a source of social norms, it makes a difference that a judge wields the power of the state.[6] When a judge appeals to the legal community's conventional understandings of what the law does or should permit or require, the appeal is in part to understandings about the proper role of the state in U.S. society, as well as about stare decisis, legislative supremacy, and other relevant matters. The appeal is to conventional understandings of what are or should be the limits of state authority and the realm of human freedom from coercion by the state—to theories about legitimacy itself.

Thus, the moral law cannot be used to establish the legitimacy of adjudication, within the framework of legal formalism, because it cannot dictate the results in cases and leave no logical room for personal values to intrude. The moral law may not exist independently of individual views and moral conventions. If it does exist, it may not be possible to know what it says. If it were possible to know what it says, it could not yield a sound decision in a particular case by deduction. The requirements of a moral law are too controversial for the moral law to serve as a legitimating foundation for judicial decisions. And conventional morality should not be used as conventional understandings of the law are used, if individual moral autonomy and limitations on the coercive power

---

[6]For a classic debate on the scope of this point, see P. Devlin, The Enforcement of Morals (1965); H. Hart, Law, Liberty and Morality (1963).

of the state are to be retained. Accordingly, a judge's moral views generally are treated as a personal, not a legal, matter.

2. Democratic Legitimating Foundations

In modern U.S. society, the persistent concern to know by what right a judge wields the power of the state in a case results in great part from well-accepted theories of democratic government. It is not so troubling that the Congress or a state legislature may enact laws that will make some people rich and some people poor, some people free and some people fettered, even some people live and some people die. Laws enacted by such institutions are made by people who are elected to perform the lawmaking function, within constitutional constraints. They are elected by a majority for limited terms of office and must face the people for reelection. All citizens can communicate their views to their elected representatives, who have reason to listen. The lawmakers' decisionmaking procedures and power to make law are set forth explicitly in the U.S. Constitution and the constitutions of the several states. The Constitution and state constitutions, in turn, were approved by the people through democratic procedures. The participation and consent of the governed, and the direct accountability of elected representatives of the people, are thought to confer legitimacy on the lawmaking functions of Congress and the state legislatures: They make law by the right that flows from a democratic mandate.

Judicial power would not be so troubling if the decision in a case were derived as required by legal formalism from rules duly enacted by democratic processes. In theory, then, the courts would not themselves create law to any degree, but would apply the law created by the democratic institutions in all respects. Their decisions would derive legitimacy from the same democratic mandate that supports the lawmaking institutions. In a less direct way, comfort could be taken in the thought that Congress and the state legislatures acquiesce in the rules and principles of the common law, which they can at any time nullify by statute. If the judicial decision in a case were derived as required by legal formalism from such rules and principles, the acquiescence of the elected representatives could be treated as transferring the democratic mandate to the courts. On this basis, judges would decide cases in accordance with the law, and the legitimacy of adjudication would rest on a democratic foundation within the framework of formal legitimacy.

However, judicial decisions necessarily involve a degree of

creativity, albeit an often trivial degree. The judicial power to interpret and apply the rules in a case — to make the judgment of importance — is in a limited sense a power to make the law for that case and potentially for other like cases. A court that reasons in the analogical and deductive forms makes the judgment of importance in part by deciding what the law ought to be in the case. The power to declare a statute unconstitutional or to overrule the common law precedents are more dramatic examples of the judicial power to make law independently of the more democratic branches of government.

Within the framework of legal formalism, it is the judicial lawmaking power itself that stands in need of legitimating foundations. The judicial lawmaking power often is thought not to be adequately supported by an independent democratic mandate, though the problem varies from more troublesome for federal judges to less troublesome for some state court judges. Judges do not entirely lack a democratic mandate because they are appointed by elected representatives or, in some states, elected by the people. In cases of extreme misbehavior, judges can be removed from office by Congress, the state legislatures, or sometimes the people. The precedential effect of most of their decisions can be nullified by subsequent legislation, and even decisions based on the Constitution can be nullified by constitutional amendment. Though these are significant democratic checks on judicial power, however, the accountability of judges to the people often is far more tangential than that of the other branches of government.

Paradoxically, judicial independence from political pressure is thought to be necessary to preserve the rule of law. The U.S. legal and political tradition does not require that judges be controlled by majoritarian politics as is a legislator. It holds that legal rights should not be the subject of political lobbying directed at courts or be subject to the cross-currents of public opinion. Thus, federal judges are guaranteed lifetime tenure by the Constitution; other judicial terms of office are long or, in practice, virtually unlimited. Judges normally do not hear the views of citizens who are not parties in the case before the court but may be affected by the precedential effect of the decision. They do not take the pulse of constituents before making their decisions, and even the parties are limited to proving the facts and arguing the law. However, the courts' power to make law in cases is not explicitly set forth in the Constitution or state constitutions, or approved formally by the people by some other method. It is hard to see how many judges are effectively accountable to the governed for the law they create.

It should be emphasized that the courts create law in a limited sense, by contrast with a legislature's wider lawmaking power. The problem of importance, and the judicial practice of accommodating each decision with the facts and the legal experience in light of the totality of the legal community's theories about law, leave logical room for judicial views of what the law ought to be in many cases. But the judicial power to make law is limited to the case and like cases. The judges do not decide what cases they shall decide; perhaps with a few exceptions, their jurisdiction depends on statutes, and the initiative in particular cases lies with the parties. A judge's decision creates law only as necessary to decide the case before the court, though it must be generalizable in principle to some other like cases.

More important, appellate court decisions have uncertain implications until other members of the legal community react. The effect of a precedent on other cases depends on other judges who may reinterpret, distinguish, or sometimes overrule a precedent or bypass a case of statutory or constitutional interpretation. Except in cases where a statute is declared unconstitutional, the legislature may nullify the precedential effect of a judicial decision by enacting subsequent legislation. Some judicial decisions find quick acceptance by lawyers and other judges, and at least acquiescence by Congress or the state legislatures. A few of these decisions have a substantial impact on the law. Others, however decisive they may be to the parties in the case, wither from inattention though they remain on the books or die by overruling or subsequent legislation. Most cases have a modest effect on the law, through their incremental contribution to the legal experience and the legal community's theories about law. Because the legal implications of a judicial decision depend on how members of the legal community treat the decision, rather than on how any one judge characterizes the decision, its effects on the law are beyond the control of any one or two judges and within the control of the legal community.

Nonetheless, the checking power of the legal community does not establish the legitimacy of the judicial lawmaking power as required by the democratic theory of legitimacy within the framework of legal formalism. Many influential members of the legal community are not themselves effectively accountable to any electorate, and the legal community has not been a fair cross-section of the public at large.[7] Moreover, an aberrant judicial decision is the only law that matters to the parties before the court in a particular case. The parties seek justice according to the law and normally are unconcerned about its broader legal implications. Many come to the court claiming their rights and conceive of their rights as a function of law that existed at the time of the events in question, not as a function of a creative judicial decision after the fact.[8] The legitimacy of the judicial lawmaking power should extend to the law made to decide a particular case and, by the democratic theory of legitimacy, this requires that the judges have a democratic mandate to create law.

Analytically, even easy cases do not satisfy the strong requirements of legal formalism together with democratic foundations. The lack of an adequate democratic foundation for a judicial lawmaking power, however, is not thought to be troublesome in such cases as a practical matter. The decision in such cases often is in the deductive form, leaving the impression that it is required by the logic of an authoritative rule. So long as the rule has been enacted or acquiesced in by the Congress or state legislatures, or is part of the Constitution or state constitutions approved by the people, its apparent logical implications in the case are accepted as legitimate. Pragmatically speaking, there is no reason to question whether the result was dictated by the rule, or whether the rule was properly authoritative, because the totality of plausible theories about law converge to suggest a single result. Such cases pass without objection because it would serve no useful purpose to question their legitimacy, even if they are analytically questionable.

The lack of an adequate democratic mandate for the judicial lawmaking power is thought to be more troublesome in harder cases. A few prominent but unpopular judicial decisions produce a strong and hostile public reaction, especially on matters of constitutional law. In recent decades, segments of the public have been harshly critical of a number of Supreme Court decisions, including those striking down congressional efforts to deal with the Great

---

[7]See Brest, Interpretation and Interest, 34 Stan. L. Rev. 765, 770-772 (1982).
[8]The "rights thesis" is put forward most forcefully in R. Dworkin, supra note 3. This problem is not solved by the theory of law and legal reasoning set forth in this book or by any other theory, to this author's knowledge. See Kress, Legal Reasoning and Coherence Theories: Dworkin's Rights Thesis, Retroactivity, and the Linear Order of Decisions, 72 Calif. L. Rev. 369 (1984).

Depression, requiring desegregation of the public schools, and recognizing a limited right for women to obtain abortions. Critics of such decisions challenge not only the wisdom of the Supreme Court's judgments. They often challenge the legitimacy of the Supreme Court's power to make such judgments, pointing to the "nine old men" who were not elected and the extreme difficulties of changing the law by constitutional amendment.

The rightness of decisions in harder cases cannot be proved to those who disagree because they often would be satisfied only with a justification that meets the strong requirements of legal formalism. The totality of the legal community's theories about law have multiple implications in the circumstances of harder cases. Strong critics of a judicial decision are able (logically) to accommodate the decision they favor by making the necessary adjustments to their webs of beliefs about law, even if the necessary adjustments would alter radically most conceptions of the U.S. legal system. Some will claim that the judicial decision was a product of the personal values of the judges, ignoring the fact that the judicial decision, too, can be accommodated coherently with the law, perhaps with less disruption to the law in its entirety than the available alternatives. The difference between a court and its critics is not a difference between right and wrong in any absolute sense, but a difference about which decision can be better accommodated coherently with the law in its entirety.

Harder cases often do not pass without objection. The judgment of importance leaps into prominence; it is apparent that *this* fact is important by one plausible theory while *that* fact is important by another plausible theory. The choice to emphasize one theory over another determined the result in the case and therefore how the coercive powers of the state would be used. But it is not possible to demonstrate rigorously that the choice was dictated by democratically adopted rules or made by electorally accountable judges.

Consequently, democratic principles cannot solve the problem of legitimacy in adjudication, if legal formalism is taken to be the meaning of legitimacy, by serving as a legitimating foundation from which judicial decisions or the judicial lawmaking power can be derived. The democratic theory of legitimacy is reassuring as a practical matter in many cases, and it will be seen that it plays a major role in alternative approaches to legitimacy. But the formalist model of legal justification requires that judges decide cases independently of political pressure. Judicial independence at the same time removes many judges to a large extent from the direct accountability to the people that is the mark of a democratic mandate.

C. The Analytical Critique of Formalism

Probably few legal thinkers today embrace a hard version of legal formalism.[9] The requirements of this abstract model are too strong to function as a workable model of legitimacy for adjudication in real-world situations, whatever legitimating foundations could be imagined. To produce an analytically sound theory of legitimacy within the formalist framework requires a legitimating foundation that both (1) itself is justified and (2) has the logical capacity to transfer its legitimacy content to authoritative rules or principles, and particular judicial decisions, without at any step appealing to the opinions of any person or group of persons. Because neither condition can be fully satisfied for analytical reasons, legitimacy necessarily is dependent on the views of some person or group of persons. Consequently, formal legitimacy fails to deliver what it promises—the logical exclusion of personal value preferences from judicial decisions.

It is easy, in a politically stable nation like the contemporary United States, to lose sight of the fact that candidates for the role of legitimating foundations can be controversial in real-world settings. In the Western tradition, the two most prominent candidates for legitimating foundations have been democratic principles and several versions of the natural law. Contemporary democratic principles tend to be widely accepted as legitimating principles, while the moral law is less widely accepted, but it has not always been so. Indeed, King George III ruled by the "divine right of kings"— a claim under natural law—and saw the American revolutionaries as lawless rebels. The American revolutionaries included rights of self-government prominently among the legitimating foundations underpinning the new American nation.

More important for present purposes is the fact that basic legitimating foundations can be controversial intellectually. Within the framework of hard legal formalism, any candidate for the role

---

[9]Contemporary manifestations of arguably formalist views are canvassed in Moore, The Semantics of Judging, 54 S. Cal. L. Rev. 151, 154-167 (1981). "Soft" versions of legal formalism are considered in Chapter 10 §A.

of legitimating foundation cannot perform the legitimating function so long as it remains itself questionable. A particular judicial decision based on a rule or principle that is claimed to be authoritative cannot be justified, in the formalist sense, by appealing to an authorizing principle (or set of consistent principles) that itself is not known to be sound. The authorizing principle remains unjustified within this framework so long as doubt about its soundness as a foundation is intellectually possible. Such doubt is always possible intellectually, as evidenced by the centuries of controversy among qualified political theorists. Consequently, any known candidate for the role of legitimating foundation cannot satisfy the strong requirements of legal formalism.

Pragmatically speaking, it may be that some legitimating principles in fact are so widely accepted within a society that, though intellectually questionable, they are not questioned. Some legal thinkers try to build a modified theory of formal legitimacy in which the foundational authorizing principles are legitimate by virtue of popular consent or social consensus, but the authoritative rules and decisions are legitimate by virtue of the foundational principle. Professor H.L.A. Hart, for example, believes that each mature legal system has a "rule of recognition" that itself rests on social consensus but that identifies the authoritative rules within the system.[10] Some constitutional scholars believe that the Constitutional text, together with the intentions of the Framers as evidenced by the constitutional history, is a legitimating foundation that itself rests on the ratification process, but from which judges can derive authoritative rules and legitimate decisions.[11]

Even if a principle (or set of consistent principles) could be recognized as a legitimating foundation, however, it still could not perform its function within the formalist model if the principle is not capable of transferring its legitimacy content to rules, principles, and particular judicial decisions without again appealing to what some person or group of persons thinks. The foundation is meant to serve as a basis for constructing an operational legal structure that, in all respects, is supported by the legitimating content of the foundation, rather than the opinions of people. The legitimating principle must be "stated" — cast in a language — in order to be capable of transferring its content to other statements,

---

[10]H. Hart, The Concept of Law 42-93, 97-100 (1961).
[11]See R. Berger, Government by Judiciary (1977).

such as legal rules and holdings, without appealing to the assent of an audience. Logical proof is the mechanism by which the content of one statement can be thus transferred to another statement, and logic operates only on statements or propositions in a language.

But once the legitimating principle is cast in a language, other problems appear and undermine the venture. The language of a legitimating principle will be general and susceptible to conflicting interpretations in particular situations, especially when cases are alike only as the members of a family are alike. Choosing among the possible interpretations itself requires justification. Because an interpretation cannot be justified by appealing to the very principle that is being interpreted, recourse to a different stated principle is necessary. The second principle then itself requires justification, and interpretation with reference to yet another stated principle, which then itself requires justification, and interpretation, and the process continues without end.[12]

Such an endless analytical process obviously is not characteristic of the way we think or could think in real-world situations. We would be disabled from acting if we questioned everything at once. We know that a logically consistent and complete justification for a particular decision either could not be stated or, if stated, would be incomprehensible for all practical purposes. Rather, even if we work within the formalist framework, we rely on intuition and the hopefully noncontroversial opinions of other persons or groups of persons both to establish a legitimating foundation and to trace out its implications for legal rules, principles, and particular decisions.[13] But it must be recognized that formal legitimacy has failed once we acknowledge that it is dependent on the opinions of people at each step in the analysis. The point of formalism, after all, is to rely on logic to exclude the personal value preferences of people from the judicial decision in order to ensure that the decision in every respect is required by the law.

The analytical failure of legal formalism has extensive implications. The magnitude of potential implications can be seen if the failure of formalism is expressed in a syllogism:

---

[12]See Burton, Comment on "Empty Ideas": Logical Positivist Analyses of Equality and Rules, 91 Yale L. J. 1136, 1140-1147 (1982).

[13]The point is not a characteristic peculiar to law. See, e.g., S. Fish, Is There a Text in This Class? (1980); T. Kuhn, The Structure of Scientific Revolutions (2d ed. 1972); R. Rorty, Philosophy and the Mirror of Nature (1980); McCloskey, The Rhetoric of Economics, 21 J. Econ. Lit. 481 (1983).

MAJOR PREMISE: Judicial decisions are legitimate uses of the coercive powers of the state only if they are in accordance with the law as required by legal formalism, which requires that the decision be dictated only by authoritative rules and principles derived from legitimating foundations.

MINOR PREMISE: Judicial decisions in fact are not dictated only by authoritative rules and principles derived from legitimating foundations.

CONCLUSION: [Judicial decisions are not legitimate uses of the coercive powers of the state.]

The conclusion is bracketed because, though it follows logically from the premises as stated, logic does not compel adoption of the distressing conclusion that appears to follow. A conclusion is only as good as its premises. As always, the premises can be questioned. Concluding that judicial decisions are not legitimate implies that the practice of adjudication should be abandoned. Both premises should be scrutinized intensely before such a radical conclusion is adopted.

The explanation of legal reasoning in Parts I and II, along with the conventional wisdom of the profession, accepts the truth of the minor premise: It seems undeniably a fact of the legal experience that the justifying connection between the law and a particular judicial decision always is analytically questionable. However, it is possible to drop or modify the major premise, which is an interpretation of the demand for legitimacy, not an immutable principle of any higher law. The next chapter explores alternative interpretations of the demand for legitimacy and thus alternative theories of legitimacy.

D. Summary

The problem of legitimacy in adjudication is the problem of showing how it is possible for judicial decisions to be justified. Judges wield the coercive powers of the state. The demand for legitimacy requires that they do so in accordance with the law and not as a product of personal value preferences. Legal formalism interprets the demand for legitimacy to require that, to be legitimate, the decision in each case be the single decision that is logically required by authoritative rules and principles that, in turn, are logically derived from a legitimating foundation. Anything less than certainty in legal reasoning is thought to leave logical room for judicial choice, into which the personal value preferences of the judges can intrude.

Analysis of the forms of legal reasoning casts doubt on whether any judicial decision can be justified so as to satisfy the strong requirements of legal formalism. Whether legitimating foundations are sought in principles of moral law, principles of democracy, principles supported by a social consensus, or any other imaginable candidate for the foundational position, judicial decisions remain dependent on the opinions of some person or group of persons in key respects. By the formalist theory of legitimacy, it follows that judicial decisions are not legitimate and, by implication, that adjudication should be abandoned.

Such a conclusion is distressing because it cannot be accommodated coherently with the legal experience and the totality of our theories about law. To maintain coherence among our experiences and theories, we either must abandon the demand for legitimacy in adjudication, abandon adjudication because it is not legitimate, or abandon formal legitimacy as a theory of legitimacy. Whether we should abandon formal legitimacy as the theory of legitimacy depends, of course, on the availability of an alternative theory of legitimacy that, together with its implications, can be better accommodated coherently within our webs of beliefs about law.

CHAPTER TEN

Alternatives to Formal Legitimacy

IN LARGE PART FOR THE reasons given in Chapter 9, members of the legal community now generally recognize that it is impossible for any working legal system to satisfy the strong requirements of formal legitimacy. Few persons, however, are willing to conclude that adjudication is not legitimate and therefore should be abandoned, or that the demand for legitimacy should be abandoned. Rather, the search is on for alternative theories of legitimacy that better capture our intuitive sense that at least much adjudication is legitimate.

The failure of formalism leaves a number of alternatives to be considered, only some of which can be explored in this introduction. One is *legal skepticism,* which doubts that law binds judges in cases and consequently holds that judges decide whatever they want to decide. Legal skeptics defend their position largely by pointing to the analytical critique of legal formalism and either abandon the demand for legitimacy or interpret it to require majoritarian political control of the judiciary. Another alternative could be called *soft formalism* because it relaxes the rigor required by hard legal formalism while otherwise retaining the formalist framework. Soft formalists accept the analytical critique of formalism insofar as it denies the possibility of authoritative rules or principles that dictate the single correct result in each case, but interpret the demand for legitimacy to be satisfied by such rules and principles that adequately limit the decisions that judges can reach. Though each of these two alternatives is supported by respected members of the legal community, neither approach in my view is successful in satisfying the demand for legitimacy.

This chapter suggests that these approaches are not successful because they suffer from legacies of formalism in ways that leave them predestined to inadequacy as theories of legitimacy. Taking the death of formalism seriously suggests that we enter a post-formalist world, in which the demand for legitimacy can be interpreted contextually to require that the people generally recognize an obligation to abide by the law within a legal and political system that merits their allegiance. The legitimacy of adjudication would depend on its contribution to the legitimacy of the legal and political system in its social, historical, and cultural context. From this perspective, there is good reason to believe that adjudication in the U.S. context is legitimate because it contributes to the contextual legitimacy of the legal and political system as a whole.

A. The Legacies of Formalism

The death of formalism has many implications, some of which are more easily appreciated than others. It is relatively easy, for example, to appreciate that legitimacy no longer can require that each judicial decision must be deduced from authoritative rules and principles that, in turn, must be deduced from a foundational authorizing principle. Unless we are prepared to abandon adjudication itself, a different conception of legitimacy is needed. It is perhaps less easy to appreciate that, having buried formal legitimacy, we may continue to worship formalism as an implicit standard for criticism or as an ideal to be mimicked imperfectly. Taking the death of formalism seriously suggests that we should dispense with formalism in these more subtle roles, too.

1. Legal Skepticism

Many lawyers and judges today believe, or at least will say, that judges in cases decide whatever they want to decide and then rationalize the result with reference to the precedents and legal rules.[1] The implication is that judges are imposing their personal value preferences on individuals under the guise of law. In reality, these legal thinkers assert, there is no law that binds judges; judicial decisions are products of the personal value preferences of those who hold the reins of official power. This theory about law will be called *legal skepticism.*

Legal skepticism poses a powerful challenge to the legitimacy of adjudication in a democratic society, which depends on some

---

[1]See, e.g., J. Frank, Law and the Modern Mind (1930); W. Twining, Karl Llewelyn and the Realist Movement (1973); Cohen, Field Theory and Judicial Logic, 59 Yale L.J. 238 (1950); Hutcheson, The Judicial Intuitive: The Function of the "Hunch" in the Judicial Decision, 14 Cornell L.Q. 274 (1929). See also Symposium: The Critical Legal Studies Movement, 36 Stan. L. Rev. 1 (1984).

sort of consent of the governed to the laws that govern. It is far-fetched to think that the American people in any sense have consented or would consent to be governed in significant measure by the personal value preferences of judges, rather than by law. It is hard to imagine why, in a democratic society, the people should consent to such unbridled power in any office that is not politically responsible to the electorate at frequent intervals. If judicial decision were a matter of personal value preferences, there would seem to be no good reason why the preferences of judges should prevail over the preferences of the elected representatives of the people or, in the absence of a clear political expression of majoritarian preferences, the autonomous decisions of individuals.[2]

Accepting legal skepticism implies one of three possible consequences for legitimacy. The first is that the demand for legitimacy is meaningless and should be abandoned. Few contemporary legal thinkers advocate this view.[3] The second is that adjudication is not legitimate and, in its present guise, should be abandoned. Some radical critics of the U.S. legal system seem to take this position.[4] The third is a reinterpretation of the demand for legitimacy, requiring at least in necessary part that the lawmaking that results from adjudication be reversible by majoritarian lawmaking. Adjudication on the basis of a judge's personal value preferences thus would be legitimate if those preferences appear to conform to the preferences of a majority of the people. Many legal thinkers seem to be willing to trust judges to exercise good judgment so long as a majoritarian political check is available.[5] In addition, there probably are some legal skeptics who take none of the above positions and maintain the demand for legitimacy, resigning themselves to an incoherent, if not cynical, posture toward the legal system.

---

[2]The counter-majoritarian difficulty often is thought to be a problem in justifying the Supreme Court's power of judicial review but not common law or statutory adjudication because judicial lawmaking in the latter settings can be reversed by ordinary legislation. See, e.g., M. Perry, The Constitution, the Courts, and Human Rights 28n. (1982), and sources cited therein. For reasons that will appear, I disagree, though I would not equate the problems of constitutional and nonconstitutional adjudication in all respects.

[3]Possible exceptions include R. Unger, Knowledge and Politics (1975) (challenging the classical liberalism in which legitimacy is of concern).

[4]See Symposium, The Critical Legal Studies Movement, 36 Stan. L. Rev. 1 (1984).

[5]See, e.g., G. Calabresi, A Common Law for the Age of Statutes 91-120 (1979); Sandalow, Judicial Protection for Minorities, 75 Mich. L. Rev. 1162 (1977).

In my view, legal skepticism itself is a theory about law that should be accepted only if supported by adequate grounds. There is no good reason to treat this theory about law as the presumptively correct theory about law and thus as the theory that one should hold if all other theories prove to be questionable. Rather, legal skepticism should be held to be true only if the reasons that can be given in defense of this theory make it a stronger theory than the available alternatives.[6]

In general, two sorts of arguments have been made by those who advocate legal skepticism, both of which are familiar. One points out that it is always logically possible for judges to manipulate the facts and the law to hide the role of their personal value preferences. This is surely true, for the reason already given, though it is a different matter to assert that judges habitually or necessarily do so. Another argument, which is related to the first, observes that in fact judges decide cases in ways that cannot be explained by deduction from legal rules and therefore must be explained with reference to the judge's own values.

Legal skepticism does not follow from these observations alone, even if both were true. It follows only if one adopts a premise that, together with the facts stated, leads to the conclusion that judges decide whatever they want to decide. The premise that seems to be presupposed by legal skepticism is something like the following dualism: Judicial decisions either (1) are dictated by authoritative rules as required by legal formalism and hence are legitimate or (2) are a product of the personal value preferences of the judges. The skeptic's observations establish that judicial decisions cannot be, and in fact are not, dictated by authoritative rules as required by legal formalism. From this dualist premise and the skeptic's observations, it would follow logically that judicial decisions are a product of the personal value preferences of the judges and, by implication, are not legitimate.[7]

Legal formalism thus serves as an implicit standard of criticism in the legal skeptic's argument. Once its role in skepticism is made

---

[6]See W. Bishin & C. Stone, Law, Language and Ethics 539-541 (1972).

[7]The logical relationship between formalism and skepticism is apparent from some theories that posit "plain" or "easy" cases, in which the results are dictated by the law formalistically, and "penumbral" or "hard" cases, in which judges legislate in the gaps or enjoy unbridled discretion. See, e.g., B. Cardozo, The Nature of the Judicial Process 113-114 (1921); Hart, Positivism and the Separation of Law and Morals, 71 Harv. L. Rev. 593, 607-608 (1958).

explicit, it can be seen that formalism and skepticism are two sides of the same coin. Both operate within the same formalist world, employing the same concept of what it means for judges to decide cases in accordance with the law. A skeptic differs from a formalist only because a formalist would believe that formalism is possible while a skeptic believes that formalism is not possible. The skeptic's charge that judicial decisions are a product of the judge's personal value preferences is a logical consequence of the failure of formalism so long as the dualist premise is axiomatic. Rejecting the dualist premise, and thus legal formalism as a standard of criticism, leaves legal skepticism inadequately supported.

The dualist premise that supports legal skepticism should be rejected. It is indefensible today to equate all legitimate law and legal reasoning with the formalist model and, in light of the critique of formalism, to throw almost everything into the trash heap of personal value preference.[8] For one thing, there simply are too many easier cases in which lawyers and judges generally would make the same predictions and decisions.[9] Easier cases generally cannot be explained by legal formalism,[10] and the skeptical view of decision by personal value preference implies an arbitrariness in judicial decision that is not reflected in the legal experience. Something else is going on.

Moreover, there is an alternative to formalism and skepticism as explanations of the judicial process—that judges decide cases so as to accommodate a decision coherently with the facts and the legal experience in light of the totality of the legal community's theories about law. This conventionalist alternative neither promises the certainty required by legal formalism nor resigns us to the arbitrariness implied by legal skepticism. It offers the possibility of decisions based on legal reasoning, where reasoning is dependent on the conventions of an interpretive community. Assuming the good faith of judges, the essential interpretive role of the legal community effectively constrains judicial decision sufficiently to distinguish adjudication from idiosyncratic fiat, without satisfying the requirements of hard legal formalism.[11] *Conventionalism* thus

---

[8]See Burton, Comment on "Empty Ideas": Logical Positivist Analyses of Equality and Rules, 91 Yale L.J. 1136, 1147-1150 (1982).
[9]See Chapter 5 §C.
[10]See Chapter 7.
[11]See Bennett, Objectivity in Constitutional Law, 132 U. Pa. L. Rev. 445 (1984); Fiss. Objectivity and Interpretation, 34 Stan. L. Rev. 739 (1982).

falls in neither category recognized by the formalist/skeptical concept of legitimacy.

Once this third alternative is recognized as a possibility, skepticism does not follow from the critique of formalism. Judges may decide cases in accordance with the law in its entirety even if their decisions are not dictated by sound legal syllogisms based sufficiently on authoritative rules and principles. To be sure, this third possibility does not itself suffice to establish the legitimacy of judicial lawmaking in a democratic society. The legal community is not sufficiently accountable to the people to establish the consent of the governed to the laws that govern. But it suffices to deprive legal skepticism of the traditional supporting grounds identified above.

Additionally, the implications of legal skepticism for legitimacy cannot be accommodated coherently within our webs of beliefs about law. Legal skepticism, even if true, establishes only that adjudication fails to satisfy the requirements of hard formal legitimacy. But the demand for legitimacy is not only academic; it is meant to say something about what should be done in real-world situations. It should not follow that adjudication should be abandoned unless alternative methods of dispute settlement are available and would do the job better. Most members of the legal community are unwilling to abandon adjudication because of a thoughtful intuition that it is a better way to settle at least some persistent disputes than the available alternatives, such as duels, jousts, feuds, trial by ordeal, flipping a coin, or letting a "wise" person decide.[12]

It also should not follow that adjudication should be tolerated only to the extent that the law made by judges is reversible by majoritarian lawmaking. Judicial lawmaking by personal preference is objectionable even if a majority approves or acquiesces.[13] No court could legitimately award a cash subsidy from the state treasury to a hard-pressed industry even if the court truly and accurately believed that the legislature would not override them; no court could legitimately suspend the writ of habeas corpus even if it truly and accurately believed that a majority would not object. The legitimacy of judicial lawmaking is not a question of what a court can get away with in relation to majoritarian politics.[14] Also,

---

[12]See Introduction, §B.

[13]See Fiss, The Forms of Justice, 93 Harv. L. Rev. 1 (1979).

[14]"Democracy" need not be equated with majoritarianism. See Bishin, Judicial Review in Democratic Theory, 50 S. Cal. L. Rev. 1099 (1977).

the principle of majoritarian rule may be taken to include, as a corollary, a principle of individual autonomy when a majority has not acted clearly. Judicial lawmaking in cases intrudes on individual autonomy in the absence of a majoritarian mandate, and subsequent inaction by majoritarian lawmaking processes often reflects political inertia far more than it reflects majoritarian preferences. Consequently, majoritarian political control of the judiciary would not seem to be necessary or sufficient to legitimate judicial lawmaking in cases.

In sum, legal skepticism is a legacy of formalism because it is intelligible only if a formalist concept of law and legal reasoning is taken to be axiomatic. Legal formalism, however, can be rejected and replaced, as a conception of the judicial process, by a conventionalist approach to law and legal reasoning. The death of formalism as a model of legitimacy consequently should lead to the death of formalism as an implicit standard of criticism. In light of the large number of easier cases, our commitment to adjudication for at least some disputes, and our commitment to individual liberty and a government of limited power, it seems that neither legal formalism nor skepticism any longer can be accommodated coherently within our webs of beliefs about law.

2. Soft Formalism

It should be apparent that legitimate adjudication is possible only if the degree of needed rigor is relaxed from what is required ideally by legal formalism. There are two principal ways to do so without abandoning the demand for legitimacy. One is to shift the meaning of legitimacy to something altogether different from formal legitimacy. This alternative will be considered in the next section. A second is to retain formal legitimacy as the meaning of legitimacy, but to treat formal legitimacy as an ideal to be mimicked imperfectly. This soft formalist alternative, which seems to be taken by a number of respected legal thinkers,[15] will be considered in this section.

Soft formalism retains the formalist framework in all respects except the requirement that decisions be *deduced* from authoritative rules that, in turn, are *deduced* from legitimating foundations. It would continue the search for legitimating foundations to sup-

---

[15]E.g., J. Ely, Democracy and Distrust (1980); H. Hart, The Concept of Law (1961); Moore, The Semantics of Judging, 54 S. Cal. L. Rev. 151 (1981).

port authoritative rules and principles, and particular decisions, but the relationships among the legitimating foundations, rules, principles, and decisions would not need to be logically airtight. The logical room that is left ungoverned by the legitimating foundations, rules, and principles would be a realm of limited judicial discretion. The decisions in cases would have to be *adequately* supported by authoritative rules and principles resting on a legitimating foundation, where adequacy is something less rigorous than logical necessity.

To illustrate, consider the case of *Trop v. Dulles*.[16] The Nationality Act of 1940[17] provided that a member of the armed forces who was convicted by court-martial for wartime desertion and dishonorably discharged thereby lost his U.S. citizenship. Trop was with the armed forces in Africa during World War II and escaped from a stockade, but voluntarily surrendered himself the next day while headed back to the camp. Though he had not deserted to the enemy, he was convicted of desertion, sentenced to three years of hard labor, and given a dishonorable discharge. Some years later, he applied for a passport and it was denied for lack of citizenship. Trop brought an action in which he sought a judicial declaration that the Nationality Act's provision for denationalization was invalid because denationalization for desertion was a cruel and unusual punishment within the prohibition of the eighth amendment to the U.S. Constitution.

Soft formalism recognizes that the Court's decision in this case or any other case cannot be justified, as required by hard legal formalism, by deduction from the cruel and unusual punishments clause: "nor [shall] cruel and unusual punishments be inflicted." The Court must decide whether denationalization is a member of the class of cruel and unusual punishments designated by the eighth amendment. Within soft formalism, the classification can be made only on the basis of the justices' own values or some additional constitutional principle found outside the constitutional text. Analogously to hard formalism, soft formalism requires a search for legitimating foundations that support constitutional principles used to interpret and apply the constitutional text. A number of such foundations have been suggested,[18] including (1) the inten-

---

[16]356 U.S. 86 (1958).
[17]54 Stat. 1168, amended by 58 Stat. 4 (1940).
[18]A critical survey of foundations is given in J. Ely, supra note 15.

tions of the Framers, as evidenced by the constitutional text and its histories,[19] and (2) the conventional morality of the American people in contemporary times.[20]

In a case like *Trop v. Dulles,* for example, a soft formalist of one kind might look to the constitutional history of the eighth amendment to ascertain the intention of the Framers. Unlike the history of many constitutional provisions, the history of the eighth amendment seems relatively straightforward. By the common version,[21] the cruel and unusual punishments clause was copied from the English Bill of Rights of 1689 and was intended to have largely the same meaning. The English Bill of Rights, in turn, was a response to the tortures inflicted on criminals during the reign of the Stuarts, some of whom practiced burnings at the stake, breaking on the wheel, boiling in oil, drawing and quartering, and other atrocities. What constitutional principle emerges from this history?

It may be said that the Framers intended the eighth amendment to constitutionalize a principle outlawing torture. The question in *Trop* would be whether denationalization is a member of the class of tortures within that principle. But this hardly limits judicial discretion at all. If the class "cruel and unusual punishments" does not have the same members as the class "tortures," then a soft formalist would have to search for additional principles outside the constitutional text and its histories to determine whether one class is smaller or larger than the other and in what ways. Even if the two classes do have the same members, then interpreting one term as meaning the other does not tell us which particular punishments are members of either class. The analysis still remains in the realm of abstractions and must be brought into the realm of concrete particulars in order to decide a case.

The constitutional history does provide a number of examples of particular punishments that are members of the class, from which a court could reason analogically. But the range of analogies is potentially unlimited and can be broadened or narrowed as a judge might prefer. It may be suggested, for example, that the eighth amendment was aimed solely at the tortures practiced by

---

[19]E.g., R. Berger, Government by Judiciary (1977); Bork, Neutral Principles and Some First Amendment Problems, 47 Ind. L.J. 1 (1971).

[20]E.g., A. Bickel, The Least Dangerous Branch (1962); Wellington, Common Law Rules and Constitutional Double Standards: Some Notes on Adjudication, 83 Yale L.J. 221 (1973).

[21]See J. Story, Commentaries on the Constitution 650 (5th ed. 1891).

the Stuarts in England,[22] though the constitutional history does not establish that the Stuart atrocities are the only examples of unconstitutional torture. By this interpretation, denationalization would not be torture and would be constitutional in *Trop*. One wonders whether poaching prisoners in water, rather than boiling them in oil, would be constitutional if the Stuarts used only boiling oil. Presumably, even this approach would allow some analogies.

The Court has said that "punishments of torture, such as those [practiced by the Stuarts], and all others in the same line of unnecessary cruelty, are forbidden."[23] By this interpretation, denationalization could be so unnecessarily cruel as to be analogous to the Stuart tortures in the important respect and therefore unconstitutional in *Trop*. But one can imagine a wide range of punishments that someone would consider unnecessarily cruel in some cases, including the death penalty, solitary confinement, and perhaps even imprisonment or probation. The eighth amendment could not be interpreted legitimately to hold unconstitutional any punishment that a judge may, as a matter of personal values, consider to be unnecessarily cruel in a case.[24]

Once one starts from the constitutional history down the road of analogies, in order to reach the poaching in water case, there are no stop signs within soft formalism. The Court easily can take its pick among close and remote analogies, decide *Trop* whichever way it likes, write an opinion setting forth the argument that supports its decision, and place a cloak of legitimacy over a decision in fact reached on the basis of the judges' own values. It is hard to believe that a constitutional principle, based in the constitutional history, is constraining judicial discretion at all.

A soft formalist of another kind might look to the conventional morality of the American people—the moral experience and the totality of our theories about morality—as if conventional morality could serve as a foundation supporting constitutional principles. A plurality of the Supreme Court seemed to take this approach in *Trop* when they said that "[t]he [Eighth] Amendment

[22]Cf. In re Kemmler, 136 U.S. 436, 446 (1890); R. Berger, supra note 19.
[23]Wilkerson v. Utah, 99 U.S. 130, 136 (1878).
[24]A contrary view seems to be taken in M. Perry, supra note 2. But see Lynch, Constitutional Law as Moral Philosophy, 84 Colum. L. Rev. 537, 556 (1984) (review of M. Perry, supra) ("More is required before people can be expected to adopt a theory that has generally been treated as the *absurdum* to which other theories should be reduced in order to be refuted").

must draw its meaning from the evolving standards of decency that mark the progress of a maturing society."[25] From this putative foundation, too, it might be said that the cruel and unusual punishments clause should be taken to outlaw torture. Again, however, it is hard to believe that such an approach constrains judicial discretion adequately to satisfy the demand for legitimacy.

It is easy to doubt that there is a significant set of moral principles that are held by a consensus of the people in a society as pluralistic as the United States or that such principles can be equated with constitutional law. The Court's appeal to conventional morality is likely in many cases to be little more than a projection onto the American people of the judges' own value preferences. Even when a consensus of the people would agree on the abstract formulation of a principle, such as a principle outlawing torture, it is doubtful that a consensus would support many particular applications of the abstract principle in cases. In a case like *Trop,* it seems far more likely that very few people outside the legal community have even thought about the question whether denationalization as a punishment for desertion is a member of the class of tortures that should be unconstitutional. Even on a question that many people have thought about, such as whether the death penalty should be unconstitutional, a judge may be likely to get it wrong because judges have no means of taking the pulse of the people.[26]

In my view, these two approaches to the problem of legitimacy are inadequate for similar reasons. By retaining the formalist framework in all respects other than the requirement that legitimate decisions be *deduced* from authoritative rules that can be *deduced* from legitimating foundations, soft formalism retains the formalist dualism that produces legal skepticism. If judicial decisions must either be dictated by the authoritative rules and legitimate principles or be a matter of personal value preferences, and if soft formalism admits that judicial decisions are not dictated by the authoritative rules or

---

[25]356 U.S. 86, 101 (1958).
[26]In Furman v. Georgia, 408 U.S. 238, 257, 314 (1972), two justices voted with the majority that the death penalty, as theretofore administered, was unconstitutional, basing their votes largely on the claim that the death penalty was out of accord with conventional morality. There followed a spate of legislation reenacting the death penalty in a large number of states, to the justices' embarassment. See also J. Ely, supra note 15, at 218 n.112 (identifying a scholar's misperception of conventional morality on the abortion issue).

legitimate principles, then soft formalism has no logical alternative but to admit that the decisions are a matter of the judges' own values in determinative part. Similarly, by retaining formal legitimacy as an ideal to be mimicked imperfectly, soft formalism continues to treat as legitimate only decisions that are dictated by the rules or principles. If judicial decisions are not dictated by the rules or principles, then soft formalism has no logical alternative but to admit that the decisions are not legitimate.

Soft formalism seeks to avoid this dilemma by relaxing the rigor required by hard formalism and thus attempting to legitimate judicial lawmaking that is *adequately* supported by authoritative rules and principles. Alas, the demand for legitimacy cannot be satisfied through such piecemeal adjustments within the formalist framework. Any claim of adequate support can be challenged because it falls short of the formalist ideal. There is no yardstick for measuring how far short of the formalist ideal an argument must fall before it becomes inadequate support for a judicial decision. It is simply too easy to treat judicial decisions (or sets of judicial decisions) with which one disagrees by a standard more rigorous than is used to treat judicial decisions with which one agrees. Accordingly, the suspicion seems unavoidable that the accordion-like quality of the realm of legitimate discretion leaves judges and their critics sufficient leeway to make or approve of judicial decisions on the basis of their own moral, religious, economic, or political values, rather than the values embodied in the law.

There are, of course, other and more sophisticated versions of soft formalism.[27] As long as legitimacy is taken to mean formal legitimacy, it seems that each would be vulnerable to the kind of criticism to which these two caricatures of soft formalism are vulnerable. To avoid such criticism, a soft formalist theory must collapse into hard legal formalism. If it does not, it admits logical room for the judges' personal value preferences to intrude and to control judicial decisions. Once it thus falls into legal skepticism in determinative part, soft formalism loses its capacity to legitimate because, like legal skepticism, it retains the formalist framework in significant respects. Soft formalism fails as a theory of legitimacy because it is impossible for any working legal system to satisfy the requirements of hard formal legitimacy.

---

[27]E.g., sources cited supra note 15.

B. Contextual Meaning of Legitimacy

Taking the death of formalism seriously frees us to enter a post-formalist world in which formal legitimacy is neither a model of legitimacy, a standard for criticism, nor an ideal to be mimicked imperfectly. In such a post-formalist world, the demand for legitimacy takes on a wholly different character. One possibility is that the meaning of legitimacy shifts from a demand for antecedent legitimating foundations for each particular judicial decision to a demand for a legal and political system that, on the whole, enjoys and merits the allegiance of the people. The legitimacy of adjudication would depend on its contribution to the legitimacy of the legal and political system as a whole in its social, historical, and cultural context. The remainder of this chapter elaborates on this alternative to formal legitimacy, which will be called *contextual legitimacy*.

The judicial decision in a case cannot be understood or evaluated in isolation from the institution of adjudication within a larger legal system, which cannot be understood and evaluated in isolation from the political system in which it operates. The legal and political system, in turn, cannot be understood and evaluated in isolation from the social, historical, and cultural context in which it functions. Evaluating the legitimacy of judicial lawmaking in particular cases in isolation from (or in relation only to isolated parts of) a system, rather than the legitimacy of judicial practices in their full systemic contexts, would be an artificial exercise of dubious intellectual value and little real concern to the American people. Though it is not my purpose to set forth a general theory of the legitimacy of legal and political systems, an outline of such a theory in the U.S. context will set the stage for a theory of the legitimacy of adjudication within the same context.

In a democratic society like the United States, contextual legitimacy requires that the people generally recognize an *obligation* to abide by the law, because it is the law, within a legal and political system that merits their allegiance. This interpretation of the demand for legitimacy has both factual and normative aspects. Whether the people generally recognize an obligation to abide by the law is a question of social fact. Whether the legal and political system merits their allegiance is a normative question. Neither aspect alone is sufficient to establish contextual legitimacy, and the two together imply a tension between the search for a more orderly and just society and the requirements of democracy.[28]

The factual question is important in U.S. society because the consent of the people to the laws that govern in some sense is required by all theories of democratic government. Contextual legitimacy requires their assent to an obligation arising from the system, rather than their assent to each particular law or judicial decision. We generally believe that a judicial decision is not illegitimate (or even unwise) solely by virtue of its unpopularity; indeed, judicial independence is valued precisely to protect legitimate adjudication from majoritarian politics. Adjudication faces the tribunal of democracy, not on a case-by-case basis, but within a corpus of law and politics.

Legal and political systems lack legitimacy when large numbers of people in fact cease to recognize an obligation to abide by laws or decisions with which they disagree, as in times of revolution, civil war, or civil disobedience. Real claims of illegitimacy are fighting words: The American revolutionaries stood on a claim of the illegitimacy of continued rule by the British crown, and Martin Luther King sat in on a claim of the illegitimacy of Southern Jim Crow laws. Claims of illegitimacy may, of course, also extend to situations that are not so dramatically evidenced.

Due to certain conceptual difficulties, it is not easy to determine when the factual condition for contextual illegitimacy is met by an existing legal and political system.[29] Whether the American people in fact accept the legitimacy of the system depends on observations of social facts that would manifest recognition or rejection of an obligation to abide by the law, because it is the law. The fact that most of the people comply with the law most of the time, for example, is evidence of their acceptance of an obligation to abide by the law because it would be hard to imagine a people accepting such an obligation and, at the same time, generally disobeying the law. But the fact of widespread obedience would not be dispositive of the question.

There is a good deal of obedience to the law in the United States. It is probably so, however, that some people abide by the law out of a sense of obligation, others from a fear of sanction for

---

[28]For a discussion of the implications of this tension, see Chapter 11.

[29]See generally, H. Hart, The Concept of Law 109-114 (1961); J. Raz, A Theory of Legal Systems 203-209 (2d ed. 1980); Hale, Bargaining, Duress and Economic Liberty, 43 Colum. L. Rev. 603 (1943).

disobedience, and many from a combination of both motives. To the extent that obedience is coerced by the threat of the state to use force, if necessary, to enforce the law, such obedience probably should not count as manifesting a voluntary acceptance of legitimacy. It may manifest only the effectiveness of a police state. Yet it is unclear how one would ascertain reliably the extent to which obedience is not coerced. Many of us would be hard put to distinguish with confidence the roles of obligation and fear in our own law-abiding behavior.

There also is a good deal of disobedience to the law in the United States, as indicated by the crime rate and the large number of persons who are incarcerated. It seems far-fetched to interpret the disobedience of the typical mugger or tax cheater as a rejection of the legitimacy of the U.S. legal and political system as a whole, rather than a manifestation of its partial ineffectiveness. Probably not all disobedience should count as evidence of a rejection of legitimacy, but distinguishing between disobedience that does or does not count involves the observer in subjective judgments that seem to defeat the purpose of looking at the evidence. The observer's predispositions would seem inevitably to affect the distinctions that would be made.

The presence of coercion in the system thus makes it difficult to justify the system only on the fact that the people do or will continue to abide by the law. In part because of these conceptual difficulties, the normative question — whether the legal and political system as a whole merits the allegiance of the people — is also important. Contextual legitimacy requires more than that the legal system be effective in securing the obedience of the people in general. It also requires that the law deserve the respect of the people.[30] Consequently, persons within the system who are concerned about legitimacy may focus on whether the people ought to recognize an obligation to abide by the law, even though an affirmative answer to that question also is not sufficient to establish legitimacy in a democratic society like the United States.

To assert that the American people ought not to accept the legitimacy of their legal and political system is not an idle act or merely a strong form of rhetoric to be used when advocating legal reform. Mere disagreement with one or many laws does not sup-

---

[30]See generally R. Dworkin, Taking Rights Seriously (1978); L. Fuller, The Morality of the Law (1963); P. Soper, A Theory of Law (1984).

port a claim of illegitimacy because, in any legitimate system of law, the obligation to obey will extend to those who disagree and, at least in any diverse society, there will be some who disagree. Mere disagreement with particular laws and a lack of success in changing those laws often can be dramatized rhetorically to look like severe usurpation or oppression. But the rhetoric may in fact reflect the disappointment of losers in a large, complex and pluralistic society in which all persons sometimes are and must be losers. A dissenter who bases a claim of illegitimacy on mere disagreement with the laws does not deny the legitimacy of a particular legal and political system, but denies the very possibility of law.

Within the American tradition, the normative aspect of contextual legitimacy seems to depend on whether the system as a whole adequately contributes to a more orderly and just society in light of contemporary circumstances and evolving notions of justice. Probably no one would assert that the U.S. legal and political system as it stands is a perfect legal and political system. Just about anyone could point to a law or practice that they believe should be changed, and many could point to a large number of laws or practices that they believe should be changed. In general, however, one can acknowledge a need for legal reform without thereby challenging the legitimacy of the system as a whole.

Claims of illegitimacy are justifiably made when the legal and political system as a whole denies the most basic rights and interests of significant segments of society to a large extent and roads to changing the law within the system are substantially closed to those groups. This was largely the American colonists' view of continued British rule, and it was the civil rights movement's view of Southern Jim Crow laws. The claim, in each instance, was one of persistent oppression without hope of change through argument and lawful action within the legal and political system. The only alternatives were to submit to injustice or resort to a contest of physical power in place of law and politics. The oppressors, in each instance, were hard pressed to say credibly to the oppressed group that they had an obligation to abide by the law because it was the law; to the oppressed group, the "law" was indistinguishable from domination by the powerful under a transparent cloak of legitimacy. A crisis of legitimacy occurs when the legal and political system breaks down and tests of physical power replace legal and political argument.

Crises of legitimacy probably can be avoided justifiably so long as the legal and political system as a whole respects the most basic rights and interests of all significant groups in the society and contains open avenues of legal change that permit each significant group to believe reasonably that it can change the law better to protect its most basic rights and interests. A legal and political system that satisfies these substantive and process-oriented conditions is engaged meaningfully in the search for a more orderly and just society with respect for all members of the body politic. Even if one can imagine a system that better contributes to a more orderly and just society, the venture deserves the people's respect as law. Such a legal and political system welcomes criticism and proposals for legal reform from all members of the body politic and, it is hoped, evolves progressively on the whole. Especially in a pluralistic society like the United States, all groups know that they will lose a few. Each will continue its participation in the system—will not turn to violence or widespread civil disobedience—as long as it also wins a few and believes that it can win a few more.[31]

The difference between contextual legitimacy and illegitimacy is one of degree in the extent to which a system treats all persons fairly and is so perceived by the people, not in the success or failure of a system to satisfy all demands—even all majoritarian demands—for reform. At some point, a system may treat some groups of persons unjustly so consistently, and with so little prospect of change by legal and political processes, that the system loses its claim to being engaged in a meaningful search for a more orderly and just society with respect for all persons. Such a system also loses its normative claim to the people's obedience from a sense of obligation, as distinguished from fear. This, as much as anything, underlay the Declaration of Independence and justified the civil disobedience of the civil rights movement.

From this contextual perspective, the legitimacy of adjudication in particular lies in its contribution, if any, to the legitimacy of the legal and political system as a whole, not in the justifiability of a particular judicial decision (or set of decisions) with reference to antecedent legitimating foundations or in majoritarian political agreement with the results of the judicial process. Unlike legal skepticism or soft formalism, contextual legitimacy transcends both formalism and the legacies of formalism and takes us into a post-formalist world. Though further elaboration would be necessary to

---

[31]See also The Federalist No. 10 (Bicentennial ed. 1976) (Madison).

work out a full theory of contextual legitimacy, one virtue now in evidence is its direct connection to matters of constitutional concern. The U.S. system of government, if it stands for anything of constitutional dimension, must, in respect of all segments of society, be distinguishable from the British colonial rule against which the American revolutionaries acted.

C. The Contextual Legitimacy of Adjudication

Certain highly stable characteristics of U.S. society provide a basis for claiming that the institution of adjudication is legitimate because it contributes to the legitimacy of the U.S. legal and political system as a whole. There are two steps to the argument. First, legal reasoning in cases makes judicial lawmaking different from lawmaking by the legislative and executive branches of government because it is not a matter of the personal value preferences of the judges, their (nonexistent) constituencies, or their (nonexistent) favored lobbies. As suggested by Part II of this book, the legal community plays the role of an interpretive community that constrains judges to decide cases in accordance with the law in its entirety, in a continuing effort to work out the implications of order and justice contextually in cases. Second, as suggested below, a legal community is the proper community to play the interpretive role in a large, complex, and pluralistic society like the United States. Members of the legal community cannot themselves legitimate the role of the legal community within the legal and political system; though the legitimacy of that role also depends on the American people, there is good reason to believe that it merits their support.

1. The Legal Conversation

The role of the legal community in legal reasoning distinguishes adjudication from political lawmaking or decision by personal value preference. Analysis of the forms of legal reasoning demonstrates that every legal argument, as stated, contains logical gaps. The existence of so many easier cases within the legal experience suggests that only some gaps in some arguments are problematic. The difference between a logical gap and a problematic gap can be explained only in the context of a case with reference to the conventions of the legal community, as indicated by the legal experience and the totality of our theories about law. Unproblematic gaps are gaps that pass without objection in an extended legal conversation about order and justice in cases.[32]

Consider, preliminarily, a nonlegal example. A construction worker may have no difficulty whatsoever knowing what is meant by *straight line* when asked by a foreman to mark off the plan for a wall. A mathematician working with non-Euclidian geometries may find the concept *straight line* among the most troublesome and easily may be able to identify many gaps or contradictions in the construction worker's concept. Only a pedant would challenge the construction worker's concept of *straight line* with the arguments of the mathematician. The lay notion is wholly adequate in the construction setting to accomplish the relevant purpose to the satisfaction of those who are concerned. It is as if the concept were used in a conversation, and the participants allow it to pass without objection. The worker, the foreman, the building contractor, the architect, the owner, and the city building inspector are the principal participants in the (metaphorical) conversation. The mathematician is not a participant in that conversation. His identification of gaps is simply unwelcome and unimportant for the practical purpose at hand; it does not affect what any of the participants will or should do.

Within the U.S. legal system as it currently operates, the logical gaps in legal reasoning rarely arise in the abstract in a way that requires some course of action. They arise with practical significance in particular cases, when courts decide whether the coercive powers of the state should be used to settle a particular dispute. The cases set the context that determine who will be the participants in a legal conversation about which of the available courses of action shall be taken. The cases are decided in accordance with the law in its entirety when the judicial decision fits harmoniously with what members of the legal community generally will take to be required by an orderly and just society in the case and like cases, as indicated by the legal experience and the totality of our theories about law.

Conversations about legal problems that acquire some action take place in a variety of settings, including courts, administrative agencies, the halls of Congress and the state legislatures, law offices, legal publications, the news media, and the family dinner

---

[32]The metaphor is adapted from R. Rorty, Philosophy and the Mirror of Nature (1980).

table. The actual participants in the conversations vary with the problem and setting, and the persons who influence each conversation are larger in number than the actual participants. Substantially the same legal question moves from one setting to another before it is settled in one case and also arises repeatedly in a series of similar cases. What was said in a prior conversation, or is expected to be said in a subsequent conversation, influences the course of a present conversation and consequently its outcome.

For example, a husband and wife at the dinner table may discuss the desirability of obtaining a divorce. To trace out the implications for their family, they may introduce into the conversation what the family lawyer has told one of them, or what they expect their lawyer to tell them, about the division of their property. They may go to their lawyer's office to pursue the matter further and be told that they each must seek legal advice from a different attorney.[33] What the two lawyers say in the conversations in their offices will reflect what they have read in legal publications, including relevant case reports expressing the views of a number of judges, relevant statutes expressing the views of past and present legislatures, and scholarly works expressing the views of legal observers. The lawyers' contributions to the conversation also will reflect what they expect the local civil trial court to say if the parties seek a divorce, and what the trial court will say reflects what it expects the highest appellate court in the jurisdiction to say if an appeal were taken. What the appellate court will say reflects what the judges have read in the relevant legal publications and the legal briefs of counsel, what the trial court said in its judgment in the case, and what the parties said to the trial court through their presentations of evidence.

Metaphorically, a particular question concerning the implications of a divorce for the spouses is the subject of a single, extended conversation that moves from setting to setting and, in sum, involves all the the participants in each of the actual conversations. Each actual conversation in a case—the one at the dinner table and the ones in the law offices, the trial court, and the appellate court—involves the voices of all of the participants in the extended conversation, through their influences on what is said

---

[33]A lawyer is ethically required to avoid representing two or more clients whose interests are adverse whenever such representation might impair the lawyer's independent professional judgment in relation to each client. American Bar Association, Code of Professional Responsibility DR 5-105 (1976).

by the actual participants. The dynamics of a participant's voice varies from one actual conversation to another: The appellate court's voice may be nearly inaudible at the dinner table, faint in the law office, stronger in the trial court, and dominant in the appellate court; the spouses' voices may be dominant at the dinner table, strong at the law office, faint in the trial court, and nearly inaudible at the appellate court. But all of those who influence what course of action will be taken in the particular case as a consequence of the entire conversation are, directly or indirectly, participants in the conversation.

Each case also is a phase in a broader legal conversation about order and justice in cases. The broader conversation extends over a lengthy period of time, with each case providing an occasion for the conversation to continue. Writings preserve the voices of the past; some judicial opinions from fifteenth-century England continue to affect problem cases in the United States, as do statutes from the middle ages and the writings of Roman jurists. Though a judge today rarely would read such legal materials in the original, the ideas they express reflected or influenced the outcome of cases decided long ago that, in turn, influenced precedents and ideas that are used with full consciousness today. Some of today's opinions by judges, enactments by legislatures, and commentaries by scholars probably will continue to influence law cases in the distant future. Each judicial opinion concludes a phase of the legal conversation and makes a contribution that will be available for use in the next round.

Many logical gaps that would bother a philosopher or legal theoretician do not bother the participants in many legal conversations. A conversation can proceed rationally if it starts with ideas that all participants accept for the purpose and maintains the support of its participants as the conversation proceeds. Truncated arguments are put forward on the assumption that the gaps can be filled in if a participant balks. Discussion occurs when a speaker glosses over a problematic gap, another participant requests clarification, and the request for clarification is of interest to the participants. The discussion focuses on finding common ground among the participants, from which they can reason together to close problematic gaps or clarify their differences.

In a legal conversation, there is much common ground for participants to draw on from the legal experience and the totality of the legal community's theories about law. The precedents, common law rules, and enacted texts with their contexts, together with many normative theories explaining and evaluating these legal materials, predictably occupy positions within the webs of beliefs about law that are held by the participants in legal conversations. They can be used in the analogical and deductive forms, through interpretation in accordance with the conventions of the legal community, to bring what is not now in question to bear on what is now in question. Problems of importance in legal reasoning are resolved, through conversation about a case and like cases, by the legal community's effort to accommodate the decision in each problem case coherently with the law in its entirety.

Thus, the court's opinion in a case in large part depends on its legal reasoning, which will contain logical gaps that are unproblematic if they pass without objection in the metaphorical legal conversation. In a law case before a court, the participants in the conversation include, most directly, the lawyers and judges assigned to the case and, indirectly, the members of the legal community whose views are brought to bear on the matter in dispute by the actual participants. The views of absent persons are brought to bear, in the familiar manner, when the actual participants cite parts of the legal experience and the totality of the legal community's theories about law. The participants use the legal materials to compose coherent legal arguments that place the case in its context in the broader legal conversation.

Though a consensus will not always emerge from a good conversation, many logical gaps will be unproblematic because left unquestioned or filled in to the satisfaction of the persons participating. On remaining differences, the judge in a case will have no alternative but to offer an opinion, supported by the best available legal reasoning, to settle the immediate dispute. The best available legal reasoning normally will support the decision that requires the least disruption to the law in its entirety in order to be accommodated coherently. At least in appellate cases, such judicial opinions make a contribution to a broader conversation that will, in any event, continue in the next similar case. Some such opinions will fail to interest the participants and be neglected, some will continue trends previously established and have little creative significance, and a few will be insightful and change the course of the conversation to varying degrees. The significance of judicial lawmaking in a case, as lawmaking affecting the future, is dependent on how it is received by participants in the broader legal conversation.

Consequently, legal reasoning in practice depends on what members of the legal community generally let pass without objection as acceptable legal reasoning for the purposes of a case. The lawyers and judges participate in a conversation about order and justice in cases. Judicial lawmakers and the legal community that supports them in each generation constitute an interpretive community whose job is to interpret the legal experience—the views of their predecessors about order and justice, as expressed in the legal materials—in light of contemporary circumstances and evolving notions of justice. Nonjudicial lawmakers and theorists may seek to write novel laws on a relatively clean slate; judicial lawmakers, together with the legal community, make law as necessary to decide a case in accordance with the law in its entirety.

The legal conversation thus requires sufficient common ground to enable members of the legal community to understand and converse about judicial decisions intelligently. The resulting social objectivity distinguishes judicial decision, on the basis of legal reasoning in cases, from political lawmaking or idiosyncratic fiat.[34] Legislative and executive lawmakers properly make law in general terms, absent a problem case, on the basis of their preferences and the preferences of their constituencies or favored lobbies. Judges properly make law only as necessary to decide a case and in accordance with the law in its entirety—what members of the legal community generally will take to be required by an orderly and just society in the case and like cases, as indicated by the legal experience and the totality of our theories about law.

In my view, however, such objectivity is necessary but not sufficient to establish the legitimacy of adjudication.[35] Any interpretive community and backdrop of experience and theory might introduce similar objectivity. What distinguishes the legal community from other interpretive communities is the presence of order and justice at the center of our webs of beliefs about law, the principles of legitimacy, stare decisis, and legislative supremacy near the center, and the commitment to legal reasoning in bringing these values and principles to bear in particular cases. The legal conversation is a conversation about the implications of these values and principles in particular cases. The demand for legitimacy

---

[34] See sources cited supra note 11.
[35] See Brest, Interpretation and Interest, 34 Stan. L. Rev. 765, 770-772 (1982); Levinson, Law as Literature, 60 Texas L. Rev. 373, 386 (1982).

poses the additional question whether, thus constituted, the legal community is an appropriate interpretive community to support adjudication.

2. The Legitimacy of the Legal Conversation

In a democratic society like the United States, contextual legitimacy requires that the people generally recognize an obligation to abide by the law, because it is the law, within a legal and political system that merits their allegiance. It does not require that a majority of the people accept that each law or judicial decision is a good law or judicial decision, nor does it require that each law or decision be subject to majoritarian control through the political process. The contextual legitimacy of the legal conversation depends on its contribution to the legitimacy of the U.S. legal and political system as a whole in its historical, social, and cultural context.

Once the problem of legitimacy is placed in context, the nature of the legal community's contribution to the legitimacy of the legal and political system can be explained. The historical, social, and cultural context includes three stable features that serve as appropriate starting points: U.S. society is a large and complex society, a pluralistic society, and a society in which the people want the legal and political system to contribute to order and justice, as well as to reflect the majority will. These three facts generate three functional characteristics of the U.S. legal and political system and, at the same time, support the legitimacy of the role of the legal community in that system.

First, it is not feasible for the people or their elected representatives to make or pass judgment on each legal decision that must be taken in a large and complex society like the United States. No one person could read all of even the appellate court decisions that are made every day, and the appellate court decisions are only the uppermost tip of a gigantic iceberg. The people must delegate responsibility for operating and monitoring the legitimacy of the legal system in its details to a smaller community of persons.

The people's elected representatives in Congress or the state legislatures are smaller communities. As members of the legal community, such representatives participate in the monitoring function. But they are too small in number to make and monitor the huge number of decisions that are taken each day. Legislators normally respond to those decisions that are brought to their attention by other members of the legal community, constituents and lobbyists. Though legislation changing the law made by judges is enacted each year, it may be enacted either because a judge did not get the law right or because change was indicated for political reasons. Legislators monitor the judicial system from a political perspective that enhances its legitimacy but, as an expression of presumably majoritarian preferences, is not adequate to establish legitimacy for the full range of cases. As indicated, the legitimacy of judicial lawmaking is not a question of what a court can get away with in relation to majoritarian politics.

Lawyers and judges are society's experts on when—in what cases—the state may use its coercive powers legitimately. The legal community is a smaller community than the general population and involves a larger number of persons than could be elected feasibly. Almost every legal decision is subjected to scrutiny by one or more lawyers. Though for the most part motivated to scrutinize decisions from the standpoint of their clients' interests, the lawyer's goal is to protect a client's legal rights. Legal decisions thus are scrutinized from the standpoint of the law that provides for legal rights. The case orientation of the legal profession seems well designed to monitor the legitimacy of a legal system in its details. In any large and complex society concerned about law, some such professional community would be necessary to run and watch the legal system on a case-by-case basis.

Second, it is not realistic to believe that strictly majoritarian politics would produce a legal and political system that could satisfy the demand for legitimacy, with respect for all significant segments of society, in a pluralistic society like the United States. U.S. society is composed of a large number of groups with differing perceptions, values, and interests. During large parts of American history, majorities have been able to enslave or oppress substantial racial, religious, ethnic, political, and other minorities. Today's majority can become tomorrow's minority. Contextual legitimacy requires that significant minorities, too, recognize the legitimacy of the legal and political system on the whole. This, in turn, requires that majoritarian politics sometimes be qualified so that all persons are treated fairly within the legal and political system as a whole.

A professional community that operates at some distance from majoritarian politics is well positioned to maintain and enhance sometimes unpopular rights so that all persons and groups in society are treated fairly. Adjudication provides an avenue of legal protection and legal change to all persons at their own initiative, regardless of their political clout. The legitimacy of the system is enhanced if some such avenue is available to persons who seek justice but may be unable to protect their most basic rights and interests through majoritarian politics. Adjudication, as part of a legal conversation about order and justice in cases, thus provides a meaningful alternative to disobedience manifesting a rejection of legitimacy.

Third, it is not desirable to base legitimacy solely on majoritarian practices in a society that wants its legal and political system to contribute to a more orderly and just society, as well as to reflect majority preferences. One should resist the skeptical temptation to equate majority preferences, or the preferences of any particular person or group, with what will contribute to a more orderly and just society. We know that majoritarian politics often are driven by passing cross-currents of public opinion or by coalitions of special interest groups; the preferences of persons and groups often reflect personal experiences and values or narrow self-interest. We need not know what Order and Justice require, in an absolute sense, in order to know that it would often be different from the preferences of people or groups on particular occasions. We may quite rightly believe that a legal conversation, as described above, is more likely than other available alternatives to make a meaningful contribution toward that highly valued end.

An orderly and just society may encompass ample room for majoritarian or other political preferences to be heard and felt in the legal and political system. Yet it also may encompass room for a legal conversation using legal reasoning in a continuing effort to work out the implications of order and justice in cases. A professional community whose job is to worry about order and justice, as part of a larger system of law and politics, augments majoritarian politics so that the system as a whole includes the pursuit of a more orderly and just society through law.

In sum, the legal conversation contributes to the legitimacy of the U.S. legal and political system as a whole because it serves these three functions within the system. The legal conversation is conducted by the members of a legal community and focuses heavily on cases in a way that no other community of persons could, without being transformed into the functional equivalent of a legal community. It is oriented toward what a court will or should do in a case; courts are significantly independent of the political process and well positioned to protect unpopular rights so that all persons and groups in society are treated fairly. The legal conversation operates on the basis of legal reasoning in cases and, consequently, is less influenced by political power or passing idiosyncratic preferences than the available alternatives.

At the same time, legal reasoning takes place in legal conversations that are cabined within the legal and political system to prevent or correct abuses by members of the legal community. The conversations focus on what a court will or should do in a case. Judges are appointed by elected officials or elected themselves, and they generally must sign and publish their opinions to take public responsibility for their decisions. Judges do not decide what cases they shall decide, but must react to the initiatives of people who find themselves in disputes. The judges must hear and respond to the arguments of the parties, who introduce the conventions of the legal community through citations to the legal experience and our theories about law. No one judge can make effective law without substantial support among many judges; any judicial decision can be overruled or confined to the facts of the case in which it was made, and almost any legal question surfaces in a series of cases before different panels of judges. No group of judges can escape from the highly democratic checks of subsequent legislation or constitutional amendment and, ultimately, removal from office for misbehavior.

When thus placed in context, the legitimacy of the role of the legal community seems relatively unproblematic. It is only when the demand for legitimacy is interpreted to require that legal reasoning satisfy the requirements of hard formal legitimacy, or analogous searches for foundations for each decision, that the lack of an absolute assurance of legitimacy in legal reasoning is troubling. Within the formalist world, any logical room in legal reasoning presumptively will be used by judges to impose wholly personal preferences on others. If judicial decisions were a matter only of the judges' preferences, there would be little reason not to insist that each decision and each judge reflect majoritarian preferences or refrain from wielding official power.

Within a post-formalist world, however, the same logical room makes it possible for a society to continue a legal conversation that seeks to find outcomes in cases that may be thought better to contribute to a more orderly and just society in light of contemporary circumstances and notions of justice. The demand for legitimacy can be interpreted to require that judges decide cases in accordance with the law in its entirety, as indicated by the conventions of the legal community, because the legal community contributes to the contextual legitimacy of the legal and political system as a whole in its social, historical, and cultural context. So long as the legal conversation takes place in a system that insists on the public responsibility of judges, and the American people want a legal and political system that in part seeks a more orderly and just society independently of popular preferences at any moment, the legal community would seem to contribute to a system that, on the whole, better merits the allegiance of the American people.

D. Summary

This chapter has reviewed three alternatives to hard formal legitimacy. Two of these alternatives—legal skepticism and soft formalism—were seen to be hampered by the legacies of legal formalism in significant ways. Thus, legal skepticism follows from the failure of formalism so long as the formalist framework is otherwise retained. If judicial decisions must be either a product of formalist reasoning or a product of idiosyncratic value preferences, and judicial decisions are not a product of formalist reasoning, then judicial decisions must be a product of idiosyncratic value preferences and, by implication, are not legitimate. Soft formalism attempts to relax the rigor required by hard legal formalism while otherwise retaining the formalist framework, making it possible to claim that some adjudication satisfies the demand for legitimacy. Within that framework, the meaning of legitimacy remains a formalist meaning, and soft formalism on analysis falls into either hard formalism or legal skepticism. It is hard to see how either legal skepticism or soft formalism, much less hard formalism, responds satisfactorily to the demand for legitimacy.

A third alternative is to enter a post-formalist world in which legal formalism is neither a model of legitimacy, an implicit standrad of criticism, nor an ideal to be mimicked imperfectly. Instead, the demand for legitimacy can be interpreted contextually to require a legal and political system that, on the whole, enjoys and merits the allegiance of the people. The legitimacy of adjudication, in turn, depends on its contribution to the legitimacy of the legal and political system as a whole, in its social, historical, and cultural context.

In the U.S. legal system, adjudication may be legitimate in this contextual sense if it is based on legal reasoning within a metaphorical legal conversation involving members of the legal community as an interpretive community, and if the legal community is the proper community to play the interpretive role. Members of the legal community hold the values of order and justice at the center of their webs of beliefs about law, hold the principles of legitimacy, stare decisis, and legislative supremacy near the center, and are committed to legal reasoning in bringing these values and principles to bear in particular cases. Judges make law only in cases in accordance with the law in its entirety—what members of the legal community generally will take to be required by an orderly and just society in a case and like cases, as indicated by the legal experience and the totality of our theories about law.

There are reasons for believing that the legal community contributes to the contextual legitimacy of the system: U.S. society is a large and complex society, a pluralistic society, and a society in which the people want the legal and political system to contribute to a more orderly and just society, as well as to reflect majoritarian preferences. The pursuit of order and justice in cases thus would seem to require a professional community of sufficient size to run and watch the legal system on a case-by-case basis, institutions like courts that can protect unpopular rights and offer an avenue of change independently of politics, and a legal conversation in place of personal value preferences to augment majoritarian politics. For these reasons, it would seem that adjudication supported by the conventions of the legal community contributes to a legal and political system that, on the whole, better meits the allegiance of the people.

Judicial lawmaking in cases, however, can range in significance from the trivial to the revolutionary. What has been said in this chapter may be adequate to legitimate adjudication as an institution, but it surely does not legitimate substantial judicial lawmaking in all cases, and it says little about which cases are appropriate for substantial judicial lawmaking. The next chapter focuses on judicial lawmaking when it is more than trivial and effects a substantial change in the law, and it further elaborates on the tension between a search for order and justice and the requirements of democracy.

CHAPTER ELEVEN

Judicial Lawmaking and Democracy

THE LEGISLATIVE, executive, and judicial branches of U.S. government often are said to perform entirely different functions: The legislative branch makes the law, the executive branch enforces the law, and the judicial branch applies the law. What has been said about law and legal reasoning suggests that this simple tripartite division of governmental functions is too simple. Judges make law, albeit often trivial law, in the course of adjudication. This chapter focuses on judicial lawmaking when it is more than trivial and effects a substantial change in the law. The contextual theory of legitimacy implies that such judicial lawmaking should satisfy three conditions: The judicial lawmaking power should be exercised in a case on the basis of legal reasoning, serve the functions in the system that support the legitimacy of the legal conversation, and be cabined within the system to prevent or correct abuses by members of the legal community. These three conditions can be satisfied in the U.S. legal and political system.

Legal reasoning can generate arguments supporting substantial legal change, at least by appellate courts, when the law as changed would improve the coherence of the legal experience and the totality of the legal community's theories about law, given the centrality of order and justice. Arguments advocating legal change, however, may be rejected by the judicial branch of government because principles of legitimacy and legislative supremacy are near-central and often require the judges to defer to the lawmaking prerogatives of the more democratic branches of government. There nonetheless are cases in which the courts act properly to change the law in order to keep it consonant with contemporary and foreseeable circumstances and evolving notions of justice. In such cases, judicial lawmaking is legitimate because it contributes to the contextual legitimacy of the U.S. legal and political system as a whole.

A. Judicial Change and Legal Reasoning

By the contextual theory of legitimacy, as well as most other theories of legitimacy, judicial lawmaking is not legitimate in a case unless needed to decide the case and supported by legal reasoning. As Charles Breitel, then Chief Judge of the New York Court of Appeals, put it:

> The judicial process is based on reasoning and presupposes — all antirationalists to the contrary notwithstanding — that its determinations are justified only when explained or explainable in reason. No poll, no majority vote of the affected, no rule of expediency, and certainly no confessedly subjective of idiosyncratic view justifies a judicial determination. Emphatically, no claim of might, physical or political, justifies a judicial determination.[1]

It might be thought that legal reasoning is not capable of supporting substantial judicial lawmaking, as if legal reasoning only could draw the connection between the decision in a case and law that existed before the case materialized. However, legal reasoning is capable of supporting substantial legal change by judicial decision in appropriate cases.

1. Retrospective and Prospective Aspects of Legal Reasoning

Legal reasoning could be used in ways that minimize the scope of judicial lawmaking, as by emphasizing the legal experience and only explanatory theories already embedded in the legal experience. Such legal reasoning would be conceivable because it would have both a form and an interpretive method, with the method requiring judges to decide cases so as to accommodate their decisions coherently with the legal experience and some of the legal community's theories about law. It would be reasoning with a retrospective emphasis because it would purport to foreclose judges from determining which decision better fit with the legal experience in light of the totality of our theories about law, including evaluative theories emphasizing what would be required by a more orderly and just society for the present and forseeable future.

Reasoning retrospectively would not extinguish the need for judicial lawmaking in cases; though conceivable, it may in practice be unachievable. Even within such a past-oriented conception, the

---

[1]Breitel, The Lawmakers, 65 Colum. L. Rev. 749, 772 (1965).

decision in a case requires a judge to elaborate on the legal experience, in light of sometimes multiple and conflicting explanatory theories, to reconcile the decision with what has gone before. The decision necessarily is creative to the extent that each case sheds new light on the legal experience and presents a question that had not theretofore been decided. Each time that an appellate court makes a judgment of importance and decides a case accordingly, it adds something new to the legal experience—a new base point from which arguments by analogy then can be made and new dicta that may affect the rules and our theories about law. Consequently, judges, without ceasing to be judges, cannot escape from making a little law in each case.[2]

The retrospective aspect of legal reasoning nonetheless often is emphasized by lawyers and judges, especially in families of cases where the social interest in order is paramount. Such an emphasis, however, is not made exclusively either by judges popularly called "conservatives," "liberals," "strict constructionists," or "judicial activists." Judges vary in the extent to which they reason retrospectively, but probably all good judges at times employ reasoning that is oriented toward the future. Like the retrospective approach, reasoning with a prospective emphasis encompasses the legal experience and the explanatory theories embedded in the legal experience. Additionally, it encompasses newly conceived theories explaining the legal experience and, more important, other normative theories evaluating it in light of contemporary and forseeable circumstances and evolving notions of justice.

To evaluate a law is to offer a judgment as to its merits—to determine whether it is a good law or a bad law. Pragmatically speaking, evaluating the goodness or badness of a law presupposes two sorts of relationships. First, the law being evaluated must be compared to alternative possible laws under the circumstances. It is a good law if it is better than the available alternatives and a bad law if it is worse than an available alternative. Second, the comparison must be made in relation to a web of beliefs from which the evaluation of goodness or badness can be made and defended in reason. It will not do for judges or legal observers to announce simply that they do not like a particular law; the evaluation is of interest to participants in a legal conversation about a judicial decision only if supported by good legal reasoning.

---

[2]See Chapter 6.

The reasons offered in support of a proposal for a judicial change in the law will be recognized as good reasons if they start from common ground with those participating in the conversation. A judge considering a proposal for legal change reasons from a web of beliefs about what members of the legal community generally will take to be required by an orderly and just society in cases. The conventions of the legal community are evidenced not only in the legal materials that constitute the legal experience, together with treatises giving conventional wisdoms explaining the legal experience. They also may be evident in a number of publications that advocate what the law ought to be for the present and forseeable future, while normally recognizing that lawmaking is necessary to make a proferred alternative into the law. Theories about what the law ought to be — evaluative theories about law — can be found in the dissenting and concurring opinions of judges, dicta in majority opinions, treatises going beyond the conventional wisdoms, "Restatements" of the law, scholarly journals, and other publications.

Legal reasoning in part draws on what members of the legal community generally will take to be required by an orderly and just society in cases for the present and forseeable future. The judicial decision in a case is made, through legal reasoning, by determining which decision can be better accommodated coherently with the facts and the legal experience in light of the totality of our theories about law, including, at times, well-supported evaluative theories about law. From a web of beliefs recognizing both kinds of theories, legal reasoning with a prospective emphasis can justify a substantial change in the law by judicial decision in an appropriate case.

2. Change and Prospective Legal Reasoning

It is helpful to think of judicial lawmaking as being of two kinds, though the difference in some respects is one of degree. Much judicial lawmaking takes place incrementally on a case-by-case basis via the judgment of importance. Some judicial lawmaking is far more abrupt and dramatic, as when a statute is declared unconstitutional or a common law precedent is overruled. Prospective legal reasoning can be used to justify either kind of legal change by judicial decision.[3]

---

[3]The appellate courts play a far stronger role than trial courts in both kinds of legal change.

To illustrate the process of incremental change by judicial decision, consider a summary of the evolution of the law concerning the liability of a manufacturer for defectively manufactured products that cause harm to consumers and others. The law did little in the nineteenth century to provide compensation to persons who were injured by defectively manufactured products, even if the products also were negligently manufactured, unless the injured person was a party to a contract with the manufacturer.[4] The prevailing slogan was "Buyer beware!" Of course, consumers now typically buy products from retailers who themselves do not manufacture products and may not know of manufacturing defects in their products. Most injuries caused by defects in products consequently would go uncompensated today if the law had not changed.

In the United States the process of change began subtly in 1852, when the New York Court of Appeals announced an exception to the contract requirement for "imminently dangerous products" that were negligently manufactured.[5] That case involved a defectively labeled jar of belladonna, a poison. The exception later was broadened also to incude "inherently dangerous products" that were negligently manufactured.[6] This "exceptional" class of cases grew to include, at times, an imperfect hair wash, a coffee urn, a scaffold, and chewing tobacco, all of which were deemed to be "inherently dangerous" if defectively manufactured. Manufacturers were held liable to consumers in such cases if the product also was negligently manufactured and the cause of harm, whether or not there was a contract between them.

The courts eventually recognized that the exception was swallowing up the general rule precluding a consumer from recovering from a manufacturer unless there was a contract between them.[7] As a practical matter, manufacturers increasingly were being held liable for injuries to consumers caused by negligently manufactured products. Today it is said still more broadly that any seller of goods is strictly liable for all injuries proximately caused to a user or consumer, or to his property, by any product sold in a defective condition unreasonably dangerous to the user or consumer.[8] In

---

[4]Winterbottom v. Wright, 152 Eng. Rep. 402 (1842). The complexities of the privity rule are passed over in the text.
[5]Thomas v. Winchester, 6 N.Y. 397 (1852).
[6]Torgerson v. Schultz, 192 N.Y. 156 (1908).
[7]McPherson v. Buick Motor Car Co., 217 N.Y. 382 (1916).
[8]Restatement (Second) of Torts §402A (1965).

California and some other jurisdictions, it is not necessary that the product be "unreasonably dangerous."[9] Manufacturers and other sellers generally are liable to consumers and others for injuries caused by defective products whether the defect is a result of negligence or not, and whether the seller had a contract with the injured party or not.

When viewed from the perspective of a century of judicial decisions, the law governing a manufacturer's liability to persons injured by defectively manufactured products has taken a complete 180 degree turn to "Seller beware!" Such an evolutionary development of the law, which occurs in many areas of the law at differing paces, could not be explained by wholly retrospective legal reasoning. As will be seen, however, legal reasoning with a prospective emphasis can explain such a development.

To illustrate an abrupt and dramatic judicial change in the law, consider the great case of *Brown v. Board of Education.*[10] The U.S. Supreme Court there held that legally compelled segregation of public school systems by race was unconstitutional under the equal protection clause of the fourteenth amendment to the U.S. Constitution: "nor shall any state . . . deny to any person within its jurisdiction the equal protection of the laws." Fifty-eight years earlier, in *Plessy v. Ferguson,*[11] the Supreme Court had held that legally compelled segregation by race of public accommodations (railroad facilities) was constitutional under the equal protection clause as long as the accommodations were "separate but equal." If there had been any doubt after *Brown* that *Plessy* had been overruled, several decisions following *Brown* quickly made it clear that all legally mandated racial discrimination was now unconstitutional.

The Court in *Brown* and its progeny in a few years nullified a large number of state and federal statutes that discriminated on racial grounds, effecting a revolutionary change in the law. It could hardly be maintained that the decision in *Brown* could be at all well accommodated with the then-existing legal experience and explanatory theories then embedded in the legal experience, though a few cases prior to *Brown* had hinted at the change to come. Wholly retrospective legal reasoning could not justify the Court's decision, though *Brown* now is almost universally ap-

---

[9]Cronin v. J.B.E. Olson Corp., 8 Cal. 3d 121 (1972).
[10]347 U.S. 483 (1954). See also Bolling v. Sharpe, 347 U.S. 497 (1954).
[11]163 U.S. 537 (1896).

plauded. Of course, the decision could not be justified by reasoning only deductively from the text of the equal protection clause because a judgment of importance was required: If public facilities were "separate but equal," was the fact of inequality implied by racial segregation or the fact of equality of facilities more important under the circumstances? It was necessary to justify the judgment of importance through legal reasoning, not by appealing to the judges' personal value preferences, the then-evident majority will, or the Court's belief that it could get away with the decision in the political context.

Legal reasoning with a prospective emphasis explains both kinds of lawmaking by judicial decision. The judge imagines the law as it would be if a portion of existing law (precedents, rules, and theories) were replaced with a proffered alternative and its probable implications for the present and foreseeable future (different possible precedents, rules, and theories). It can be concluded with reason that the law would be better as changed if the imagined law in its entirety, including the portions that would be changed and those that would be retained, would more coherently contribute to a more orderly and just society than the existing law in its entirety. From this perspective, the difference between the legal reasoning that supports incremental and more abrupt change in the law is one of degree. Incremental change implies that a small portion of existing law would be replaced with a proffered alternative while abrupt change implies that a large portion would be replaced at one time.

The commitment to order and justice remains stable at the center of our webs of beliefs about law. It would be hard even to imagine a system of law that denied the centrality of these values or treated them as mere rhetorical flourishes without practical implications for the rules and cases that fill out a working system of law. The remainder of the web continually changes as members of the legal community work out the implications of order and justice as cases arise in the social, historical, and cultural context. Legal reasoning often emphasizes the strong role of order in the system and resists legal change. At times, it emphasizes the equally strong role of justice in a system that must change to maintain its contextual legitimacy as circumstances change and notions of justice evolve.

Thus, the judges in cases that contribute to the evolution of the law of products liability decided the cases before them in light of the legal experience and the totality of the legal community's theories about law, including evaluative theories indicating what members of the legal community generally would take to be required by an orderly and just society in the case and like cases, under contemporary circumstances and evolving notions of justice. Circumstances in the U.S. economy were changing as the law evolved—the industrialization of the U.S. economy led to much division of labor with many more persons buying many more products from retailers, rather than making their own or buying from local small manufacturers as in more agrarian days. Notions of justice also were evolving as the law evolved, from the "rugged individualism" of the nineteenth century, epitomized in part by "Buyer beware!," to the Welfare State of the twentieth century, symbolized in part by popular movements for greater corporate responsibility and consumer protection. The law of products liability evolved on a case-by-case basis along with the social, historical, and cultural context to maintain and enhance its contribution to a more orderly and just society.

The Court in *Brown v. Board of Education* similarly decided the case in light of the legal experience and the totality of our theories about law, including evaluative theories. Unlike the law of products liability and most other examples of judicial lawmaking, however, the law against legally compelled racial discrimination did not evolve along with contemporary circumstances and evolving notions of justice in the society at large. The Court, acting unanimously, spearheaded massive changes in U.S. society and helped lead the evolution of notions of racial justice. With hindsight, few would doubt that the Court's decision contributed in a major way to a more orderly and just society. The Court's vision of a more orderly and just society, one whose law condemned racial discrimination, lay behind and supported its decision. Given our webs of beliefs about law, in which the values of order and justice occupy the central positions and should support all of the beliefs in the web, it is hard to doubt that the law in its entirety after *Brown* more coherently contributes to a more orderly and just society than the law in its entirety before *Brown*.

Accordingly, legal reasoning is capable of supporting a judicial decision that makes a substantial change in the law. It has a retrospective aspect, emphasizing the legal experience and the explanatory theories embedded in the legal experience. It also has a prospective aspect, additionally drawing on evaluative theories about law. Evaluative theories—theories about what the law ought to be for the present and foreseeable future—are eligible for incorporation into the law as it is by judicial decision in appropriate cases when the theories are supported by members of the legal community. Legal change by judicial decision in a case depends on legal reasoning that accommodates the decision in the case coherently with the facts and the legal experience in light of the *totality* of our theories about law.

B. Change and Deference to Democracy

Even though legal reasoning is capable of supporting legal change through adjudication, insofar as the substantive question is concerned, proposals for legal change often are rejected by judges for institutional reasons. The principal lawmaking branches of government are the legislative and executive branches, which are the more democratic branches and go a long way toward maintaining and enhancing the contextual legitimacy of the system as a whole. The system encompasses ample room for majoritarian or other political preferences to be heard and felt, whether or not those preferences support laws that also can be justified by legal reasoning. The judicial lawmaking power cannot be exercised in every case without reducing substantially the room for majoritarian and other political lawmaking. Consequently, judges often defer to the more democratic lawmaking processes.

To illustrate, consider *San Antonio Independent School District v. Rodriguez,*[12] in which a state's legislative and administrative scheme organizing school districts was challenged as unconstitutional under the equal protection clause in the fourteenth amendment. Texas's system provided for a large number of public school districts to be financed in major part by property taxes on property within each district. The state provided some additional funds, in part to help offset disparities in local spending in order to guarantee a minimum or basic educational offering for each child. But there were substantial disparities in the funds available for education in different school districts, depending largely on whether the property values within the district were higher or lower than in other districts. The lawsuit was brought by parents of children in the less affluent districts, who claimed that their children were

---

[12]411 U.S. 1 (1973).

being discriminated against on the basis of wealth in violation of the equal protection clause.

The judicial practice of deference to democracy is reflected in the Supreme Court's doctrines under the equal protection clause by a multitiered standard of judicial review.[13] At the time *Rodriguez* was decided, it appeared that there were only two tiers. First, the Court would uphold the constitutionality of most state action so long as it was rationally related to any legitimate state interest. This standard of review sometimes is said to establish a presumption of constitutionality. In very few cases has the Court held state action to be "irrational" and, for that reason, unconstitutional. Second, the Court would subject the state action to "rigorous scrutiny" if it operated to the disadvantage of certain constitutionally suspect classes, such as classes defined by the race of its members, or impinged upon a fundamental right that is protected by the Constitution, such as the freedom of speech. This standard of review sometimes is said to establish a presumption of unconstitutionality and requires the state to justify its action as being necessary to protect a compelling state interest. Very few state actions survive rigorous scrutiny by the Court.

A major issue in *Rodriguez* was whether the Texas system of financing public education operated to the disadvantage of a suspect class or impinged upon a constitutionally protected fundamental right, requiring rigorous scrutiny by the Court. A three-judge district court had held that the system's financing practice discriminated on the basis of wealth, which it held to be a suspect classification, and that education was a constitutionally protected fundamental right. The district court consequently determined that the Texas system could be sustained only if the state could show that it was premised on some compelling state interest. It found that the state had failed to carry that heavy burden and held the state's system unconstitutional. An appeal was taken to the U.S. Supreme Court.

Justice Powell, writing for the Court, upheld the Texas system's constitutionality because wealth in itself was not a suspect classification, education was not a constitutionally protected fundamental right, and the financing scheme was rationally related to the legitimate end of ensuring a large measure of participation in and control of each district's schools at the local level. In so holding, Justice Powell did not deny that the Texas system might

---

[13]See Bice, Standards of Judicial Review, 50 S. Cal. L. Rev. 689 (1977).

unfairly provide inferior educations to the less affluent or that education was an important value in U.S. society. Rather, he was careful to distinguish the Court's proper function from those of the legislature, school boards, and other elected representatives responsible for education policy:

> [T]his Court's action today is not to be viewed as placing its judicial imprimatur on the status quo. The need is apparent for reform in tax systems which may well have relied too long and too heavily on the local property tax. And certainly innovative new thinking as to public education, its methods and its funding, is necessary to assure both a higher level of quality and greater uniformity of opportunity. . . . But the ultimate solutions must come from the lawmakers and from the democratic pressures of those who elect them.[14]

Among Justice Powell's reasons for limiting the Court's function were concerns relating to the precedential effect of a contrary decision, the Court's competence to deal with the problems, and principles of federalism.

The problems involving the precedential effect of judicial decisions under the equal protection clause are especially important to the Court. All laws treat some persons unequally in a literal sense, but rigorous scrutiny of all state laws would have the Court substantially displace elected state officials in all matters for which those officials are responsible. Justice Powell thus looked beyond *Rodriguez* to a large family of cases that might be legally indistinguishable from the case at bar:

> No scheme of taxation, whether the tax is imposed on property, income, or purchases of goods and services, has yet been devised which is free of all discriminatory impact. In such a complex arena in which no perfect alternatives exist, the Court does well not to impose too rigorous a standard of scrutiny lest all local fiscal schemes become subjects of criticism under the Equal Protection Clause.[15]

At the same time, the court has recognized that it has a duty to enforce the equal protection clause in appropriate families of cases. Refraining from giving rigorous judicial scrutiny to all state action would be no more justifiable than giving such scrutiny to all state action. Among the considerations that help the Court to determine which cases are appropriate for rigorous scrutiny is the

---

[14]San Antonio Indep. School Dist. v. Rodriguez, 411 U.S. 1, 58-59 (1973).
[15]Id. at 41.

Court's circumspection regarding its own competence. Thus, Justice Powell indicated that rigorous scrutiny in the case at bar and other like cases would go beyond the competence of the Court, without implying that there are not other families of cases that are within the competence of the Court:

> [T]his case also involves the most persistent and difficult questions of educational policy, another area in which this Court's lack of specialized knowledge and experience counsels against premature interference with the informed judgments made at the state and local levels. . . . The very complexity of the problems of financing and managing a statewide public school system suggest that "there will be more than one constitutionally permissible method of solving them," and that, within the limits of rationality, "the legislature's efforts to tackle the problems" should be entitled to respect.[16]

Another consideration that influences the Court's judgment in determining which families of cases are appropriate for rigorous judicial scrutiny is the Court's institutional relationship to the organ of government whose action is challenged as unconstitutional. The principles of separation of powers and federalism often are called on to help justify a court's deference to the more democratic branches of government. In *Rodriguez,* Justice Powell related concerns about federalism to the interpretation of the Court's doctrines concerning standards of review:

> It must be remembered, also, that every claim arising under the Equal Protection Clause has implications for the relationship between national and state power under our federal system. Questions of federalism are always inherent in the process of determining whether a State's laws are to be accorded the traditional presumption of constitutionality, or are to be subjected instead to rigorous judicial scrutiny.[17]

In this connection, it is notable that the California Supreme Court reached the opposite conclusion in a case very similar to *Rodriguez,* based on the California Constitution.[18] The California decision remained good law after the Supreme Court's decision in *Rodriguez* because it was a matter of state law not in violation of the federal Constitution.

The Court's opinion in *Rodriguez* is to be understood in sig-

---

[16]Id. at 42.
[17]Id. at 44.
[18]Serrano v. Priest, 5 Cal. 3d 584 (1971).

nificant part not as a judgment concerning the wisdom of financing public school education heavily by a property tax within the school district, but as a judgment concerning the proper role of the federal courts, in relation to electorally accountable state officials, in constitutional cases. The Court's judgment was controversial. Three dissenting Supreme Court justices (and three lower court judges) would have subjected the Texas system to a more intensive judicial scrutiny and would have held it unconstitutional.[19] Their opinions indicate that the opposite decision, too, could be supported by good legal reasoning. For the majority, however, concern for limiting the legitimate role of the Court and deferring to the more democratic lawmaking processes loomed larger in the context of the case and like cases.

The problem of legitimacy and theories of the proper judicial role similarly influence decisions in statutory and common law cases. Justice Holmes's opinion in *McBoyle v. United States*, discussed in Chapter 4,[20] exemplifies a case in which the problem of legitimacy influenced the Court to defer to the expressed views of Congress and to its primary responsibility to change federal statutory law. The common law, of course, is in all respects a law made by judges. Sometimes, however, courts asked to reform the common law refuse to do so on the ground that the legislature is better situated to effect a desired reform.[21]

The problem of legitimacy and theories concerning the proper judicial role in the U.S. legal and political system often are a most important influence on judicial decisions. Principles of legitimacy and legislative supremacy occupy a near-central place in our webs of beliefs about law and support much of the web. Consequently, a judicial decision is not well supported by legal reasoning unless it can be accommodated well with theories of the legitimate judicial lawmaking role. Judges often defer to the lawmaking prerogatives of the more democratic branches of government, even when a change in the law otherwise is supported by good legal reasoning.

---

[19]San Antonio Independent School District v. Rodriguez, 411 U.S. 1, 60, 72 (1973) (dissenting opinions of Justices Brennan and Marshall, joined by Justice Douglas).

[20]See Chapter 4 §C.

[21]E.g., Murphy v. American Home Prod. Corp., 58 N.Y. 293 (1983) (held, discharged "whistle-blower" under employment contract terminable at will failed to state a claim for breach of contract; whether limitations on employer's right to terminate should be implied in law is a question for the legislature).

C. Legitimate Lawmaking by Judges

The U.S. legal and political system encompasses ample room for majoritarian or other political lawmaking, but the system as a whole also encompasses room for the legal conversation concerning order and justice in cases. To preserve that room, courts in some cases do not decline to make law as needed, subject to the democratic checks of subsequent legislation or constitutional amendment and the less formal checking power of the legal community. The judicial lawmaking power is exercised legitimately when, in addition to being supported by good legal reasoning, legal change by judicial decision in a case serves the functions within the system that support the legitimacy of the legal conversation.

Recall that the contextual legitimacy of the legal conversation depends on its contribution to the legitimacy of the legal and political system as a whole in its social, historical, and cultural context. The legitimacy of the system as a whole requires that it enjoy and merit the allegiance of the American people. The legal system better merits the support of the people if it includes components that serve three functions related to stable features of the social, historical, and cultural context: (1) a professional community to run and watch the system on a case-by-case basis, (2) institutions that operate at some distance from majoritarian politics, and (3) a legal conversation that uses legal reasoning in the search for a more orderly and just society, to augment lawmaking processes that reflect majoritarian and other political preferences. The judicial lawmaking power can be used in adjudication to serve these functions both in cases effecting incremental changes and in cases effecting abrupt and dramatic changes.

Incremental change by judicial decision proceeds on a case-by-case basis, at some distance from majoritarian politics, and in a cautious search for order and justice in a case and like cases. It is necessitated by the indeterminacy of language and the family-style relations among cases, and better contributes to order and justice if it sometimes employs legal reasoning with a prospective emphasis. The legitimacy of the legal and political system as a whole does not depend only on the highly visible or otherwise political matters that are the subjects of legislation or constitutional amendment; it also depends on how the system treats individual cases that may not be reported in the popular press. The cumulative effect of hundreds of thousands of decisions in particular cases affecting ordinary citizens helps give the law its public character. The contextual legitimacy of the system, in turn, is affected.

In a large and complex society like the United States, many legal issues will arise in cases that do not attract the substantial public or political attention needed to move a legislature to act. The avenues to legal change by the more democratic branches of government may be too broad to notice, in a timely way, small matters of significance in their cumulative effect. Incremental change by judicial decision keeps the law up to date on a case-by-case basis in a way that augments the more democratic avenues of legal change. The courts learn of contemporary circumstances from the congeries of facts in the series of cases before them, and they learn of evolving notions of justice through the claims of litigants, the reactions of juries, and commentaries by members of the legal community. The road to legal change by judicial decision is available to those who seek justice in particular cases, whether or not their claims attain significant public prominence or gain the support of the politically powerful.

More abrupt and dramatic change by judicial decision occurs in a particular case, also at some distance from majoritarian politics, and also in a search for order and justice in the case and like cases. Judicial lawmaking may be justified in some cases because they exemplify a much broader and more significant grievance that may not lend itself to effective change by only incremental judicial development and may not be redressed by the more democratic branches of government. Dramatic judicial decisions can address the broader and more significant situation and thus better contribute to a more orderly and just society when the other branches of government are less well positioned to do so.

The more democratic branches of government tend to respond to the majority will or political alliances of well-organized interests and can be used by the majority or politically powerful interests to deny generally the rights of minorities or the politically weak. In a case like *Brown v. Board of Education,* for example, the white majority in state legislatures, by legally mandating racial segregation in education and otherwise, were dominating a black minority in virtually all phases of life. The facts of *Brown* exemplified a broad social problem: The most basic rights and interests of blacks were being persistently denied. Only a bold legal response could address the real problem, but the minority then could not hope realistically to change the law by democratic processes of legislation or constitutional amendment. The legitimacy of the system as a whole was seriously affected. Surely the Court's decision in *Brown* contributed substantially to a more orderly and just society in which the legal and political system as a whole better merits the allegiance of all significant groups in U.S. society.

The more democratic branches also tend to respond to the politics of the moment, leaving areas of the law untouched for long periods of time while the courts wait for the legislature to respond to a need for change. During the interim, the courts may have no realistic choice but to make law in the political vacuum or allow disorder or injustice to prevail. For example, Congress enacted a Copyright Act in 1909,[22] providing authors and some other creators with exclusive rights to market their artistic creations. It was not revised until 1978. The courts in the interim were asked to decide numerous questions concerning forms of artistic expression not contemplated in the 1909 act, including technological innovations like talking movies, radio and television, audio and video tapes, the photocopy machine, and computer programs. The courts did not decide that such forms of expression could not be copyrighted, or could not be copies in violation of a copyright, because they were not within the letter of the statute or congressional intent in 1909. Rather, they interpreted the 1909 act in many creative ways to further the purposes of the act coherently in light of contemporary and foreseeable circumstances, contributing to order and justice in the artistic and entertainment worlds.

Some areas of the law, such as much of the common law, traditionally have been thought to be subjects of judicial expertise. The more dramatic branches of government often expect the courts to continue their stewardship of these areas of the law, through both incremental and more abrupt moves when needed. Incremental change may culminate in a dramatic decision by which the cumulative effect of the slow process of change is fully recognized by the rules and explanatory theories about law. The progressive decline of the rule insulating manufacturers of products from liability to consumers who had no contract with the manufacturer culminated in a dramatic decision that finally overruled the increasingly obsolescent precedents that supported the rule.[23] The end of the rule limiting a manufacturer's liability for injuries

---

[22]60 Stat. 1075 et seq. (1909).
[23]McPherson v. Buick Motor Car Co., 217 N.Y. 382 (1916).

caused by negligently manufactured products, and imposing a rule of strict liability, came more abruptly;[24] a shift of theory and principle probably cannot be accomplished incrementally. Until recent years, legislatures had done almost nothing concerning liability for defective products, but apparently were content to leave the matter to judicial lawmaking. Judicial lawmaking kept the law up to date in light of contemporary circumstances and evolving notions of justice concerning the responsibilities of manufacturers in a highly developed market economy.

Thus, there are cases in which the courts properly defer to the lawmaking prerogatives of the more democratic branches of government and cases in which they do not, subject to checks both within and external to the legal community. It might be thought that one could state a formal rule or principle, in the form of necessary and sufficient conditions, that would identify cases in which the judicial lawmaking power is exercised legitimately and those in which it is not. Except for vague and question-begging generalities, it cannot be done because cases of legitimate judicial lawmaking are alike as the members of a family are alike; there is no fact or facts in common among them.[25] Rather, theories of legitimacy call attention to the proper judicial role in each case and organize the easier cases that can be used as base points for analogies in harder cases.[26] Though theories of legitimacy may be many, it often is possible to accommodate a decision in a problem case coherently with the law in its entirety.[27]

Of course, the legal experience and theories of legitimacy may have conflicting implications in ways that produce harder cases concerning the relationship between adjudication and democratic politics. In such cases, the judges must choose from among the available alternatives. The only practical alternative is to look to what some group of people think—in most cases, to what members of the legal community, including lawyers, judges, legislators, and others, generally will take to be required by an orderly and just society in the case and like cases.[28] If the decision remains controversial when viewed from this perspective, the judge may have no alternative but to give an opinion, supported by the best

---

[24]See Greenman v. Yuba Power Prod., 59 Cal. 2d 453 (1963).
[25]See Chapter 5.
[26]See Chapter 6.
[27]See Chapter 7.
[28]See Chapter 9.

available legal reasoning, to accommodate the decision in the case with the facts and the legal experience in light of the totality of our theories about law, including principles of legitimacy and legislative supremacy. The opinion then serves as a contribution to the broader legal conversation, which may be continued by the more democratic branches of government and, in any event, will continue in the next similar case before a court.[29]

The conventions of the legal community in U.S. society thus reveal an unresolved tension between commitments to law and democracy. The search for a more orderly and just society requires legal reasoning that distinguishes law from the preferences of people. At the same time, the sovereignty of the people requires their consent, in some sense, to the laws that govern. In theory, one can say that legitimacy requires the legal and political system as a whole to comport well with both commitments — that it both enjoy and merit the allegiance of the people. In practice, however, there are cases in which the available alternatives require judges to uphold law or democracy. In U.S. society, we are simply unwilling to exalt theoretical consistency at the cost of jettisoning one or the other of these deep commitments. Rather, we live with uncertainty in a legal and political system that nonetheless achieves a remarkably large measure of both.

D. Summary

To preserve its contextual legitimacy, the U.S. legal and political system as a whole must enjoy and merit the allegiance of the people. This implies that the law must change because social, historical, and cultural circumstances change and notions of justice evolve. In a large, complex, and pluralistic society in which the people want the legal and political system to contribute to a more orderly and just society, as well as to reflect majority preferences, judicial lawmaking contributes to the legitimacy of the system if three conditions are satisfied: Judicial lawmaking must occur in a case on the basis of legal reasoning, must serve the functions in the system that support the legitimacy of the legal conversation, and must be cabined within the system to prevent or correct abuses by members of the legal community.

All three conditions can be satisfied in the U.S. legal system.

---

[29]See Chapter 10.

Legal reasoning can be used to justify both incremental and abrupt legal change by judicial decision in an appropriate case. A case is appropriate for judicial lawmaking if, in addition to good legal reasoning supporting legal change on the substantive question, judicial lawmaking in the case can be accommodated well with principles of legislative supremacy. This near-central principle often requires courts to defer to the lawmaking prerogatives of the more democratic branches of government. Courts nonetheless make law legitimately when doing so in a case would enhance the contextual legitimacy of the system as a whole.

The legal conversation, unlike political conversations, must concern order and justice centrally if it is to concern law at all. Adjudication affords occasions for the legal conversation to continue while resolving disputes with real-world implications. The American people seem to welcome the search for a more orderly and just society through law and legal reasoning, which can serve the purposes they are called on to serve within the U.S. legal and political system.

INDEX

Adjudication. *See* Judicial decision; Legitimacy, problem of
Advocacy. *See* Lawyers, functions of
Analogical form of legal reasoning. *See also* Forms of Legal Reasoning
  cases in, 28-29, 68-77, 140-142
  easier cases, in, 63-64
  enacted law, and. *See* Enacted law
  facts in, 25, 29-31, 95
  functions of, 25, 40, 163-164
  harder cases, in, 69, 140-142
  importance in, 27, 31-40, 83, 95, 165
  limitations of, 31-40, 43, 77-82
  normative theories, and, 111-116
  rules, and, 31-38, 59-68, 87
Analogy. *See* Logic
Auster's case, 45-53, 116-121
Authority. *See also* Legitimacy, problem of
  foundational approach, 169-184
  judges at common law, of, 36-38
  precedents, of, 28-29
  rules, of, 44-48, 169-170, 181-184

Brown v. Board of Education, 222, 224, 231-232

Case law. *See* Common law
Cases. *See also* Precedent
  classification of. *See* Rules
  defined, 11-13
  family-style relations among, 91-94, 102, 230, 233
  functions of, 21-24, 69-78, 110, 211
  rules contrasted with, 14-15, 37, 55-56
  synthesis of. *See* Synthesis
Church of the Holy Trinity v. United States, 73-76, 79-80
Coercion, 12-13, 23-24, 168-169, 175-176, 200-211
Coherence. *See* Logic
Common law. *See also* Cases; Lawmaking
  defined, 25
  enacted law, contrasted with. *See* Enacted law
  legitimacy, and, 229
  normative theories, and, 111-116
  process illustrated, 32-39

rules, 31-38, 41, 59-67
synthesis of. *See* Synthesis
Constitutional interpretation, 69-73, 76-77, 194-197, 225-234. *See also* Enacted law; Language
Conventions of the legal community. *See also* Legal community
  defined, 96-97
  democratic theory, and. *See* Democratic theory
  functions of law, and, 96-98, 110, 111, 167, 204-214
  functions of lawyers, and, 95-98, 110
  judicial decision, and, 95-98, 136-143, 204-208
  legitimacy, and, 170-171, 204-214
  limitations of, 124, 170-171, 234
  webs of beliefs about law, and, 136-143, 209
Counseling. *See* Lawyers, functions of
Courts. *See* Judicial decision
Critical legal studies movement. *See* Legal skepticism

Deduction. *See* Logic
Deductive form of legal reasoning. *See also* Forms of legal reasoning
  cases and, 64-77
  easier cases, in, 60-64, 125-130
  facts in, 48-53, 83, 85-91, 165
  functions of, 44, 47, 56, 60-68, 81-82, 150
  importance in, 44, 50-57, 59, 68, 77, 82, 83, 165
  limitations of, 31-38, 44, 47, 49-57, 85-91, 171-184
  rules in, 37, 44-48
Democratic theory. *See also* Legitimacy, problem of
  contextual legitimacy, and, 199-215, 225-230, 233-235
  conventions of the legal community, and, 117, 210-214, 215, 225-235
  formal legitimacy, and, 171, 176-181
  judicial lawmaking, and, 77-81, 176-181, 225-234
  legal skepticism, and, 188-189

237